Sustainable Societies in a Fragile World

Perspectives from Germany and Japan

Edited by Carola Hommerich & Masato Kimura

上智大学出版
Sophia University Press

Sustainable Societies in a Fragile World

Perspectives from Germany and Japan

Edited by
Carola Hommerich & Masato Kimura

Sophia University Press

One of the fundamental ideals of Sophia University is "to embody the university's special characteristics by offering opportunities to study Christianity and Christian culture. At the same time, recognizing the diversity of thought, the university encourages academic research on a wide variety of world views."

The Sophia University Press was established to provide an independent base for the publication of scholarly research. The publications of our press are a guide to the level of research at Sophia, and one of the factors in the public evaluation of our activities.

Sophia University Press publishes books that (1) meet high academic standards; (2) are related to our university's founding spirit of Christian humanism; (3) are on important issues of interest to a broad general public; and (4) textbooks and introductions to the various academic disciplines. We publish works by individual scholars as well as the results of collaborative research projects that contribute to general cultural development and the advancement of the university.

Sustainable Societies in a Fragile World: Perspectives from Germany and Japan
© Eds. Carola Hommerich & Masato Kimura, 2024
Published by Sophia University Press

Printed and distributed by GYOSEI Corporation, Tokyo
ISBN978-4-324-11375-2
Inquiries: https://gyosei.jp

In memory of
Prof. Dr. Dr. h.c. Hans-Joachim Kornadt

Table of Contents

List of Contributors vii

Introduction

Where Are We Headed? The Role of Social Science Research
in Working Towards a Sustainable Future
Carola Hommerich, Masato Kimura 1

Transition to an Environmentally Friendly Society

Chapter 1   Kamikatsu as a Zero Waste Role-model?
Lessons for Future Zero Waste Cities
Regina M. Bichler 15

Chapter 2   Paving the Way for Carbon-neutral Schools:
Getting Students Actively Involved in Climate
Protection Measures
Lotte Nawothnig, Oliver Wagner, Sebastian Albert-Seifried,
Lena Tholen 39

Chapter 3   A Revolution in Consciousness?
Changes in Environmental Attitudes and Behaviours
in Germany and Japan
Carola Hommerich, Joanna Kitsnik 61

Sustainable and Resilient: Regional and Urban Development

Chapter 4   Sustainability and Adaptation in Planning:
Community Resilience Against Accelerating
Environmental Change
Christian Dimmer, Mark Kammerbauer 95

Chapter 5   Sustainable and Resilient Societies?
Comparing Notions of the 'Smart City' in Germany
and Japan
Andrea Hamm, Yuya Shibuya, Christoph Raetzsch 123

Inclusive Societies: Leave No One Behind

Chapter 6   The Urban Poor Under the COVID-19 Pandemic:
The Case of Tokyo
Masato Kimura 151

Chapter 7   Cyber- and Traditional Bullying as Global
Challenges?
Findings from Germany, Hong Kong, and Japan
Fabian Schunk, Gisela Trommsdorff, Natalie Wong,
Gen Nakao 177

Chapter 8   Sustainable Democracy and Value Change:
Europe, East Asia, and Southeast Asia in
Comparison
Carmen Schmidt, Defny Holidin 203

Epilogue

Sustainable Societies: Moving Forward With No Time to Waste
Masato Kimura, Carola Hommerich 231

List of Contributors

Sebastian Albert-Seifried is Co-CEO of energy consulting office Büro Ö-quadrat. Sebastian obtained a doctoral degree in physics from the University of Cambridge with a research focus on new generation solar photovoltaic technology. Following Cambridge, he worked in a multinational business consulting firm with experience in diverse business and technology sectors. With a strong scientific background, analytical skills and first-hand business experience, Sebastian joined Büro Ö-quadrat in 2017 and since then, has initiated and led a number of research projects, development and demonstration projects on the topics of energy and climate change in Germany and abroad. His current research focus covers the topics of energy-efficiency, renewable energy and climate change mitigation in schools. He is an active member of the Entrepreneurs for Future, which supports climate protection through business innovations. Recent publications include 'Making School-Based GHG-Emissions Tangible by Student-Led Carbon Footprint Assessment Program' (*Energies* 14 (24): 1-20, 2021, with Oliver Wagner, Lena Tholen, Lotte Nawothnig) and 'Secondary school student participation in Carbon Footprint Assessment for Schools' (*Conference Proceedings* 'ECEEE 2022 summer study on energy efficiency' (6-11 June 2022): 743-748 (with Lotte Nawothnig, Lena Tholen, Dieter Seifried, Amelie Straßen, Amelie Vogler, Maike Venjakob and Oliver Wagner).

Regina M. Bichler is a Doctoral candidate in Environmental Humanities at the Rachel Carson Center for Environment and Society at the Ludwig Maximilian University Munich. She has studied Chemistry, Biochemistry, and Japanese Studies in Munich, Pavia, and Osaka. After working in a Japanese chemical company, she decided to dedicate herself to the relation between society and waste. As a visiting scholar at Kyoto University in 2022 and 2023, she studied zero waste measures in both Kamikatsu and Kyoto. She analyses how waste prevention, re-use, and recycling are organized in daily life through social practices on the one hand, and materials and technologies on the other. Her most recent publication 'Harm and Harmony—Concepts of Nature and Environmental Practice in Japan' is a contribution to the *Histories* special issue 'Images of Nature—From the Middle Ages to (Non-)Western Modernities' (*Histories* 3(2): 62-75, 2023).

Christian Dimmer is Associate Professor for Urban Studies at Waseda University's School of International Liberal Studies (SILS) since 2021. He graduated with honours from the Spatial and Environmental Planning program of the Technical University of

Kaiserslautern. Christian earned his PhD from The University of Tokyo on the emergence of public space ideas in Japanese modern urban planning. As a JSPS post-doctoral fellow at Tokyo University's Interfaculty Initiative in Information Studies he researched the politics and media representations of public space. Christian served as an Assistant Professor for Urban Design Studies at The University of Tokyo between 2012 and 2016 and for Urban Studies at Waseda University between 2016 - 2021. He also taught urbanism courses at Keio University and Sophia University. He is co-founder of the charitable disaster response organizations Tohoku Planning Forum as well as the Alliance for Humanitarian Architecture. His research interests are urban commons, transition design and community design.

Andrea Hamm is a Postdoc researcher in the group 'Digitalization, Sustainability, and Participation' at the Weizenbaum Institute for the Networked Society, Berlin, Germany, and a research associate at the University for Sustainable Development Eberswalde, Germany. She received her PhD at the Faculty of Political and Social Sciences of the Free University Berlin, Germany, in the subject of Media and Digital Technologies. Her work focuses on the socio-political dimensions of digitalization, sustainability transitions, and the role of digital technologies, such as the Internet of Things, among civic actor groups in city governance and urban innovation.

Defny Holidin is a Doctoral Candidate in Social Sciences at Osnabrück University, working on comparative institutional analysis and postmodern approach to non-western government system reform in Indonesia and the Philippines. He secured research funding from the Indonesian Higher Education Commission (DIKTI). He is a lecturer in public administration at the University of Indonesia and a guest lecturer at the Development Academy of the Philippines while providing policy advice to the Government of Indonesia and leading national NGOs. He also researched with the National Graduate Institute for Policy Studies (GRIPS Tokyo) and currently serves as a country expert on Indonesia's democracy with the Varieties of Democracy (V-Dem) Institute at the University of Gothenburg. His publications include 'The Compatibility of Islam and Pancasila in Indonesia's Declining Democracy' (*Politics and Religion Journal* 16:2, 2022) and Emerald Publishing's *Public Policy and Governance* series (vol. 30, 2018) among others.

Carola Hommerich is Professor of Sociology at the Department of Sociology, Faculty of Human Sciences, at Sophia University, Tokyo. In the past, she has served as Associate Professor of Sociology at the Graduate School of Letters of Hokkaido University, Sapporo, and as Senior Research Fellow at the German Institute of

Japanese Studies (DIJ), Tokyo. She holds a PhD in Sociology from the University of Cologne. Her current research focuses on subjective well-being and social inequality, especially on the interrelation of experiences of precariousness, status anxiety and feelings of exclusion, and their impact on behavioral outcomes. Recent publications include 'Impact of COVID-19 Pandemic on Household Income and Mental Well-Being: Evidence from a Panel-Survey in Japan' (*Sociological Theory and Methods* 36(2): 260-278, 2021, with Hiroshi Kanbayashi & Naoki Sudo) and *Social Change in Japan, 1989-2019: Social Status, Social Consciousness, Attitudes and Values* (Routledge, 2021, edited with Naoki Sudo & Toru Kikkawa).

Mark Kammerbauer is an urbanist researcher, educator and author. Mark held research and teaching positions at the University of Queensland (School of Geography, Planning and Environmental Management), Lund University (Centre for Sustainability Studies), Tulane University (Center of Bioenvironmental Research) and Technical University of Munich (Faculty of Architecture). He received his Doctorate in Urban Studies from the Institute for European Urban Studies at the Bauhaus University Weimar. His main research interest is post-disaster recovery and its socio-spatial impact. He has published extensively on case studies in the USA, Germany, Australia and the Philippines, including 'Natural Hazards Governance in Germany' (In: *Oxford Research Encyclopedia of Natural Hazard Science*, 2019, eds. B. Gerber, C. Wamsler) and *Planning Urban Disaster Recovery. Spatial, institutional and social aspects of urban disaster recovery in the USA* (VDG, 2013). In 2020 he founded the Nexialist Agency for Research and Communication with clients in architecture and urban planning and design.

Masato Kimura is Professor of Sociology at the Department of Sociology, Faculty of Sociology, at Toyo University, Tokyo. In the past, he has served as Professor at the Human Sciences Department of Takachiho University, Tokyo, and Research Associate at Waseda University, Tokyo. His current research focuses on phenomenological theory of collective action, and social movements of the poor in Tokyo. Recent publications include 'Privatization and Protest of 'Commons': On the Gentrification and Homeless Movement in Shibuya' (*Space, Society, and Geographical Thought* 22: 139-156, 2019) and 'Collective Action and Recurrence of Expectations' (*Annual Review of Phenomenological Association of Japan*, 34: 15-25, 2018).

Joanna Kitsnik is a Japan Society for the Promotion of Science (JSPS) funded postdoctoral researcher at Sophia University, Tokyo. Her research investigates and compares the function of individual-level ideas about justice and fairness principles and the role they play in the normative assessment of wealth inequality across economically developed societies. She holds a PhD in Sociology (2022) from the Graduate School of Letters, Kyoto University. Her PhD dissertation project was funded by the Ministry of Education, Culture, Sports, Science, and Technology in Japan (MEXT) and explored the factors affecting tolerance of unequal income distribution in post-industrial societies. Her other ongoing research topics are related to the comparative aspects of attitudes towards wealth and income inequality, environmental attitudes, and lifelong learning. Her recent publications include 'Why We Don't Mind the Gap: The Robust Role of Individual Beliefs in Enduring Unequal Income Distribution—Evidence from 34 Countries' (*Comparative Sociology* 22(4): 589-630, 2023) and 'Untangling the Tolerance of Socio-economic Inequality: Comparing Japan, the United States, South Korea, and the People's Republic of China' (*Japanese Journal of Sociology* 31(1): 86-109, 2021).

Gen Nakao is a social/cultural psychologist who currently works as Lecturer at the Faculty of Management, Otemon Gakuin University, in Osaka, Japan. He obtained his BA in Intercultural Education at Sophia University, his MSEd in Mental Health Counselling from Fordham University in New York, and his PhD in Social/Cultural Psychology from Kyoto University. Nakao's research interests center around acculturation, intercultural competence, marginalization, mental health, and quantitative and qualitative research methods. His cross-cultural studies also examine the relationship between popular culture and well-being. Recent publications include 'Struggles and Strategies of Foreign-born Counsellors: A Qualitative Inquiry into Japanese Counsellors' (*Múltiplas faces de pesquisa japonesa internacional: integralização e Convergência*. Campinas: Pontes Editores: 516-533, 2022) and 'Cultivating the Sense-of-the-Other/Sense of Community: An Autoethnographic Case Study of Psychotherapy with High-Risk, Urban Adolescents' (*Current Urban Studies* 9: 196-205, 2021).

Lotte Nawothnig is a researcher at the Wuppertal Institute for Climate, Environment and Energy in the research division 'Energy, Transport, and Climate Policy' since 2021. She holds a M.A. in political science, and a Master of Science in 'Sustainability, Society and the Environment'. In the past, she has lived and worked in Japan as interpreter and language instructor. Her current research encompasses climate protection measures at schools and comparison of energy policies in Germany and Japan.

Christoph Raetzsch is Associate Professor at the Department of Media and Journalism Studies of Aarhus University (Denmark). He works in journalism studies and researches history and theory of media development and practice in journalism, public spheres and urban spaces. Previously, he was a postdoctoral researcher in the project OrganiCity at Aarhus University. His recent research deals with interpretations of smartness to animate civic innovation in cities, the interfaces and infrastructures of publics besides journalism, and the emergent potential of quotidian media practices to shape public discourses.

Carmen Schmidt is Professor of Political Sociology at the Faculty of Culture and Social Sciences at Osnabrück University and the speaker for the Japan Research Center there. She is a member of the International Advisory Board of the *Journal of Japanese Sociology*. She has been President of the German-Japanese Society for Social Sciences (GJSSS) since 2019. She researches and teaches at the Japanese Studies Seminar of the Ruprecht Karls University Heidelberg, the Institute for Political Science at the University of Hildesheim, the Graduate School of Social Sciences at Hitotsubashi University (Tokyo), the Institute of Social Sciences at Tokyo University, and the Faculty for International Studies at Bunkyo University (Chigasaki), Yokohama National University, and Osaka National University, the Institute for Social Science at Chung-Ang University (Seoul), the School of Labor and Human Resources at Renmin University of China (Beijing). Her research foci include smart cities, social transformation, comparative participation, digital modernity, comparative analysis of political systems, electoral and political party systems, politics and society in modern Japan.

Fabian Schunk received his PhD at the Department of Psychology, University of Konstanz. His research focuses on the interplay of emotion regulation, psychological well-being, and social interaction, especially in terms of aggressive behaviour (e.g., bullying), across different cultural contexts. He published research on emotion regulation and cyberbullying in journals such as *Cognition and Emotion* and *Computers in Human Behavior*. He is currently a member of the International Association for Cross-Cultural Psychology (IACCP), German-Japanese Society for Social Sciences (GJSSS), German Psychological Society (DGPs), and International Society for Research on Aggression (ISRA).

Yuya Shibuya is Associate Professor at the Center for Spatial Information Science at The University of Tokyo, Japan. Her interests lie in how the virtual and real worlds interact with one another. She has investigated how democratic participatory structures have changed in the digital era and the impacts on people's behaviour change. She is the author of the book Social Media Communication Data for Recovery:

Detecting Socio-Economic Activities Following a Disaster (Springer, ISBN 978-9811508240).

Lena Tholen studied Environmental Sciences at the Leuphana University of Lüneburg with a focus on energy policy, environmental law and sustainability communication. She joined the Wuppertal Institute for Climate, Environment and Energy in 2008 and works as a Researcher in the Division 'Energy, Transport and Climate Policy'. Lena Tholen is involved in different national and international research projects, mainly focusing energy efficiency policies, low-carbon schools and education for sustainable development.

Gisela Trommsdorff is Professor Emerita for Developmental and Cross-Cultural Psychology at the Department of Psychology, University of Konstanz. She is Research Fellow at the German Socio-Economic Panel, Research Fellow at the International Society for Developmental Psychology, as well as Honorary President of the German Japanese Society of Social Sciences GJSSS). She holds the Federal Cross of Merit, 1st Class, of the Federal Republic of Germany, is a member of the Academy of Sciences, Erfurt, and has received the 'Minister of Foreign Affairs Commendation' (*Gaimu daijin hyōshō*). She is a member of several national and international advisory and editorial committees, and has authored numerous publications on socialization, value change, socioemotional development, and intergenerational relations in cultural contexts, e.g., recently: 'Values, religion, and culture in adolescent development; 'The influence of socio-economic change and culture on intergenerational relations'; 'Cultural psychology, socialization and development in changing contexts'.

Oliver Wagner is co-head of the research unit 'Energy Policy' in the research division 'Energy, Transport and Climate Policy' at the Wuppertal Institute for Climate, Environment and Energy and holds a Master's degree (Diploma) in social sciences. Since 1995, he has been working on various issues related to climate protection and energy conservation. His work focuses on municipal energy saving and climate protection policies as well as environmental and climate protection-related strategy options of municipal enterprises and instruments for increasing energy efficiency. In numerous publications and climate protection concepts, Oliver Wagner has highlighted the importance of the municipal level for the success of the energy transition.

Natalie Wong is a Post-Doctoral Fellow at the Department of Educational Psychology at The Chinese University of Hong Kong, from where she also received her PhD. She has published theoretical and intervention research on cyberbullying and social development in journals such as *Computers in Human Behavior, Personality and Individual Differences,* and the *Journal of Cross-Cultural Psychology.* She is particularly interested in the multi-method approach and the cross-cultural perspective in the research of cyberaggression and social development in the internet era. Her current project involves developing an eye-tracking assessment of social information processing in cyberaggression.

Where Are We Headed?
The Role of Social Science Research
in Working Towards a Sustainable Future

Carola Hommerich
Masato Kimura

The unidimensional focus on economic growth followed by most societies up until now has created a deeply unequal global landscape, puts undeniable strain on our planet and has generated severe risks to our lives and livelihoods. The imminent need for new approaches and solutions to economic, social, and political organization becomes ever more visible, as the existential threat posed by inequality and the climate crisis become tangible all over the world. After decades of carefree affluence, also industrialized nations of the Global North – that have mainly pushed this global development – have seen the rise of new inequalities caused by neoliberal policies created to foster continuous economic growth and start to experience unprecedented extreme weather events. The COVID-19 pandemic has further revealed the fragility of our current system – especially in the way it aggravates the position of the most vulnerable between but also within societies. While posing an opportunity for cooperation, the global interlinkages of our economies and societies have become more complex than ever, creating enormous challenges in steering humankind towards a sustainable future.

That there are 'Limits to Growth' (Meadows et al. 1972) has been known since the publication of the report of the same title commissioned by the Club of Rome half a century ago. Its authors convincingly showed how uncontrolled growth would inevitably collide with Earth's finite resources, leading to future overshoot and collapse of the world as we know it. At the same time, it has become evident that economic growth does not equate well-being for all. Instead, the unequal distribution of economic gains has resulted in huge inequalities in income and wealth across but also within societies (Milanovic 2016, Sachs 2015).

Some claim that only a fundamental transformation of our socioeconomic systems, could effectively mitigate the impact of the crisis we have caused (Stuart 2021: 104). This would mean a shift away from growth-dependent capitalist ideology towards alternative visions of social organization, which subordinate economic goals to social and ecological well-being, as, for example, eco-socialist solutions (Foster 2010, Saito 2017) or approaches focusing on degrowth (Rosa & Henning 2018, Schor & Jorgenson 2019). However, this kind of 'metamorphosis of the world' (Beck 2016) does not seem likely to happen, at least not soon enough. Climate scientists are growing increasingly pessimistic about our ability to limit global warming to 1.5 degrees Celsius above pre-industrial levels and are calling for rapid, deep, and immediate action (IPCC 2022). At the same time, the authors of the World Inequality Report (Chancel et al. 2022) call for governments to take action to reduce the extreme concentration of wealth in the hands of a few Billionaires, after their share of global wealth increased even further during the COVID-19 pandemic.

So, what is to be done? For one, giving up is not the answer. On the contrary, defeatism would likely lead to a worse future outcome than currently predicted, as it would mean business as usual, with further economic growth, resulting in more consumption, more pollution, more inequality, and destruction. While we should not give up, we need to 'stop pretending' (Franzen 2021). It is too late to stop climate change, but we can still try to mitigate the effects as much as possible. As suggested by Stiglitz et al. in 2009, utilizing indicators which go beyond GDP, and which instead focus on the measurement of economic inequality and vulnerability, is part of our journey in moving towards a more sustainable and inclusive way of life.

To give direction in this endeavour, the United Nations General Assembly has instilled 17 sustainable development goals (SDGs) to be reached by 2030, which emphasize the interlinkage of global challenges posed by uncontrolled economic growth, environmental degradation, inequality, and poverty (United Nations 2022). The 2030 Agenda has set globally shared norms, for developing and developed countries alike (Stiglitz et al. 2019: 22). They holistically address the confluence of crises we are facing today, giving us a roadmap to lead us towards a better and more sustainable future for all.

Working towards achieving the goals we have set for ourselves in this way, actors from all backgrounds and levels need to come together. In this endeavour, social scientists are specifically called on to take responsibility not only as researchers, but also as communicators and connectors between different disciplines and actors. Radtke and Renn (2022) plead for topics of sustainability to become an integrative part of any social research (ibid: 313) and encourage social scientists to be more daring in entering cross-disciplinary cooperations. Klinenberg et al. (2020), similarly, urge social scientists to contribute to identifying exist paths from the high-carbon, low-equity social structures that currently organize our global world. Like Eric Olin-Wright's (2010) 'Real Utopias Project', they claim, social scientists need to take a core role in documenting problems and successes, to stay relevant as a discipline, and useful to policy makers who rely on their work (Klinenberg et al. 2020: 662).

The present volume is a collection of papers by social scientists who act in this spirit. It brings together analyses of topics that threaten the sustainability of our social organization and approaches to tackling these problems, all the while focusing on Japan and Germany.

1. Working towards sustainability – comparing Germany and Japan

While the fight for a sustainable future is a global endeavour, the responsibility to push for the necessary changes lies especially with rich industrialized nations in the Global North. The affluent lifestyle and consumer dependent economic system of the latter has caused the crises we are facing today. In this volume, we circle in on two of them, namely Germany and Japan. As third (Japan) and fourth (Germany) largest economies in the world[1], the two nations take on prominent positions in the global order.

As members of the Paris Agreement adopted in 2015[2], both nations declared

---

1 At the time of writing, the International Monetary Fund has projected for Germany to overtake Japan as the third largest economy in 2023 (IMF 2023).

2 https://unfccc.int/sites/default/files/english_paris_agreement.pdf

to swiftly reduce carbon emissions to achieve carbon-neutrality over the next three decades. In October 2020, then Prime Minister Yoshihide Suga declared that Japan would aim to become a carbon-neutral society by 2050[3]. Several months later, in April 2021, Japan announced to raise its previously set goal to reducing emissions to 46% of 2013 levels by 2030. Germany, based on decisions of the European Union and a recent ruling of the German Federal Constitutional Court (2021), also raised its original climate goal, and now aims at a reduction of its greenhouse gas emissions of at least 65% by 2030 compared to 1990 levels, and to achieve carbon neutrality by 2045.

At the same time, both societies are committed to the UN's SDGs and are actively working on implementing policies directed at various sustainability aspects across ministries and at different levels of political authority. The German government has published and regularly updates a 'Sustainable Development Strategy', which is guided by a focus on intergenerational justice, quality of life, social cohesion, and international responsibility[4]. The Japanese government set up a 'SDGs Promotion Headquarter' which is led by the Prime Minister and is attended by all Ministers, with the goal of monitoring and steering the implementation of SDGs across all government bodies[5]. Voluntary self-evaluations carried out by the governments of both nations in 2021 sound promising[6]. Still, there is reasonable doubt whether the proclaimed goals are realistically achievable within the announced time frame. In its report on 'Measuring Distance to the SDG targets', the OECD (2022) once more demonstrates the complexity of the task at hand. While both Germany and Japan, as virtually all OECD countries, have already met most targets related to securing basic needs, challenges remain. Both countries struggle with unequal opportunities for women and minorities, among other problem areas. Overall, both countries are projected to achieve only a small share of the 169 targets underpinning the 17 SDGs. Nevertheless, while large transitions take time, we

---

3 https://www.meti.go.jp/english/policy/energy_environment/global_warming/roadmap/innovation/jctgi.html

4 https://www.bundesregierung.de/breg-en/issues/sustainability/germany-s-sustainable-development-strategy-354566

5 https://www.kantei.go.jp/jp/singi/sdgs/index.html

6 Germany: https://sustainabledevelopment.un.org/memberstates/germany

Japan: https://sustainabledevelopment.un.org/memberstates/japan

do see initiatives of change, a selection of which are presented and analysed in this volume.

2. Structure and purpose of the book

First steps towards this volume were taken at the 16th Meeting of the German-Japanese Society of Social Sciences[7], which was organized by the editors and held in online format in March 2022, focusing on 'Sustainable Societies'. The inspiring presentations and discussions between the participants led to the conviction that we should keep working together on the topic of sustainability. Since then, additional researchers have joined the group, resulting in this edited collection of approaches to various aspects of sustainability in Germany and Japan.

While we are far from covering all aspects of sustainable development stipulated in the UN's SDGs, our volume targets three core areas, which are examined through case studies and survey research from a comparative point of view: 1. Transition to an environmentally friendly society (waste management, education, and environmental attitudes); 2. Sustainable and resilient: regional and urban planning (disaster resilience, smart cities); and 3. Inclusive societies: leave no one behind (welfare, education, and democracy). This volume brings together a wide range of experts from sociology, education, psychology, and urban engineering, with most of the research being interdisciplinary and collaborative in nature, paired with the goal of making concrete policy suggestions.

Transition to an Environmentally Friendly Society

Regina M. Bichler (Chapter 1) starts off this section with a case study of a 'zero-waste' initiative in the town of Kamikatsu, Tokushima Prefecture, Japan, from a sustainability perspective. The town with a population of 1,500 people, which once prospered through forestry, has successfully reduced the amount of household garbage by 80% since 2003, when it first declared its zero-waste policy. This was achieved by implementing 45 different categories of separate

---

7 https://gjsss.org/

garbage collection and thorough recycling. Bichler introduces various systems, start-ups, and projects which all aim to not only reduce garbage, but also to utilize what used to be considered garbage as resources and to promote interaction among residents. She concludes that Kamikatsu succeeded in revitalizing the local economy, while also fostering communications among residents. This makes this case interesting not only in terms of waste disposal, but also as an attempt to revitalize small municipalities after the decline of the traditional industry.

In Chapter 2, Lotte Nawothnig, Oliver Wagner, Sebastian Albert-Seifried, and Lena Tholen turn to the education system, with a discussion of the importance of climate change education in schools. Specifically, they introduce several initiatives from Germany and Japan, which aim at reducing the carbon footprints of schools. The specific focus of the analysis is on a German initiative called 'Schools4Future', which actively involves students in the evaluation and reduction of their schools' carbon footprint. Compared with Japanese projects, specifically the 'eco school program', which was merely directed at reconstruction measures, 'Schools4Future' fosters students' self-efficacy and empowers them to implement changes for climate protection. In conclusion, the authors recommend an implementation of 'Schools4Future' also in Japan as an example of education for sustainable development. This might even pose an opportunity for cross-cultural exchange between German and Japanese students involved, thereby also strengthening an understanding for the importance of global cooperation to achieve climate goals.

In Chapter 3, Carola Hommerich and Joanna Kitsnik compare how environmental attitudes and pro-environmental behaviour have changed in Germany and Japan over the past three decades. Analysing data of the Environment module of the International Social Survey Project (ISSP) spanning from 1993-2020, they find a general upsurge in environmental concern in both countries, and country specific differences by age, in how this translates into willingness to act and actual behaviour. In Japan, it is mainly the over 65-olds, for whom increased concern is also connected to heightened behavioral initiatives. Among Japan's younger age groups, on the other hand, willingness to make sacrifices for the environment is shrinking. This trend is reversed in Germany, where it is specifically the younger age groups who have grown most aware and willing to make changes. Hommerich and Kitsnik conclude that these attitudes to some extent mirror and are mirrored in the sociopolitical approaches to the climate crisis to be found in the two countries.

Sustainable and Resilient: Regional and Urban Planning

Christian Dimmer and Mark Kammerbauer (Chapter 4) lead into this topic with an examination of how urban and regional planning can be the context and instrument to create and foster resilience in post-disaster situations. Revisiting interrelated concepts of planning, sustainability, and resilience, they develop analytical criteria to evaluate the performance of post-disaster urban planning interventions, which they then apply to an analysis of the recovery and reconstruction efforts in Deggendorf, Germany, after the 2013 Danube floods and Onagawa, Japan, after the 2011 Great East Japan Earthquake and tsunami. Their case studies show that adaptation efforts oriented towards environmental risk are dependent on the degree to which residents and communities accept institutionalized urban planning as being in the community's best interest and not being imposed 'from those above'. After pointing out problems with highly bureaucratized mainstream policies, Dimmer and Kammerbauer introduce five theses of how an alternative place governance could bypass institutional and other organizational challenges that stand in the way of creating more resilient and sustainable communities.

Focusing on the smart city as an innovative concept and practical space to achieve sustainability, Andrea Hamm, Yuya Shibuya and Christoph Raetzsch (Chapter 5) examine two different interpretations and practices of the concept in Kashiwa-no-ha, Japan, and Cologne, Germany. Applying smart city scenario analysis, an analytical framework developed by the authors, they show how respective advantages and forms of citizens participations are shaped by their specific geolocational, historical, and economic conditions. While the Japanese smart city prioritises reducing commuting by public transport, improving public health, and providing disaster supplies, the German smart city focuses especially on mobility apps and monitoring, increasing automotive e-mobility, and raising public awareness of sustainability. Their comparative analysis indicates that the concept of the smart city generates diverse actions and involvement, depending on the specific local settings, with more or less citizen participation. Most notably, their findings suggest that efforts to increase resilience may sometimes stand in contradiction to measures aimed at a transition to more sustainable forms of social organization.

Inclusive Society: Leave No One Behind

Masato Kimura (Chapter 6) picks up the first and primary goal of the SDGs, which is aimed at solving the problem of poverty. In his chapter, he describes how the urban poor in Japan have been impacted by the COVID-19 pandemic and its economic damage. Results of his survey of private soup kitchen users show that one quarter of the users had lost their jobs or income and 10% lost their housing due to the pandemic. At the same time, among soup kitchen users overall, the proportion of those who have housing such as apartments has significantly increased compared to before the pandemic. In Japan, several income support systems have been made available to all households or low-income individuals since the beginning of the pandemic. However, the reception of such payments is based on resident registration, which means that specifically many of the needy who have lost their homes remain unable to receive this financial support. The same is true for housing security benefit, vaccinations, PCR tests, etc. Kimura's study reveals that the government's 'stay home' (home healthcare) policy has, in effect, also translated into a 'stay homeless' order for indigent people who are forced to live at a minimum. In this chapter, Kimura reveals the perceptions of the persons concerned as to why public assistance, which is supposed to guarantee a minimum standard of living, does not work well.

With an analysis of cyberbullying, Fabian Schunk, Gisela Trommsdorff, Natalie Wong, and Gen Nakao (Chapter 7) contribute to a different aspect of inclusivity. The UN emphasizes the importance of reducing bullying for attaining the SDGs, as it contributes to the promotion of safe and non-violent learning environments that the SDGs seek to guarantee and to the elimination of physical, sexual, and emotional violence. Schunk et al. present an empirical study of how cyberbullying is perceived in Japan, Germany, and Hong Kong, with focus on how it differs from traditional bullying in frequency and motivation. Among their respondents, they find cyberbullies to be more prevalent among Hong Kong Chinese than in Germany and Japan, while victims of 'traditional' non-cyberbullying were more prevalent among Germans and

Hong Kong Chinese as compared to Japanese. There, cyberbullies reported higher agreement for having perpetrated cyberbullying 'out of fun' rather than out of anger. Based on these findings, the authors emphasize the necessity to incorporate cultural factors behind cyberbullying into the development of culture-sensitive prevention and intervention measures, in order to foster a safe educational environment for all.

Finally, Carmen Schmidt and Defny Holidin (Chapter 8) discuss the impact of changing values in two stages of modernization on understandings of democracy and authoritarianism in Europe and Asia. Traditional Western discourse on democratization has held that, not only the secularization in the first modernity, but post-materialistic values of self-expression in the second modernity would promote democracy by raising educational standards. However, Confucian countries like Japan, with high support for secular-rational values and high-level education, show relatively low support for liberal democratic ideas. Southeast Asian countries such as Indonesia and the Philippines have moved closer to democratic values, having inherited institutional and socio-cultural imprints from their colonial masters, but have a tendency towards an authoritarian understanding of democracy. Against this backdrop of diverse cultural, historical, and religious values, Schmidt and Holidin claim that these different trajectories underscore the importance of pluralistic views of what forms democratic and sustainable societies can take.

We close the volume with some deliberations on how large economies like Japan and Germany can move forward to make impactful changes – both within their own society as well as for the global community.

Lastly, we would like to take the opportunity to insert a personal note. While editing this book, we were saddened to hear of the passing of our mentor Prof. Dr. Dr. h.c. Hans-Joachim Kornadt at the age of 95. He was Professor in Educational Psychology and Educational Science at Saarland University, Germany, and a founding member, President (1989-2006) and Honorary President of the German-Japanese Society for Social Sciences, which organised the conference from which this book has resulted. We dedicate this book to him in gratitude for his many years of contribution to our society and his always kind, continuous support of younger colleagues.

References

Beck, Ulrich (2016): *The Metamorphosis of the World: How Climate Change is Transforming Our Concept of the World*. Cambridge, Oxford: Polity.

Chancel, Lucas/Piketty, Thomas/Saez, Emmanuel/Zucman, Gabriel, et al. (2022): World Inequality Report 2022. World Inequality Lab. wir2022.wid.world, [Accessed 26 September 2022].

Federal Constitutional Court (2021): Constitutional complaints against the Federal Climate Change Act partially successful. Press Release No 32/2021. www.bundesverfassungsgericht.de/SharedDocs/Pressemitteilungen/EN/2021/bvg21-031.html, [Accessed 30 September 2022].

Foster, John Bellamy (2010): Why Ecological Revolution? *Monthly Review* 61(8): 1-18.

Franzen, Jonathan (2021): *What If We Stopped Pretending?* London: Harper Collins.

International Monetary Fund (IMF) (2023): World Economic Outlook: Navigating Global Divergences. Washington, D.C., October. www.imf.org/en/Publications/WEO/Issues/2023/10/10/world-economic-outlook-october-2023, [Accessed 25 October 2023].

IPCC (2022): *Climate Change 2022: Mitigation of Climate Change. Contribution of Working Group III to the Sixth Assessment Report of the Intergovernmental Panel on Climate Change* [P.R. Shukla, J. Skea, R. Slade, A. Al Khourdajie, R. van Diemen, D. McCollum, M. Pathak, S. Some, P. Vyas, R. Fradera, M. Belkacemi, A. Hasija, G. Lisboa, S. Luz, J. Malley, (eds.)]. Cambridge University Press: Cambridge, UK and New York, NY, USA. DOI: 10.1017/9781009157926.

Klinenberg, Eric/Aaros, Malcom/Koslov, Liz (2020): Sociology and The Climate Crisis. *Annual Review of Sociology* 46: 649-469.

Meadows, Donella H./Meadows, Dennis L./Randers, Jergen/Behrens, William W. (1972): *The Limits to Growth: A Report for the Club of Rome's Project on the Predicament of Mankind*, III, New York: Universe Books.

Milanovic, Branko (2016): *Global Inequality. A New Approach for the Age of Globalization*, Cambridge, Massachusetts: The Belknap Press of Harvard University.

OECD (2022): The Short and Winding Road to 2030: Measuring Distance to the SDG Targets, OECD Publishing, Paris. DOI: 10.1787/af4b630d-en.

Olin-Wright, Eric (2010): *Envisioning Real Utopias*. London: Verso.

Radtke, Jörg/Renn, Ortwin (2022): Impulse für eine Soziologie der Nachhaltigkeit. *Soziologie* 51(3): 295-327.

Rosa, Harmut/Henning, Christoph (2018): Good Life Beyond Growth – an Introduction. In: Rosa, Harmut/Henning, Christoph (eds.): *The Good Life Beyond Growth. New Perspectives*, London: Routledge, pp. 1-14.

Sachs, Jeffrey D. (2015): *The Age of Sustainable Development*. New York: Columbia University Press.

Saito, Kohei (2017): *Karl Marx's Ecosocialism. Capitalism, Nature, and the Unfinished Critique of Political Economy*, New York: Monthly Review Press.

Schor, Juliet B./Jorgenson, Andrew K. (2019): Is It Too Late for Growth? *Review of Radical Political Economies* 51(2): 320-329.

Stiglitz, Joseph E./Sen, Amartya,/Fitoussi, Jean-Paul (2009): *Mismeasuring our Lives: Why GDP Doesn't Add Up*, New York: The New Press.

Stiglitz, Joseph E./Fitoussi, Jean-Paul/Durand, Martine (2019): *Measuring What Counts: The Global Movement For Well-Being*, Paris: OECD Publishing.

Stuart, Diana (2021): *What is Environmental Sociology?*, Cambridge, Oxford: Polity.

United Nations (2022): The Sustainable Development Goals Report 2022. unstats.un.org/sdgs/report/2022/The-Sustainable-Development-Goals-Report-2022.pdf, [Accessed 26 September 2022].

Wilkinson, Richard/Pickett, Kate (2009): *The Spirit Level: Why More Equal Societies almost always Do Better*, London: Penguin.

Transition to an Environmentally Friendly Society

Chapter 1

Kamikatsu as a Zero Waste Role-model? Lessons for Future Zero Waste Cities

Regina M. Bichler

1. Introduction

'The ocean doesn't choose its waste' (*taikai ha akuta wo erabazu*) – this Japanese saying from the Edo period (1604–1858) means that you must accept the people around you the way they are (Galef & Hashimoto 2012: 129). At the same time, the metaphor demonstrates that waste from civilization has been discharged into the environment for centuries, a practice that has shaped even Japanese language. It seems all the more true in the 21st century, when the mass of waste in the oceans is expected to exceed the mass of fish by 2050 (Ellen MacArthur Foundation 2017: 12).

While proper waste management might appear as the answer to environmental pollution, it comes with multiple challenges. Burning waste releases high volumes of CO_2,[1] exacerbating climate change. Landfilling consumes space and can lead to the leakage of noxious substances (Müller 2018). Even recycling is no permanent solution, as it requires energy and additional resources, is limited to a few downward cycles for materials like paper and plastics, and has increasingly resulted in a waste stream from the Global North to the Global South, with all of the negative implications for human health and the environment (Gutberlet 2016: 1–2). In summary, waste reduction through emission prevention is the only long-term sustainable solution – especially in cities, where 70% of the global waste is produced

---

1 The incineration of household waste produces a similar volume of CO_2 as the incineration of lignite (cf. Umweltbundesamt 2021).

(Zaman & Lehmann 2013: 123).

Facing these waste issues, the 'zero waste city' that aims for complete recycling and resource recovery (ibid. 2011: 73) appears as a new spark of hope for a general waste reduction and a more sustainable way of life. Framed as an issue of urban sustainability, zero waste cities stand in for the assumption that ecological changes are especially effective at local governance level; a finding that is supported by many case studies (cf. Jaeger-Erben et al. 2017, Mattissek & Müller 2018). Following the lure of 'zero waste', cities and towns around the globe are developing zero waste strategies.

A radical example is the Japanese town Kamikatsu in Tokushima prefecture, the first Japanese town that declared its commitment to zero waste (Zero Waste Academy 2016: 7). Since 2003, by this stringent waste separation, upcycling, and waste reduction during shopping and consumption, the community has managed to decrease their household waste and recycle more than 80%–in comparison to about 20% in the rest of Japan (ibid. 2020b: 35). Its elaborate recycling system is often emphasized in both media coverage and academic literature on zero waste (Fukuoka Shin'ichi 2022; McCoy 2019; Stories 2015; The Japan Times 2017; Zaman & Newman 2021: 9–10), yet hardly any in-depth reports about the relation of local governance measures and individual lifestyle practices for achieving zero waste can be found. However, this topic remains a crucial question for future zero waste cities.

My research contributes to closing this gap by analysing the meaning of zero waste in Kamikatsu and contrasting the municipality's waste management approach with waste reduction contributions through consumption- and waste-related practices in Kamikatsu. I suggest that Kamikatsu's understanding of 'zero waste' is a technocratic fix aiming for a net-zero balance of waste, shaping a local discourse that provides little incentives for waste prevention through lifestyle change.

2. Theoretical framework: Connecting zero waste with social practices

The term 'zero waste' seems to suggest that by pursuing this concept, no waste is produced at all, yet the definition of 'zero waste' by the Zero Waste International Alliance reads differently:

'Zero waste is the conservation of all resources by means of responsible production, consumption, reuse and recovery of products, packaging and materials without burning, and with no discharges to land, water or air that threaten the environment or human health' (Zero Waste International Alliance 2018).

Accordingly, zero waste means to handle waste in a way that it will not exert a negative effect on both humans and their environment, and encompasses mainly a waste management approach. '[R]esponsible production and consumption' is mentioned, but not elaborated, and leaves ample space for interpretation. A typical reading is the connection with 'circular economy', a business principle in which material emissions from both production and consumption are valued as a resource and therefore brought back into the production process (cf. Ghisellini et al. 2016). Practically, this goes hand in hand with a variety of challenges, such as product design, networking between providers and users of a material, technical capabilities, waste management strategies, as well as the consumer's willingness to cooperate (Wilts & Gries 2017: 27). These difficulties might be easiest to overcome at municipal level–which is where the zero waste city comes in. Although there is no fixed definition of a zero waste city, its notion incorporates the zero waste concept, and according to Zaman and Lehmann (2011: 73), this 'includes a 100% recycling of municipal solid waste and a 100% recovery of all resources from waste materials'. They basically suggest a net-zero approach to waste, where all the generated waste is recycled and therefore disappears from the count. However, some zero waste cities, like Kiel in Northern Germany, are setting their focus on reduction of waste emission from households and businesses instead of recycling (Wuppertal Institut für Klima, Umwelt, Energie 2020: 87), showing the diverse strategies that zero waste concepts can comprise.

In the analysis of sustainable consumption, a range of studies has shown that many decisions in daily life are not made actively and consciously, but follow established practices, also in relation to waste (cf. waste-sorting behaviour in Katan & Gram-Hanssen 2021: 4; cf. food waste in Revilla & Salet 2018). The concept of 'social practices' sees daily actions embedded in the context of social conventions and societal norms (cf. Welch & Warde 2015: 88).

With their prominent role in consumption (Shove et al. 2012: 2; cf. Warde 2005), social practices are interrelated to the emission and handling of waste, both within individual households and organised waste management. These links in the waste chain are connected by services and infrastructure, like waste collection and waste processing facilities. Their configurations might encourage or discourage certain practices, as shown for example by the availability of kerbside recyclable collection, which promotes recycling rates, yet does not enforce them (cf. Seyring et al. 2016). The infrastructure provided not only for waste disposal, but also for consumption will affect the associated practices, as they determine where we can buy what and in which condition (old/new, wrapped/unpackaged), and how we can get rid of the leftovers afterwards (in public/at home, sorted/unsorted, bring system/collection system etc.).

3. Research question and methods

The work described in this chapter is part of my dissertation project 'Waste-Society Relations in Zero Waste Cities and their Implications for the Establishment of Sustainable Practices: A Case Study of Munich, Kamikatsu, and Kyoto'. The following case study focuses on the questions how Kamikatsu implemented its zero waste transformation, how the local zero waste concept is understood in theory and performed in practice, and if the outcome is promoting sustainability in Kamikatsu, based on qualitative interviews and participatory observation in May 2022.

In preparation of the fieldwork, academic articles, media coverage, and primary sources published by the Kamikatsu town office and Zero Waste Academy (ZWA)[2] were reviewed to get an overview of Kamikatsu's history, its theoretical understanding of 'zero waste', the local waste management system and its zero waste measures, as well as activities that shape the life in this community. This was paired with an investigation of which services and activities in Kamikatsu's zero waste concept are provided by the municipality, by volunteers, or by households to identify the different local stakeholders and

---

2 The Zero Waste Academy is a NPO in Kamikatsu that was founded in 2005 and organises most of Kamikatsu's anti-waste measures in close collaboration with the town office (Zero Waste Academy 2020b: 41).

the consumption and waste-related practices they engage in. Furthermore, due to frequent interview requests in Kamikatsu from national and international media on this topic, careful preparation was necessary to avoid asking questions that residents are answering routinely.

For explorative fieldwork, empirical qualitative data collection (cf. Przyborski & Wohlrab-Sahr 2019; Yoshida 2020) was applied to capture social life in Kamikatsu as experienced by its residents, and to question the role that waste plays in their daily practices. Due to ongoing travel restrictions during the Covid-19 pandemic, fieldwork had to be considerably shortened from several months to two weeks. Therefore, a rapid ethnography approach modified from Baines and Cunningham (2011) was employed to collect data of sufficient complexity within the limited time given. This multi-method technique included literature, media, and document review, qualitative interviews with residents, participant observation, as well as unstructured observation in Kamikatsu. Data collection was assisted by academically trained locals (Azuma Terumi, Linda Ding, and Kana Watando) who provided both field access and long-term experience of life in Kamikatsu, together with highly valuable input, discussions, and background information for data analysis.

During the two-week stay, data was continuously gathered through participation in local events and activities, interviews with citizens, and an internship at the Waste and Resource Station. Informal conversations during daily interaction and communal activities were used to get an impression of different attitudes, opinions, and life realities of Kamikatsu's inhabitants in relation to their consumption and the waste management system. In this way I aimed to experience life in Kamikatsu and to explore if the impression suggested by media and literature coincides with my observations in the field. Both participant and unstructured observations were – where possible – documented with both photos and field notes. More formal interviews were recorded or directly transcribed during the interview. To encourage my research participants to state their opinions frankly about Kamikatsu's zero waste efforts and to protect their privacy within their community, no names are indicated unless authorized or published already in other media, and I avoid providing descriptions that could reveal their identity.

I am aware of the limitations that are inherent in a short-term qualitative fieldwork approach. I was not able to observe and interview all different demographic groups in Kamikatsu, as the events I was taking part in are not frequented by all age and interest groups alike. As there are especially many elderly women engaged in zero waste and other communal activities in Kamikatsu (Fukuoka Shin'ichi 2022), their views and thoughts might be overrepresented. What is more, the social connections I could establish were influenced by the network of my gatekeepers, which might have led to me moving in a specific 'bubble' within the community. Moreover, despite the co-production approach, knowledge about hidden social relations and implicit meanings cannot be feasibly acquired during a two-week stay. These biases have always been reflected in the process of data collection and analysis, and I consider them acceptable in an explorative study. To attenuate these drawbacks, future fieldwork phases in Kamikatsu are planned to further approximate an accurate picture of life in this community.

4. Case study: The Zero Waste Town Kamikatsu

Kamikatsu town in Tokushima prefecture is a conglomerate of 55 settlements with a population of approximately 1,400 (Kamikatsu town 2022) in a mountainous area covered with forest and rice terraces. While Kamikatsu was still producing timber and citrus fruits by the start of the 1980s, decreasing competitiveness and cold weather led to a collapse of these industries (Haga 2015: 128–129). With these factors pushing especially young people into bigger cities, Kamikatsu has been hit hard by rural exodus and an aging society (Suzuki 2012: 88). Today, more than half of its population is over 65 years old (cf. Kamikatsu town 2022). Since 1986, the collection of decorative leaves for high-class Japanese restaurants mainly in the Kansai region has been established as a new source of income for many people in Kamikatsu, especially elderly women (Suzuki 2012: 90). This unusual enterprise has been the object of several studies (cf. Haga 2015; Ikegami 2010; Suzuki 2012; Tanaka 2020), yet Kamikatsu is probably most famous for its unique waste and recycling system. It is not only Japan's first zero waste town and succeeds in organising its complete waste management as a bring system, but it also integrates waste reduction and reuse measures into various aspects of daily life, which differentiates it from other Japanese municipalities with high recycling rate, like Ōzaki in Kagoshima prefecture or Toyoura in Hokkaido.

Kamikatsu has gone a long way to establish its current zero waste agenda.[3] Due to the lack of both waste collection and an incineration plant, landfilling and open burning were the most common forms of waste disposal in Kamikatsu until 1997. Only organic leftovers were separated and used as fertilizer for the fields. This practice turned into home composting when the purchase of electric composters was subsidized from 1995 onwards. With the official abolishment of backyard burning and prefectural pressure (Zero Waste Academy 2020a: 4), the sorting of several recyclable waste fractions commenced already in 1997 at the Hibigatani Waste and Resource Station (*Hibigatani gomi sutēshon*). In 1998, the waste problem appeared to be resolved after the local installation of two small incinerators, yet they had to be closed again in 2001 due to revised laws for toxic dioxin emissions. This backlash urgently required a holistic solution for Kamikatsu's waste management. The town office tried to partner with other cities and regions for incineration, but this would have meant an explosion of the waste management costs (cf. TEDx talks 2017). Instead, under the lead of Azuma Hitomi (1959–2013), the town office's person in charge for waste management, Kamikatsu's local government decided to develop a comprehensive recycling system that would save one third of the costs in comparison with complete incineration (cf. Stories 2015). Within one month of the incinerators' closure, the first 35 sorting categories were established by contracting various recycling companies in the prefecture, setting up respective collection containers at the Hibigatani Waste and Resource Station, and educating residents about the new separation rules. Since then, waste management in Kamikatsu has been directed at complete recycling of household waste. In 2003, Kamikatsu came up with the first 'Zero Waste Declaration' (*zero ueisuto sengen*) in Japan, stating the goal to stop landfilling and incineration until 2020 (Kamikatsu town 2003). Today 45 waste categories are separated at the Waste and Resource Station of the Zero Waste Center, which was opened in 2020 as a replacement for the Hibigatani site (cf. Kamikatsu Town Hall Planning and Environment Division 2020).

---

3   Unless stated otherwise, the source for Kamikatsu's waste management history in this paragraph is Zero Waste Academy (2016: 7-8).

4.1 Kamikatsu's 'Zero Waste Declaration' and 'Zero Waste Town Plan'

On September 19th, 2003, Kamikatsu's town office issued the following 'Zero Waste Declaration':[4]

'In order to pass on to future generations an environment with clean air and water, and fertile land, Kamikatsu hereby issues the Kamikatsu Zero Waste Declaration, manifesting our firm commitment to reduce waste to zero by 2020.

1. Kamikatsu will strive to foster ecologically conscience [sic] individuals.
2. Kamikatsu shall promote waste recycling and reusable resources to the best of its ability for eliminating waste incineration and landfill by 2020.
3. Residents of Kamikatsu shall join hands with people around the world for ensuring sustainable global environment.' (Zero Waste Academy 2018: 1)

The declaration was approved by the Kamikatsu town assembly on 19th September 2003 (Kamikatsu town 2003). In the preamble following the core declaration, the financial, social, and environmental challenges posed by incineration and landfilling are summarized. It calls for 'policies to prevent the generation of waste at the production and consumption stage' (*seizō ya shōhi dankai ni oite gomi no hassei wo yobō suru seisaku*) and 'the establishment of a social system in which resources circulate' (*shigen ga junkan suru shakai shisutemu no kōchiku*). It further ascribes the responsibility of collection, re-use, and recycling of valuable resources to manufacturers, and the responsibility of creating a legal framework to facilitate this to the state. Moreover, the preamble expects technological progress and a 'new system' (*atarashii shikumi*) of waste economy in this scenario (ibid. 2003).

A 'Zero Waste Action Plan Declaration' (*zero ueisuto kōdō sengen*) follows the preamble, and concrete measures that have been already taken and are in planning are formulated in the 'Zero Waste Town Plan' (*zero ueisuto taun keikaku*) that has been updated in 2015 (cf. Zero Waste Academy 2016). The Zero Waste Town Plan gives important insights into the theoretical concept of

---

4 The declaration has been renewed in 2020 until 2030 (Kamikatsu town 2021), but as the content hasn't changed substantially, the new version will not be discussed separately here.

waste in the eyes of both the town office and the ZWA and thereby the official waste discourse in Kamikatsu:

'The quintessence of zero waste is the elimination of wastefulness, or what is understood as "waste". In Kamikatsu Town, only items that must be incinerated or landfilled are perceived as "waste", and efforts are being made to turn as many of these as possible into resources. Moreover, it is important to reduce the number of items that are recognised as "waste" and destroyed.' (ibid. 2016: 34; translation from Japanese by the author)

This statement reveals a pivotal insight into the logic of Kamikatsu's waste management system: as 'waste' is only what cannot be recycled, everything that can be recycled is no waste, but a resource. Consequently, according to this assumption, if residents of Kamikatsu buy a single banana wrapped in plastic packaging (which is not an uncommon sight in Japan), they are not producing any waste, as the packaging can be recycled, and the peel composted. In summary, with this definition of waste, 'zero waste' equates to 100% reuse and recycling–and although the example of the banana might appear paradoxical, it coincides with both the aforementioned zero waste definition of the Zero Waste International Alliance, and zero waste understanding in academic literature (cf. Zaman & Lehmann 2011: 73).

This also sheds new light on the calls for producer responsibility and the emphasis of materiality and technology: if eliminating waste is only a question of recycling, then it should be possible to achieve it with a sophisticated technological fix that can be implemented top-down, relying on upcoming innovations that are supposed to be both beneficial to the economy and the environment. At the same time, with this approach, personal responsibility for one's waste is disconnected from individual lifestyle and redirected to the compliance with separation practices stipulated by industry and administration. This stands in stark contrast with the Western popular discourse on zero waste, which often emphasizes bottom-up initiatives and individual consumption decisions as the key to a waste- and especially plastic-free life, medially represented by figureheads like Bea Johnson (cf. Müller & Schönbauer 2020: 417).

In the following, I examine how this understanding of waste is translated in

Kamikatsu into measures along the waste hierarchy, whether its residents share this understanding, and how different concepts of waste convert into consumption- and waste-related practices in daily life in Kamikatsu.

4.2 Avoid and reduce

Kamikatsu offers various waste reduction measures for both public and private consumption. The ZWA has established a zero waste-label certification system for businesses in Kamikatsu (cf. Kamikatsu Town Hall Planning and Environment Division 2020), and provides rental tableware for events (Zero Waste Academy 2018: 6). Families are supported with free cloth diapers and subsidies for organic waste composters by the town (Zero Waste Academy 2020b: 40, 2020b: 7), and visitors can stay at the Zero Waste Hotel WHY. Furthermore, some residents make efforts to reduce waste from consumption, or to avoid materials that will end up as residual waste, for example by using bulk sale (*hakariuri*) options in Kamikatsu and bringing their own bag, which is rewarded with a point card system (Chiritsumo card, cf. Zero Waste Academy 2020b: 31). Research participants reported both personal motivation for waste reduction for environmental reasons, and a reduction of their labour in waste cleaning and sorting through this practice.

There is also a farmers' market that sells locally produced groceries and gifts, which would provide an easy opportunity to reduce packaging and plastic waste. However, most products – even fruits and vegetables – are packaged in plastic wrapping (**Figure 1**) such as in standard Japanese supermarkets and other shops in Kamikatsu. Upon inquiry, I found an interest in retaining the plastic packaging both from the vendor's and buyer's side. The wrapping and label were said to help keeping track of the individual sales of each farmer, for products from several local suppliers are offered in the same space, and farmers decide the packaging size and price by themselves. A farmer confirmed that the market requests pre-packaging for sale, and that she could not choose to sell her products loosely. In addition, according to several research participants, even when buying groceries directly from the producer, consumers expect a proper wrapping and a bag, which provide shopping convenience and label the goods as products of Kamikatsu, making them suitable gifts especially for people outside the area. The centuries-old Japanese convention of giving local products as souvenirs called *omiyage* when coming back from a trip, and giving

Figure 1: Locally produced vegetables wrapped in plastic packaging at the farmers' market in Kamikatsu. (Source: Regina M. Bichler, 2022)

especially groceries as gifts on a variety of formal and informal occasions is still an important part of social interactions all over Japan (cf. Cwiertka 2016: 91). This custom seems to exert a strong influence on consumption practices in Kamikatsu that are not questioned against the background of zero waste and waste reduction measures.

4.3 Reuse

There are two main institutions for reuse activities in Kamikatsu, the Kurukuru ('circular') shop (*kurukuru shoppu*), and the Kurukuru craft center (*kurukuru kōbō*). The Kurukuru shop (**Figure 2**) has been established in 2006 by the ZWA and is a free second-hand shop located in the Zero Waste Center. The BIG EYE COMPANY, a waste-conscious start-up from Kamikatsu, has taken over its monitoring in 2020. The shop encourages people not to discard unwanted items, but to pass them on to someone else (Zero Waste Academy 2020b: 6). Residents of Kamikatsu can bring unwanted objects to the Kurukuru shop, and anyone can take them home for free. It has a turnover rate of several tons per year (Zero Waste Academy 2016: 16, 2018: 5). Furthermore, there is a bulletin board where citizens can also state that they offer items or are looking

Figure 2: Interior of the Kurukuru shop. The open door allows a glimpse at the outer area. (Source: Kana Watando, 2022)

for specific articles, either for sale, giveaway, or lending/borrowing (Zero Waste Academy 2020b: 6).

The Kurukuru craft center has been founded in 2007 by the ZWA and is now managed by Hidamari, a local institution to prevent the elderly's need for nursing (*kaigo yobō seikatsu sentā Hidamari*) . It sells clothing, accessories, and gifts that are handcrafted by local women through upcycling of textiles and fabrics like the carp-shaped flags (*koi nobori*) displayed on children's day in Japan (ibid. 2020a: 16).

According to several of my research participants and my own observations, although locals are often donating items, it is rather tourists that are using the take-home options of the Kurukuru shop for consumption. In contrast, I have noticed many residents using upcycled articles from the craft center in daily life. These findings suggest that the reuse-infrastructure has successfully translated into zero waste-oriented practices among the community.

4.4 Recycle

Recycling is the linchpin of Kamikatsu's waste management strategy and was already established on a smaller scale before the zero waste declaration (ibid. 2016: 7–8). Today's 45 waste separation categories are an attempt to fully exhaust the technical possibilities of recycling. Therefore, the town office actively searched for and contacted recycling companies, inquiring about options to make use of items and materials that had ended up as residual waste before (cf. ibid. 2020a: 7; interview material). Sometimes the initiative for new categories also came from residents, the ZWA, or staff at the Waste and Resource Station, and the number might still increase in the future (cf. ibid. 2020a: 12; 17; interview material).

Disposal at the Waste and Resource Station requires a designated pre-treatment in the household, which is described in a guidebook distributed to all households (cf. Zero Waste Academy 2020b). Waste–for example, plastic food packaging–should be freed from leftovers, disassembled into its separate material components, washed to remove any impurities, dried, and is often bundled and pre-sorted into one of many categories. Depending on the material, there can also be variations from this procedure. Once enough waste has accumulated in their homes, citizens bring it to the Waste and Resource Station, where they sort it into 45 categories (metals, paper, plastics, glass, wood, cloth, hazardous waste, bulk waste, waste for burning, waste for landfilling, waste subject to charges, and respective subcategories). Each category is labeled with a sign that displays sample items for disposal, where the waste will go for recycling, what products will be made of the recyclate, and how much the disposals per kg/t costs or yields for Kamikatsu (**Figure 3**).

There are two main reasons why such an effortful procedure is considered necessary. First, the recycling companies that receive the respective waste want their material as clean as possible and free of impurities. Contaminated material would increase the recycling costs and thereby the costs for Kamikatsu, respectively. Second, bringing clean and dry waste ensures that there is neither smell, nor insects, or mould spreading at the Waste and Resource Station, as each waste fraction is only picked up by a recycling company when the storage capacity approaches its limit, which occurs usually once every few months.

The staff at the Waste and Resource Station stated that most households in Kamikatsu have adopted the requested waste treatment practices, and although residents have become used to these practices, they still see them as a source of effort. When inquiring about waste handling and separation, I often encountered the term 'annoying' (*'mendōkusai'*; interview material) as evaluation of these tasks, and how 'convenient' (*'benri'*; interview material) the open burning of the

Figure 3: Miscellaneous sorting categories (paper, bottles, metals, caps, batteries, etc.) at the Waste and Resource Station in Kamikatsu. (Source: Regina M. Bichler, 2022)

past had been. With the staff at the Waste and Resource Station both assisting and controlling the waste for cleanliness and correct sorting, it seems difficult for residents to escape the strict requirements of waste pre-treatment. However, during my internship at the Waste and Resource Station, I also witnessed people bringing unwashed and unsorted plastic waste to have it sorted by the staff (in that case, me). There are neither fines nor other forms of penalty if the waste is not in the requested condition, but in general the staff's support and supervision – in combination with the public visibility of sorting – seems to generate the desired effect of compliance, as hinted by the rising recycling rate after their employment in 2010 (ibid. 2020a: 21).

There are also other incentives to participate in the recycling system than avoiding social pressure. People often mentioned the visually unpleasant sight of the previous landfills, and the troublesome smoke and smell from open incineration, which could be abolished through recycling. Research participants also reported that coming to the Zero Waste Center had positive side effects such as meeting friends that are living in a different settlement of Kamikatsu, having a look into the Kurukuru shop, or collecting points and receiving bonuses with the Chiritsumo card. Furthermore, during my conversations with citizens, I found some are feeling that by performing the separation practices, they are reducing the burden for local health and environment through resource recovery, or are contributing actively to the smooth functioning of the town's waste management and its zero waste agenda.

5. Kamikatsu's zero waste strategy between theory and practice

The comparison of Kamikatsu's primary literature and the situation encountered during fieldwork revealed less a discrepancy between theory and practice, but more between the Western lifestyle-based zero waste discourse, and Kamikatsu's municipal top-down approach focused on waste management. The waste 'reduction' is not so much achieved by reducing waste emission, but by removing the label of 'waste' from recyclables in public perception. One research participant eloquently articulated this sentiment as 'mixed waste is rubbish, but separated waste is a resource' ('*mazeta gomi ha gomi, bunbetsu shita gomi ha shigen*'; interview material). This strongly reminds of Mary Douglas' famous concept of waste and dirt as a 'matter out of place' (Douglas 1966/2013: 41) – and in Kamikatsu, this place is the correct bin at the Waste and Resource Station.

Although the cleaning and sorting of their household waste is perceived as burdensome by many residents in Kamikatsu, associated practices might actually be not more challenging than in other municipalities. Since the 'waste management and public cleansing law' (*haikibutsu shori oyobi seisō ni kansuru hōritsu*) took effect in 1970, Japanese towns and cities have the responsibility for their waste management (Zero Waste Academy 2020a: 4) and therefore can decide the sorting categories, collection schedules, etc. While some municipalities only distinguish between burnable waste (*moeru gomi/ kanen gomi*) and unburnable waste (*moenai gomi/funen gomi*), others offer several separation categories like plastics, paper, glass, and metal, which are collected by either the municipal waste management or private recycling companies. Cleaning, drying, and bundling recyclables is a common request in Japanese cities. Incorrect sorting, insufficient cleaning, taking out waste at the wrong date or time, or using the wrong rubbish bag may result in non-collection of one's waste – a shameful experience, especially in small and well-connected neighbourhoods. In contrast to the strict schedule for most kerbside collection systems, which poses both physical and mental labour to citizens (Tompkins 2019: 81; 98), Kamikatsu residents can bring their waste almost any day of the year (Zero Waste Academy 2020b: 44), without having to store it at home for weeks. Personally, I experienced the sorting of (my and other) waste at the Waste and Resource Station as less time and effort demanding than the pre-treatment in the kitchen, which I also have to do at my home in Kyoto.

Nonetheless, recycling delays rather than avoids final disposal (Geyer et al. 2017: 2). After only a few (down-)cycles, the 'circularity' of materials like paper or plastic ends (Remondis Entsorgung 2022), describing a spiral movement instead of a circle. Yet this problem is neither addressed in Kamikatsu's zero waste literature, nor in the discourse I have encountered on-site. Instead, the 'busy-ness' of recycling practices described by MacBride as a 'fulfilling sense of work and achievement that often brings positive side effects but fails to reach the central effect' (2011: 5–6) can easily be found: engaging in laborious recycling and the various zero waste activities might be understood as an act of political participation (cf. Hawkins 2013: 79–80), environmental activity (Katan & Gram-Hanssen 2021: 4), or an adaptation to community rules and social pressure. This perception is undisturbed in Kamikatsu by the lack of a discussion of the limits of recycling, and reinforced by policy keywords like 'circular society' (*junkangata shakai*, cf. Kamikatsu town 2003; MOE 2008) suggesting that the material flow generated by individual recycling efforts were actually circular. However, considering that packaging comprises around two thirds of Japanese household waste volume, with half of this being plastic wrapping (MOE 2022), the recycling-oriented approach obscures the need for a large-scale change in production, retail, and consumption practices. Although several research participants reported their concern that recycling is stressed too much, and reuse and waste prevention too little in Kamikatsu, it appears this is not a common mindset among the majority of citizens. Rather, most citizens seem to support the idea of Kamikatsu's waste recycling in general, and seem to prefer it over the former open burning. This is seconded by the fact that in Kamikatsu's mayor election in 2021, Nitta Katsunori, the candidate who emphasized the plan to abolish the separation system in his campaign, lost the vote (Senkyo Dotto Comu 2021).

Moreover, the propagation of waste as a resource in a sustainable social and economic system strips it of its critical potential (Doeland 2019: 5; cf.

Valenzuela & Böhm 2017) and provides all the more incentives to consume without limit and second thought (cf. Catlin & Wang 2013). Yet the fixation on recycling and circularity instead of waste emission reduction is no unique feature of Kamikatsu's local governance, but a linchpin in Japanese national waste and environmental policy (cf. Brecher 2000: 21–26; Ohnishi et al. 2016: 96). Already in 2000, even before Kamikatsu's Zero Waste declaration, Japan's national government formulated the 'Basic Law for the Establishment of a Recycling-based Society' (*junkangata shakai keiseisuishin kihonhō*, Environment Agency Japan 2000) and thereby set its policy focus on recycling instead of waste reduction. Considering the available subsidies and waste management guidelines (Zero Waste Academy 2020a: 3–5), the national recycling focus probably shaped Kamikatsu's approach substantially. 20 years later, even though there are small waste reduction efforts like compulsory fees for plastic bags in Japan since July 2020 (The Japan Times 2022), the overall course hasn't changed (cf. MOE 2021).

Even in Kamikatsu, which stands out against other zero waste and recycling towns for its reuse and reduction measures like the Kurukuru shop, hardly any large-scale efforts to decrease the emission of household waste from consumption can be found. Apart from their lack of influence on industrial packaging and retail, I heard one possible reason from both local farmers and entrepreneurs: they complained that their efforts to offer environmentally friendly or reduced packaging would lead to higher costs than their competitors have–a classical problem of externalization of environmental costs in economics (cf. Rice 2007). But apart from capitalistic principles, functions of packaging like hygiene and safety perception (Hawkins 2013: 69) also play a substantial role in its proliferation, as the Covid-19 pandemic has illustrated (Kaufman 2020; Süßbauer et al. 2022). In addition, and maybe less obvious, cultural aspects influence consumption-related practices and their waste emission: in Kamikatsu's case, not only shopping convenience, but also the extensive Japanese gift (*omiyage*) culture appears to be a major factor contributing to the rejection of environmentally friendly or reduced packaging by both local and visiting customers. How difficult it is to change a cultural practice even on a local scale, is exemplified by the fact that already 30 years ago, Hendry (1993: 24) reported about the domestic critique of the wasteful practice of *omiyage* wrapping. Both research participants and literature (cf.

Budgen 2021; Daniels 2009; Hendry 1993) agreed that wrapping and packaging are too deeply rooted in the Japanese (service) culture to be easily abolished– even in a zero waste town like Kamikatsu.

On the contrary, in the German public anti-waste discourse, plastic wrapping of groceries is seen as one of the main culprits of high waste load in households (cf. Verbraucherzentrale Hamburg 2019), and has therefore been recently declining in supermarkets, while France has even introduced a ban since 1st January 2022 (BBC 2021). In Kamikatsu, I have mainly witnessed shopping and consumption practices independent of zero waste and environmental considerations, and my informants confirmed that this was the case for the majority of the local population. However, it is difficult to assess if this is rather caused by a lack of large-scale infrastructure for waste-conscious consumption, or if establishing this infrastructure is difficult because technical and cultural functions of packaging outweigh waste considerations.

In any case, environmentally motivated individuals still practice waste prevention during shopping and daily activities to not only enhance the recycling rate in Kamikatsu, but also to decrease their personal waste emission rate independent of recyclability. In my interviews, I found that residents focusing on environmental aspects were often informed about and identified with the Western popular zero waste discourse that stresses personal emission reduction over recycling. In addition, their views on sustainability and zero waste differed from the official recycling-oriented discourse in Kamikatsu, which they in some cases criticised as insufficient and ineffective. Simultaneously, others try to evade the effort of the requested waste disposal procedures and only comply to a minimal extent. This underscores the observation that Kamikatsu is not a homogenous community, but a place that hosts a variety of individual people, practices, and opinions on zero waste, which I am planning to further examine during my next fieldwork phase in Kamikatsu.

6. Conclusion

Kamikatsu is a unique zero waste town with a meticulous recycling system that has attracted the interest of both researchers and media worldwide. Although its 45 sorting categories for waste are not easily transferable (and maybe not even desirable) for other zero waste cities-to-be, there are important lessons to be learned from this small community.

The understanding of 'zero waste' is variable and must be clarified for each city individually, as this will be a prerequisite for shaping the public discourse and setting up respective measures. In Kamikatsu, 'zero' waste is understood as net-zero, following a technocratic waste management concept of diversion from incineration and landfill through recycling, but is not necessarily aiming at the reduction of individual waste emissions. The institutionalization of anti-waste measures and the setup of recycling infrastructure are meant to elicit designated behaviour in consumption and disposal, yet citizens are developing their own, sometimes deviating practices. The residents voluntarily committing themselves to waste reduction appear to be familiar with the Western lifestyle-based zero waste discourse.

Furthermore, not only technological challenges, national policy guidelines, and lack of influence on retail processes are limiting the scope of Kamikatsu's zero waste measures, but also cultural and social factors, like the example of *omiyage* detailed above. This underlines that even in a zero waste town, citizens can hardly be forced to a sustainable lifestyle, and a sole waste management approach is not sufficient for large-scale reduction of waste emissions. Local customs and needs should be identified and integrated into zero waste strategies to promote active engagement of citizens instead of mere compliance.

Therefore, also in Kamikatsu, the question remains regarding what it takes to raise awareness about the limits of recycling and transform current sorting-focused practices into practices that reduce the production of waste in the first place. Moreover, fighting waste is usually not the only challenge communities have to face, and this will certainly influence the sense of urgency and commitment that is shown towards waste-related measures. Thus, the interplay of environmental and social sustainability could provide an interesting subject for follow-up research.

Even if the zero waste measures in Kamikatsu might just be a drop in the ocean of global waste, its case shows both the power of local governance, and the importance to not only provide technologies and infrastructures, but also to consider local norms, traditions, and lifestyles in the zero waste transformation. Without addressing people's daily practices, zero waste will remain a mere policy instead of turning into a path to a sustainable future.

References

Baines, Donna/Cunningham, Ian (2011): Using comparative perspective rapid ethnography in international case studies: Strengths and challenges. In: *Qualitative Social Work* 12 (1): 73–88. DOI: 10.1177/1473325011419053.

BBC (2021): French ban on plastic packaging for fruit and vegetables begins. www.bbc.com/news/world-europe-59843697, [Accessed 30 June 2022].

Brecher, Puck (2000): *An investigation of Japan's relationship to nature and environment.* Lewiston, NY: Edwin Mellen Press.

Budgen, Mara (2021): Can Japan embrace an alternative approach to plastic? In: *The Japan Times.* 21 February. www.japantimes.co.jp/life/2021/02/21/environment/japan-plastic-alternatives/, [Accessed 30 May 2022].

Catlin, Jesse R./Wang, Yitong (2013): Recycling gone bad: When the option to recycle increases resource consumption. In: *Journal of Consumer Psychology* 23 (1): 122–127.

Cwiertka, Katarzyna (2016): Japanese Packaging: From Straw to Plastic. In: Cwiertka, Katarzyna/Machotka, Ewa (eds.): *Too pretty to throw away: packaging design from Japan.* Krakow: Museum of Japanese Art and Technology Press, 74–101.

Daniels, Inge (2009): Seasonal and commercial rhythms of domestic consumption: A Japanese case study. In: Shove, Elizabeth/Trentmann, Frank/Wilk, Richard R. (eds.): *Time, consumption and everyday life: Practice, materiality and culture.* Oxford, New York: Berg, 171–187.

Doeland, Lisa (2019): At home in an unhomely world: On living with waste. In: *Detritus* (6): 4–10. DOI: 10.31025/2611-4135/2019.13820.

Douglas, Mary (1966/2013): *Purity and danger: An analysis of concepts of pollution and taboo.* Hoboken: Taylor and Francis.

Ellen MacArthur Foundation (2017): The new plastics economy: Rethinking the future of plastics. www.emf.thirdlight.com/link/faarmdpz93ds-5vmvdf/@/preview/1?o, [Accessed 29 May 2022].

Environment Agency Japan (2000): The basic law for the establishment of a recycling-based society (junkangata shakai keisei suishin kihonhō). elaws.e-gov.go.jp/document?lawid=412AC0000000110, [Accessed 6 June 2022].

Fukuoka Shin'ichi (2022): Fukuoka Shin'ichi afoot in Kamikatsu (Fukuoka Shin'ichi ga aruku Kamikatsu). In: *The Asahi Shimbun.* January 2022, 13.

Galef, David/Hashimoto, Jun (2012): *Japanese proverbs: Wit and wisdom.* Kawasaki: Tuttle Publishing.

Geyer, Roland/Jambeck, Jenna R./Law, Kara L. (2017): Production, use, and fate of all plastics ever made. In: *Science advances* 3 (7): 1–6. DOI: 10.1126/sciadv.1700782.

Ghisellini, Patrizia/Cialani, Catia/Ulgiati, Sergio (2016): A review on circular economy: The expected transition to a balanced interplay of environmental and economic systems. In: *Journal of Cleaner Production* 114: 11–32. DOI: 10.1016/j.jclepro.2015.09.007.

Gutberlet, Jutta (2016): *Urban recycling cooperatives: Building resilient communities.* London, New York: Routledge Taylor & Francis Group.

Haga, Kazue (2015): Innovation and entrepreneurship in aging societies: Theorical reflection and a case study from Kamikatsu, Japan. In: *Journal of Innovation Economics & Management* 18 (3): 119–141. DOI: 10.3917/jie.018.0119.

Hawkins, Gay (2013): The performativity of food packaging: Market devices, waste crisis and recycling. In: *The Sociological Review* 69 (S2): 66–83. DOI: 10.1111/1467-954X.12038.

Hendry, Joy (1993): *Wrapping culture: Politeness, presentation, and power in Japan and other societies.* Oxford: Clarendon Press.

Ikegami, Jun (2010): The rural sustainability and creative cluster in Japan: With conceptual analysis on cultural capital. In: *Nōson keikaku gakkaishi* 29 (1): 12–20.

Jaeger-Erben, Melanie/Rückert-John, Jana/Schäfer, Martina (2017): *Social innovations for sustainable consumption (Soziale Innovationen für nachhaltigen Konsum).* Wiesbaden: Springer Fachmedien Wiesbaden.

Kamikatsu town (2003): Zero waste declaration (zero ueisuto sengen). www.kamikatsu.jp/zerowaste/sengen.html, [Accessed 20 June 2022].

Kamikatsu town (2021): Zero waste declaration for accomplishment until 2030 (zero ueisto sengen 2030 nen tassei ni mukete). www.kamikatsu.jp/docs/2021012600017/, [Accessed 22 June 2022].

Kamikatsu town (2022): Population state, basic resident register (jinkō jōtai, jūmin kihon daichō). www.kamikatsu.jp/docs/2011012800173/, [Accessed 7 June 2022].

Kamikatsu Town Hall Planning and Environment Division (2020): Zero waste town Kamikatsu. www.zwtk.jp/, [Accessed 20 September 2021].

Katan, Lina/Gram-Hanssen, Kirsten (2021): 'Surely I would have preferred to clear it away in the right manner': When social norms interfere with the practice of waste sorting: A case study. In: *Cleaner and Responsible Consumption* 3: 1–9. DOI: 10.1016/j.clrc.2021.100036.

Kaufman, Leslie (2020): Plastics had been falling out of favor. Then came the coronavirus. In: The Japan Times. 19 March. www.japantimes.co.jp/news/2020/03/19/world/science-health-world/plastic-coronavirus/, [Accessed 06 June 2022].

MacBride, Samantha (2011): *Recycling reconsidered: The present failure and future promise of environmental action in the United States.* Cambridge: MIT Press.

Mattissek, Annika/Müller, Simone M. (2018): Green City: Explorations and visions of urban sustainability. www.environmentandsociety.org/sites/default/files/2018_i1_final.pdf, [Accessed 22 June 2022].

McCoy, Terrence (2019): In a world drowning in trash, these cities have slashed waste by 80 percent. In: The Washington Post. 13 February. go.gale.com/ps/i.do?p=ITOF&u=lmum&id =GALE|A573949907&v=2.1&it=r&sid=bookmark-ITOF&asid=b9f09102, [Accessed 07 June 2022].

MOE (Ministry of the Environment of Japan) (2008): Towards the new challenge of a circular society: 3R (reduce, reuse, recycle). www.env.go.jp/recycle/circul/keikaku/pamph.pdf, [Accessed 23 June 2022].

MOE (Ministry of the Environment of Japan) (2021): 2021 white paper about environment, circular society, and biodiversity (reiwa 3 nenban kankyō, junkangata shakai, seibutsutayōsei hakusho). www.env.go.jp/policy/hakusyo/r03/pdf.html, [Accessed 24 June 2022].

MOE (Ministry of the Environment of Japan) (2022): Overview over the study on the situation of use and emission of containers and packaging waste in fiscal year 2021 (yōkihōsō haikibutsu no shiyō, haishutsu jittai kensa no gainen reiwa 3 nendo). www.env.go.jp/recycle/yoki/c_2_research/research_R03.html, [Accessed 6 June 2022].

Müller, Ruth/Schönbauer, Sarah (2020): Zero Waste–Zero Justice? In: *Engaging science, technology, and society* (6): 416–420. DOI: 10.17351/ests2020.649.

Müller, Simone M. (2018): The Life of Waste. www.rccve.ub.uni-muenchen.de/rccve/article/view/34/41, [Accessed 21 August 2021].

Ohnishi, Satoshi/Fujii, Minoru/Fujita, Tsuyoshi/Matsumoto, Toru/Dong, Liang/Akiyama, Hiroyuki/Dong, Huijuan (2016): Comparative analysis of recycling industry development in Japan following the Eco-Town program for eco-industrial development. In: *Journal of Cleaner Production* 114: 95–102. DOI: 10.1016/j.jclepro.2015.04.088.

Przyborski, Aglaja/Wohlrab-Sahr, Monika (2019): Research designs for qualitative social research (Forschungsdesigns für die qualitative Sozialforschung). In: Baur, Nina/Blasius, Jörg (eds.): *Handbuch Methoden der empirischen Sozialforschung*: Wiesbaden: Springer VS, 105–123.

Remondis Entsorgung (2022): Website. www.remondis-entsorgung.de, [Accessed 25 January 2022].

Revilla, Beatriz P./Salet, Willem (2018): The social meaning and function of household food rituals in preventing food waste. In: *Journal of Cleaner Production* 198: 320–332. DOI: 10.1016/j.jclepro.2018.06.038.

Rice, James (2007): Ecological unequal exchange: International trade and uneven utilization of environmental space in the world system. In: *Social forces* 3 (85): 1369–1392. DOI: 10.1177/0020715207072159.

Senkyo Dotto Comu (2021): Kamikatsu's mayor election vote of 11.04.2021 (Kamikatsu-chō chōsenkyo 2021 nen 4 gatsu 11 nichi tōhyō). go2senkyo.com/local/senkyo/20791, [Accessed 7 September 2022].

Seyring, Nicole/Dollhofer, Marie/Weißenbacher, Jakob/Bakas, Ioannis/McKinnon, David (2016): Assessment of collection schemes for packaging and other recyclable waste in European Union-28 Member States and capital cities. In: *Waste management & research the journal of the International Solid Wastes and Public Cleansing Association*, ISWA 34 (9): 947–956. DOI: 10.1177/0734242X16650516.

Shove, Elizabeth/Pantzar, Mika/Watson, Matt (2012): *The dynamics of social practice: Everyday life and how it changes*. London: SAGE Publications.

Stories (2015): How this town produces no trash. www.youtube.com/watch?v=eym10GGidQU, [Accessed 30 June 2022].

Süßbauer, Elisabeth/Wilts, Henning/Otto, Sarah J./Schinkel, Jennifer/Wenzel, Klara/Dehning, Rabea-Lorina/Caspers, Justus (2022): Way out of the one-way? Effects of the COVID-19 pandemic on the generation of waste from packaging in Germany. In: *NachhaltigkeitsManagementForum*. DOI: 10.1007/s00550-022-00525-z.

Suzuki, Nanami (2012): Creating a community of resilience: New meanings of technologies for greater well-being in a depopulated town. In: *Anthropology & Aging Quarterly* 2012 (33): 87–96.

Tanaka, Kensaku (2020): A study of the mobility of the elderly women in Kamikatsu-town, a mountainous area in Japan. In: *Geographical Sciences* 75 (1): 1–18.

TEDx talks (2017): Zero Waste–A way to enrich your life & the society: Akira Sakano, TEDxAPU. www.youtube.com/watch?v=pgRnAsK18es, [Accessed 30 June 2022].

The Japan Times (2017): Tokushima town becomes global draw with zero-waste strategy. In: The Japan Times. 23 February. www.japantimes.co.jp/news/2017/02/23/national/ tokushima-town-becomes-global-draw-zero-waste-strategy/, [Accessed 7 June 2022].

The Japan Times (2022): Plastic bags provided at Japanese stores halved due to fees. In: The Japan Times. 27 March. www.japantimes.co.jp/news/2022/03/27/national/plastic-waste-falls/, [Accessed 6 June 2022].

Tompkins, Rebecca (2019): *The waste of society as seen through women's eyes: Waste, gender, and national belonging in Japan*. Dissertation, Leiden University. Leiden.

Umweltbundesamt (2021): List of CO_2 emission factors 1990-2019 (CO_2-Emissionsfaktorenliste 1990-2019). www.umweltbundesamt.de/themen/klima-energie/treibhausgas-emissionen, [Accessed 19 August 2020].

Valenzuela, Francisco/Böhm, Steffen (2017): Against wasted politics: A critique of the circular economy. In: *ephemera* 17 (1): 23–60.

Verbraucherzentrale Hamburg (2019): Fruits and vegetables come with plastic flood (Plastikflut bei Obst und Gemüse). www.vzhh.de/themen/umwelt-nachhaltigkeit/muell-verpackungen/plastikflut-bei-obst-gemuese, [Accessed 30 June 2022].

Warde, Alan (2005): Consumption and theories of practice. In: *Journal of Consumer Culture* 5 (2): 131–153. DOI: 10.1177/1469540505053090.

Welch, Daniel/Warde, Alan (2015): Theories of practice and sustainable consumption. In: Reisch, Lucia A./Thøgersen, John (eds.): *Handbook of research on sustainable consumption*: Cheltenham, UK, Northampton, MA, USA: Edward Elgar Publishing, 84–100.

Wilts, Henning/Gries, Nadja von (2017): The hard way to circular economy (Der schwere Weg zur Kreislaufwirtschaft). In: *GWP – Gesellschaft. Wirtschaft. Politik* 66 (1): 23–28. DOI: 10.3224/gwp.v66i1.02.

Wuppertal Institut für Klima, Umwelt, Energie (2020): Zero waste concept. Preventing waste and saving resources collectively (Zero Waste-Konzept. Gemeinsam Abfälle vermeiden und Ressourcen schonen). www.kiel.de/de/umwelt_verkehr/zerowaste/zerowaste_kiel_konzept.pdf, [Accessed 19 August 2021].

Yoshida, Akiko (2020): How to collect data: An introduction to qualitative social science methods. In: Kottmann, Nora/Reiher, Cornelia (eds.): *Studying Japan: Handbook of Research Designs, Fieldwork and Methods*. Baden-Baden: Nomos Verlagsgesellschaft mbH & Co. KG, 131–141.

Zaman, Atiq U./Lehmann, Steffen (2011): Challenges and opportunities in transforming a city into a 'zero waste city'. In: *Challenges* 2 (4): 73–93. DOI: 10.3390/challe2040073.

Zaman, Atiq U./Lehmann, Steffen (2013): The zero waste index: A performance measurement tool for waste management systems in a 'zero waste city'. In: *Journal of Cleaner Production* 50: 123–132. DOI: 10.1016/j.jclepro.2012.11.041.

Zaman, Atiq U./Newman, Peter (2021): Plastics: Are they part of the zero-waste agenda or the toxic-waste agenda? In: *Sustainable Earth* 4 (1). DOI: 10.1186/s42055-021-00043-8.

Zero Waste Academy (2016): Zero waste town plan (zero ueisuto taun keikaku). www.zwtk.jp/

wp-content/uploads/2020/02/ゼロ・ウェイストタウン計画最終.pdf, [Accessed 19 August 2021].

Zero Waste Academy (2018): Zero Waste Kamikatsu: The zero waste measures of Kamikatsu, Tokushima Prefecture.

Zero Waste Academy (2020a): Kurukuru: Towards the year 2020 targeted in the zero waste declaration (zero ueisuto sengen mokuhyō no 2020 nen wo mukaete).

Zero Waste Academy (2020b): Resource separation guidebook in 2020 (reiwa 2 nendoban shigen bunbetsu gaidobukku). www.kamikatsu.jp/docs/2017040700010/file_contents/R2betsugideobook.pdf, [Accessed 7 June 2022].

Zero Waste International Alliance (2018): Zero waste definition. www.zwia.org/zero-waste-definition/, [Accessed 19 December 2020].

Chapter 2

Paving the Way for Carbon-neutral Schools: Getting Students Actively Involved in Climate Protection Measures

Lotte Nawothnig
Oliver Wagner
Sebastian Albert-Seifried
Lena Tholen

1. Introduction

The climate crisis is undoubtedly one of the most pressing problems of our time, as it risks destroying future generations' basis for a liveable life (WBGU 2021). Accordingly, Goal 13 of the UN 2030 Agenda for Sustainable Development aims at improving 'education, awareness-raising and human and institutional capacity on climate change mitigation, adaptation, impact reduction and early warning' (UN Agenda 2030 2022). Climate action is thus clearly identified as one of the 17 goals that are to ensure sustainable development.

Given the increase in extreme weather events, today's students will be significantly affected by global warming, while also shaping the future to come. In light of this, schools play an important role because they can raise awareness and explain the background of global warming to future generations. Moreover, schools can teach sustainable practices and thus change behaviour among students and possibly also their families and peer groups (Flora et al. 2014; Hungerford & Volk 1990; Mochizuki & Bryan 2015). With the 'Education for Sustainable Development' programme, introduced in 2015, the UN developed a framework to successfully integrate topics related to sustainable development into the education system through new teaching approaches, such as the cooperation of schools with stakeholders outside of schools allowing for real-life experiences (BNE Portal 2017). Such action-oriented learning, which engages students in projects in school or even in their local communities, is also crucial to increasing beliefs in 'self-efficacy' (Anderson 2012; Cantell et al. 2019; Cordero et al. 2008; Flora et al. 2014; Monroe et al. 2019).

First coined by Canadian psychologist Albert Bandura, self-efficacy expresses the positive attitude toward one's own abilities, describing the personal judgement of how well one can effectively influence the course of a given development (Bandura 1997). A strong feeling of self-efficacy can thus motivate people to become change agents who seek to directly change an undesired situation, e.g. stopping global warming (Kristof 2010; Schneidewind 2019). The issue of self-efficacy is particularly relevant for students who are still in the process of learning just how much influence they have (Pütz, Kuhnen, & Lojewski 2011). Consequently, climate protection education activities at schools that foster self-efficacy have the potential to be more motivating, therefore generating more sustainable outcomes than activities that neglect the issue of self-efficacy (Anderson 2012; Cantell et al. 2019; Cordero et al. 2008; Flora et al. 2014; Monroe et al. 2019).

Although a wealth of initiatives have been launched at schools throughout the world, climate change education to date focuses primarily on knowledge, while lacking 'connection with the current communication paradigm of young people' (Ouariachi & Wim 2020: 2). Lasen et al. (2017) identified the need to promote continuous professional learning among teachers to support students in critical and action-oriented engagement.

At the same time, the breath-taking speed at which the 'Fridays for Future' movement grew is indicative of the fact that many young people worldwide do indeed care about the future of the earth (Haunss & Sommer 2020; Wagner 2021). In Germany, the project "Schools4Future – Implementing the Joint Task of Climate Neutral Schools", led by the Wuppertal Institute and Büro Ö-quadrat, supports motivated students by showing them how to make their immediate surroundings – namely their schools – more environmentally sustainable. The three-year project which is financed with funds from the Federal Ministry for Economic Affairs and Climate Action started in May 2020 (lasting until June 2023). It addresses all types of secondary schools in Germany aiming at diversity with regard to regional representation and school types. Stressing the fact that climate protection requires the cooperation of all people, all businesses, all public institutions as well as all schools, the project aims at fostering not only structural measures, but also behavioural changes among students, teachers and parents.

Through the cooperation of school authorities, teaching staff, students, parents, caretakers, the wider school environment and if necessary, other local implementation partners such as energy cooperatives, schools are to be put on the path to becoming climate-neutral places of learning. While participation in the project does not ensure the funding of identified climate mitigation measures, the project aims at enabling all participating actors – including students – to identify and implement necessary changes themselves. In a nutshell, the goal and core concern of the project can be described as enabling students at the local level to do what Greta Thunberg succeeded in doing on the world stage of politics. They should be empowered to clearly voice their demands for climate-friendly schools.

Japan is the cradle of international agreements on climate change mitigation efforts namely the Kyoto Protocol (1997). As a technologically highly developed economy, Japan set ambitious goals to become climate-neutral by 2050 (Obane et al. 2022).[1] In the field of energy transition, there has been a lively and fruitful exchange among scholars which has emphasised how Japan and Germany – two major economies – can learn a great deal from each other (Cherp et al. 2017; Kharecha & Sato 2019; Weidner 2020). Similarly, the German Japanese Energy Transition Council (GJETC)[2] has established a framework for scientific exchange among experts from these two countries to promote reciprocal learning, as demonstrated in many examples (Kutani et al. 2021; Ninomiya et al. 2020; Thomas et al. 2022; Toyoda et al. 2020).

The energy transition paths of Germany and Japan have shown interesting parallels, most notably the decentralisation processes of the energy supply at the local level (Wagner et al. 2020). At the same time, a comparative analysis of scenarios related to the climate neutrality goals of these two countries, carried out by the GJETC, revealed that the countries' means to achieve the goal of

---

1   This goal was in line with the German goal to become climate-neutral. However, in Germany the goal of reaching climate neutrality was set to 2045 following a ruling of the German Constitutional Court in June 2021 (Constitutional Court 2021).

2   The Council has been launched in 2016 by the Wuppertal Institute, ECOS, hennicke.consult and the Institute of Energy Economics Japan (IEEJ/Tokyo).

climate neutrality differ considerably, e.g., the increase of renewable energy in Germany versus the continuous use of nuclear power in Japan (Obane et al. 2022).

Such differences in the approach of reducing the respective countries' greenhouse gas (GHG) emissions, logically affect possible measures taken to improve the performance of schools in reaching climate neutrality and enhancing climate change education. Against this backdrop, this chapter compares the above-mentioned approach of the Schools4Future project with initiatives launched at the school level in Japan. It specifically discusses the extent to which exchange between German and Japanese students on climate change measures would be beneficial for both sides.

To answer that question, this chapter first sheds light on more general differences in Germany and Japan (2), then outlines existing programmes in Japan that seek to tackle global warming (fifty/fifty, Eco-school programme) and presents initial results from the ongoing Schools4Future project (3). Based on the latter, we discuss the potential merit of exchange between German and Japanese students on climate change (4). The analysis builds upon desktop research on existing initiatives in Japan, and first results of the accompanying research of the Schools4Future project in Germany.

With that in mind, it would be a valuable endeavour to connect students across various countries, not only to increase their mutual awareness of the necessity to protect the climate as an essential global public good, but also to exchange ideas about different approaches to how this can be achieved. In addition, it could be made clear to students that climate change and climate protection is a global task that goes beyond national borders. Indeed, international cooperation, especially on the part of the industrialised nations, is required to solve this task.

2. Climate mitigation policies and political culture in Germany and Japan

While both countries strive to become climate-neutral by 2050 (Japan) and 2045 (Germany), the measures put in place to achieve this goal differ considerably. In 2020, the Japanese government declared that the country would reach climate neutrality by 2050, with an interim target of reducing GHG by 46%

of 2013 levels by 2030 (METI 2020). This goal has been further augmented by the 6th Strategic Energy Plan, published by the Japanese government in October 2021 (METI 2021): To reach its net-zero goal, the plan foresees an increase of renewable energy installations while also considering the utilisation of nuclear energy and technology for hydrogen and ammonia power plants as well as carbon capture, utilisation and storage (CCUS) (Obane et al. 2022). Apart from that, the government's focus has been on the development of enhancing efficiency through the development and improvement of new energy-saving technologies.

In addition to this, the Japanese government asks citizens to save energy by leading a more frugal life with initiatives such as *cool biz*, a campaign started in 2005 that encourages workers to dress in lighter clothes during the hot summer months to reduce air-conditioning use. Similarly, also *aiderungu stop*, a campaign that asks drivers to switch off the engine when not driving. In the aftermath of the earthquake in March 2011, the government also carried out regulated switch-offs to meet energy demand, due to the nuclear meltdown of the Fukushima Daiichi nuclear power plant. While protests against nuclear power were frequent in the aftermath of the nuclear accident (Gengenbach & Trunk 2012), these protesters 'never became players in mainstream nuclear policymaking' (Avenell 2016: 88).

In contrast to Japan, the nuclear disaster at the Fukushima Daiichi nuclear power plant triggered massive protests by German citizens calling for the phase-out of nuclear energy and led to unprecedented gains of votes for the Green party in the federal state of Baden-Wuerttemberg. Eventually, in June 2011, the Fukushima nuclear disaster even caused the German government to decide on a phaseout of nuclear energy by 2022,[3] although that same government had decided to extend the operation of nuclear power plants only months before the nuclear accident (Hennicke & Welfens 2012).

The awareness of the urgency to act against the climate crisis is high, especially among young Germans, which is evident from a youth-led constitutional complaint from 2021. Following a ground-breaking ruling of the

---

3   To counter the energy crisis induced by the Russian invasion of Ukraine, the German government decided to keep two nuclear power plants on stand-by until April 2023 (Drucksache 20/4217; Bundesregierung 2023).

Federal Constitutional Court (*Bundesverfassungsgericht*) that obliged the German state to prevent any future disproportionate restrictions in the fundamental liberties of today's young generation (Federal Constitutional Court 2021), the German government, led by then-Chancellor Angela Merkel, was forced to tighten its climate protection law (originally dating from 2019). The success of this complaint significantly shaped the German climate protection debate. First, it framed climate protection as being an integral part of protecting the civil rights of Germany's future generations (Wefing 2021). Second, it underscored the potential of young citizens to effectively advocate for the protection of the climate. Among the adjustments proposed by the cabinet of then-Chancellor Merkel was the phaseout of coal-fired plants, which was announced to be accelerated by the coalition agreement of the new government inaugurated in December 2021 (Bundesregierung 2021). Energy generated from coal was to be substituted by a significant increase in renewable energy. By 2030 up to 80% of Germany's gross electricity consumption shall be covered by renewable energy (BMWK 2022).

Overall, this indicates that climate mitigation efforts in Germany and Japan differ with regard to the instruments chosen by the political decision makers (renewable energy vs. nuclear energy), as well as the level of citizen involvement. Accordingly, Hasegawa (2021) argues that the Fridays for Future movement in Japan is considerably weak. He points out that even among Asian countries, the Japanese movement is lacking power (ibid.). Compared to 105,396 followers of Fridays for Future Germany on Facebook in September 2020 there were only 479 followers of Fridays for Future Japan, and 3,831 followers of Fridays for Future Tokyo (ibid). This suggests that either the interest in climate protection in Japan is considerably weak, or the trust in being able to make a difference, namely self-efficacy perception, is missing.

3. Climate-action programmes in Japan and the German Schools4Future project

Schools play a major role in the discussion about energy and climate protection – both as (municipal) buildings and as institutions. Schools are important as central places of education to make future generations aware of the importance of climate protection. Schools must therefore act as role models.

In Japan and Germany, the relevance of integrating the topic of climate change education (CCE) as part of Education for Sustainable Development (ESD) has generally been well understood. In a comparative analysis, Takahashi et al. (2016) compare existing Japanese programmes for CCE with German initiatives and conclude that the Japanese programmes considerably lack the integration of key competencies and connection to the local level. Instead of simply focusing on individual behaviour, Takahashi and her co-authors stress the importance of developing competencies that empower students to take action at the local level, and of integrating local data to assess the scope of possible actions to be taken (ibid.).

While addressing behavioural change that can be realised by individuals, the German Schools4Future programme focuses on the direct involvement of students and teachers to reduce the GHG emissions of the entire school, primarily by also addressing local stakeholders. This empowers students to actively participate in transformation processes and, thereby increase their self-efficacy perception. This aspect is comparable to the fifty/fifty programme, which was first conceived by the environmental department of Hamburg in 1994-1997 and has since spread throughout Germany and was later launched in Japan. The main idea of this initiative was to reduce the overall consumption of building energy (electricity and heating), as well as water by implementing behavioural change. To this end, the students first assessed the overall consumption of energy and water in their respective school. Then, after implementing relevant measures, students reassessed the school's overall resource consumption. Based on this, the amount of money that the school saved because of the reduction measures was calculated, a share of which was awarded to the school. This share often amounts to 50%, which is where the name of the programme stems from.

In Japan, an environmental programme with a long history is the so-called Eco-school programme, which has been subject of several scholarly evaluations (Okamoto & Sato 2012; Noda 2006; Song & Suzuki 2006; Qi 2012; Ikezawa & Sunaga 2009). This makes it valuable for further investigation on CCE initiatives in Japan.

In the following, the implementation of the fifty/fifty programme as well as the Eco-school programme in Japan will be outlined, before describing the implementation of the Schools4Future project in Germany in more detail.

3.1 Japan's Eco-school programme and the fifty/fifty programme

Following the success of the fifty/fifty project in Germany and Europe, the project idea reached Japan in 2005. In Germany, the programme quickly spread throughout the country with numerous organisations contributing to its realisation, out of which many continue to support today (UfU 2022). Although in some places the programme has been substituted by alternative programmes, such as in Hamburg (City of Hamburg 2022).

Since the launch of the fifty/fifty programme in Japan, it has been implemented in a total of 859 schools: 500 elementary schools, 129 middle schools, and 230 high schools (FoE 2014). Conducted by public schools in cooperation with NGOs from their respective municipalities, the programme aimed to raise climate awareness through environmental education and monitored by regular assessment of the school's electricity, gas and water consumption. For this purpose, data provided by the schools is analysed with the support of the NGO called Friends of the Earth Japan. That organisation points out that one of the core goals for the students was to better understand resource consumption through assessing it themselves (ibid.). To make the consumption transparent, prominently placed posters in the classroom further helped to visualise the development of the schools' consumption. Comparing consumption data of the past three years, charts were created that enabled a real-time assessment of the resources consumed at the schools. Further, relating the resource consumption to its monetary value, made the relevance of resource consumption reduction more tangible. The programme directly involved students and teachers to reduce the resource consumption of their schools and through that empowered the young students to take actions.

However, as the assessment is not standardised, the scope of assessment differs from school to school (FoE 2014). When comparing across schools, resource consumption of a specific school often had to be compared to another school that did not use the exact same reduction measures, which made a direct comparison between schools difficult.

With a total of 859 fifty/fifty schools in Japan, the project can be said to have been successful in terms of the reduction achieved. However, according to Friends of the Earth Japan, the project activities seem to have largely come to a halt in recent years apart from some smaller fifty/fifty events conducted by the organisation itself. One possible reason might be the reliance of the programme on public fundings.

The Japanese Eco-school programme, on the other hand, which was established by the Ministry of Education, Culture, Sports, Science and Technology (MEXT) in 1997, continues today. The central goals of the Eco-school programme have been (1) to increase the energy efficiency of school buildings while also increasing the usage of renewable energy; (2) to green the building; (3) to carry out retrofit measures such as insulation; and (4) to install facilities for students to get in touch with nature (Ecoschool 2022). Currently, a total of 1,912 schools have been designated as 'Eco-school', which include elementary, middle and high schools (MEXT 2022).

In contrast to the fifty/fifty programme, the focus of the Eco-school programme lies on construction measures, e.g., the installation of renewable energy generation sources and the improvement of building insulation, while behavioural measures are only a minor part. This approach thus reflects the aforementioned focus of the Japanese government on technological advancement instead of encouraging citizens, or students here respectively, to become active themselves.

Nevertheless, the programme's goal to increase awareness among students of all ages and teachers alike by also talking about the topic of climate change in various subjects seems to have been partially successful (Noda 2006). Suzuki & Song (2006) argue that the focus clearly lies in the retrofitting of school buildings. They stressed that the main motivation to apply for the programme seems to have been the financial support that came along with it to carry out retrofit projects, despite often only one-third to two-thirds of the amount required being granted, depending on the respective school's financial capacity. However, their analysis indicates that the overall energy consumption effectively increased due to the commissioning of new technical equipment, e.g., by the installation of air conditioning. The latter is commonly justified as a precautionary measure to protect the health of students during the increasingly hot summers in Japan, but also by the use of the facilities by people outside the school such as the fact that the gymnasiums are also used as shelters in times of natural disasters (Isaka et al. 2013; Nakamura et al. 2016). This is in line with the findings of Ikezawa & Sunaga (2009), who stated that the target of effectively reducing energy consumption was missed. Moreover, the maintenance of the newly installed equipment is more cost-intensive than running the school without any refurbishment measures would have been. Finally, Suzuki & Song (2006) further reveal that despite the installation of renewable energy sources at Eco-schools, the installed capacity only amounted to roughly 1% of the overall capacity needed.

One particularity of the Eco-school approach is that many of the activities take place outside in the great outdoors (Qi 2012). Contrary to the Chinese 'Green School' programme, which Qi compared the Eco-school program me to, the content of the Eco-school programme has not thoroughly been integrated into any school's curriculum and lacks creative approaches to better convey the content. An analysis by Okamoto & Sato (2012) of a similar programme, the 'Green Flag Award' conducted in the UK, also suggested that the Japanese programme lacked a thorough integration of the topic/content into the school curriculum. In the case of the Green Flag Award, a large number of criteria have to be fulfilled, including (1) regular meetings with the 'Eco Committees', (2) continuous assessment (of energy consumption), (3) dissemination of information outside the school context, and (4) incorporation of all grades as well as integration of the topic into at least three school subjects in order to maintain the Green Flag Award designation.

On a general note, the aforementioned study by Takahashi et al. (2016) identified a general lack of demand for effective CCE at the school as well as at the local level. The authors also stress that the focus was still on individual efforts to be taken while neglecting the importance of fostering initiatives that would involve the community level (ibid.).

3.2 The implementation of the Schools4Future programme in Germany

The German Schools4Future project seeks to achieve an overall reduction of the schools' energy consumption, partly based on behavioural change among students. At each school a small group of students and teachers is involved. This can be either an entire class, or just a group of students who meet in the format of an extracurricular school activity. The project concept consists of four pillars or stages: (1) the Carbon Footprint (CF) assessment, (2) the climate protection concept, (3) the implementation of the climate protection concepts, and (4) the rollout and networking.

Through the CF assessment conducted in the first stage, students gain a better understanding of the direct relationship between school activities and

GHG emissions. The scope of assessment includes building energy (electricity and heat), areas of transport (commuting and school trips), food (from school canteens) and procurement (here, this means only paper, including toilet paper, hand towels, and paper used for copies).

The tool makes GHG emissions tangible and thus pinpoints the areas that require particular attention in the second stage – the identification of climate protection measures and the development of a climate protection concept to reduce these GHG emissions. In addition to more comprehensive renovation measures, such as replacing the heating system or installing additional photovoltaic systems, the reduction potential through behavioural change plays an important role. Particularly when it comes to transport and (canteen) food, students and teachers have greater capabilities to make an impact than in the area of building energy. This is because the administrative barriers for renovation measures are considerably high, and renovations are time-consuming and expensive. In contrast, since barriers related to the transport situation, cafeteria food, and procurement are lower; changes can take place much faster, and students' participation is more visible.

In the third stage, students and teachers implement the measures identified. Smaller measures, such as raising awareness for saving energy, such as turning off electronic appliances when not in use, can be implemented by students and teachers alone; however, replacing the heating system or introducing regulations such as speed limits or car-free zones around school gates require cooperation with stakeholders outside the school. Here, the application for public funding as well as crowdfunding leaves two possible ways to address any lack of financial sources. While there is no official budget connected to the project that can be used for retrofitting measures, the participating schools are encouraged to apply for public funding and to address political stakeholders at municipal level. However, as approval of public funds is often a lengthy process, crowdfunding could accelerate the implementation of specific measures while contributing to raising awareness even beyond the school community.

In the final stage, the participating schools are encouraged to network with one another to facilitate peer-to-peer learning, as well as to invite other schools to become part of the project. As part of the fourth "rollout and networking" stage, for example, two online meetings with students from participating schools, as well as from schools interested in the project, were held in 2021

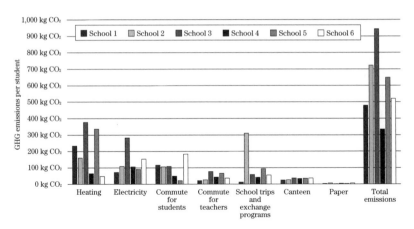

Figure 1: Comparison of GHG emissions per student for the six schools (Albert-Seifried et al., 2022)

(June 18 and December 17) during which they discussed the topics of climate-neutral food and transport. In addition, a meeting with students from a total of seven different German schools took place in May 2022 in Southern Germany, during which the participating students, who were between 14 and 18 years old, discussed challenges and opportunities that they had encountered during the implementation of the Schools4Future project.

When comparing the CF assessment of the six schools that had already completed it at the time of writing, the differences become evident (see **Figure 1**).

Such a comparison of the CF assessments of different schools can further shed light on the source of emissions in a way that students can learn from one another. Enlarging the scope of mutual learning is one of the main reasons why the project seeks to connect students from different schools. During the aforementioned on-site meeting in May 2022, the participating students were invited to discuss the differences and deduct possible solutions for their respective schools. The completed CF assessments that are partly uploaded on the project's website and are thus accessible, may trigger an increase in efforts in a particular area in which schools perform poorly.

Figure 2 shows the ranking of per-student GHG emissions in different sectors for all six schools that completed the CF assessment. It shows that the schools perform very differently across the various emission sectors, indicating

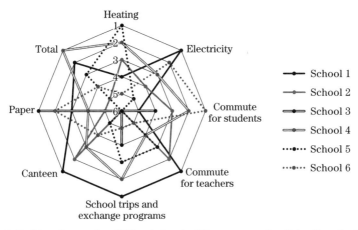

Figure 2: Ranking of per-student GHG emissions in different sectors for all six pilot schools with a completed CF assessment (Albert-Seifried et al., 2022)

that all schools have significant saving potential in one field or another and could potentially learn from each other (Albert-Seifried et al. 2022).

During the implementation of the project, students were highly motivated to be part of a specific task such as assessing GHG emissions, developing countermeasures or thinking of solutions to put these measures into place. Thanks to the work with the CF assessment tool, they gained a better understanding of where GHG emissions mainly came from. This in turn helped them to address the sources of GHG emissions with more specific countermeasures. In addition, several discussions took place with different actors, like the school management, the canteen operators, the caretakers, and others. In one school, the students independently organised a climate day, which was attended by the facility management and city officials, including the city-mayor. This climate day led to committed investments of 500,000 Euro by the city facility management for measures on the heating system and the implementation of smaller measures, such as the construction of a parking facility for bicycles. On this climate day, the students also organised a panel discussion, held a speech, and prepared a video illustrating the need to take action. At another school, students introduced the topic of climate protection by preparing a number of participatory activities (e.g., a Solar Obstacle Course, a Repair-Your-Bike Station, quizzes).

Exchange among students from different German schools during the on-site networking meeting in May 2022 set free a remarkable energy, highlighting the importance of encouraging the young generation to join forces in protecting the global public good climate. Notwithstanding the inspiring motivation of the students participating in the project, the accompanying research found that the success of such projects often depends on a number of highly motivated teachers (Nawothnig 2022; Vogler 2022). The lack of integration of climate education into the school curriculum was also identified as a major challenge.

3.3 Comparative Analysis of Climate Change Education Projects

As outlined above, the Japanese Eco-school programme differs greatly from the German Schools4Future programme. While the focus of the Schools4Future project is mainly on what the students themselves can do, the Eco-school programme focuses on construction measures. The latter does not necessitate student (or teacher) involvement. Consequently, the Eco-school programme does not contribute to any increase in self-efficacy beliefs among students and teachers at the participating schools. In contrast, Schools4Future's approach of empowering students through their quest in making their schools climate-neutral, significantly increases the self-efficacy perceptions of students and teachers alike (Albert-Seifried et al. 2022; Nawothnig 2022; Vogler 2022; Wagner et al. 2021).

Moreover, the comparisons of the Japanese Eco-school programme with counterparts in China and the UK show that much more is possible in Japan to ensure the active involvement of students and the long-lasting impact of the programme. The German Schools4Future project expressly seeks to empower students to take action and to address (local) politicians to push for fundamental change (Albert-Seifried et al. 2022; Wagner et al. 2021). In doing so, it potentially increases students' self-efficacy beliefs, which is likely to create a long-lasting impact of the project's activities.

In terms of scale, the Eco-school programme approach seems to reach a wider range of school subjects and age groups, whereas the Schools4Future project, largely only takes place among smaller groups of active students, or within a particular class (although the reason for this has partly been constraints related to the Covid-19 pandemic).

The fact that the Japanese Eco-school programme comes with a generous amount of financial support adds to its attractiveness and thus incentivises applying for the programme. Participation in the Schools4Future project, on the other hand, brings about no financial benefits. Instead, students and teachers have to make an effort to apply for financial support and/or request the school authority and other stakeholders to grant financial support to carry out any measures they have devised. While this procedure initially appears to be burdensome, it also allows for more empowerment among students and teachers alike: instead of simply receiving money and getting a number of retrofit measures done, the participants of the Schools4Future project also receive the experience of self-efficacy based on their personal efforts.

Contrary to the Eco-school programme but similar to the Schools4Future project, the implementation of the fifty/fifty project in Japan focused on the direct involvement of students in the project activities and means to visualise the resource consumption.

All approaches, nevertheless, lack a thorough enough integration of the programme into the general curriculum of the schools, which means that no large-scale long-term effects can be expected.

To ensure a long-lasting effect of CCE initiatives, schools worldwide need to develop programmes that are fully integrated into the school curriculum and empower students and teachers alike to take actions at the school level and beyond. The successful implementation of ESD in all schools could significantly contribute to students' and teachers' long-term engagement in sustainable activities such as climate protection measures. In order to keep up the motivation of the students, it seems most important to make results tangible. The assessment of GHG emissions conducted by the students themselves as part of the Schools4Future project is one way of doing this and first evaluations indicate that this had a substantial impact on their self-efficacy perceptions.

Furthermore, the experience of the Schools4Future project team with connecting students throughout Germany to discuss their CF assessment indicates that comparing the GHG emissions that the own school causes with the ones of other schools, contributes to a better overall comprehension of the main sources of GHG emissions. The peer-to-peer-learning further allowed the students to exchange ideas on possible solutions to reduce emissions and to overcome encountered barriers.

To take this result a step further, we argue that it would be beneficial to encourage students from various countries to a) assess their school's CF and b) to compare the results with those of peers from other countries and discuss approaches for how to reduce emissions. This would allow students to get a better understanding of geographical and cultural differences that influence each country's emissions and climate change mitigation strategies (e.g., level of development, dependence on energy imports, etc.).

As a first step towards taking this global approach, we argue that cross-national exchange among students from Japan and Germany could be beneficial for students' climate awareness, while also widening their perspective of what can be done and what kind of additional benefits climate protection measures might have (e.g., increasing the resilience of school buildings equipped with solar panels at times of shutdowns caused by a natural disaster). Moreover, a dialogue of this kind could further improve the mutual understanding of the cooperating countries, which is important when advocating joint efforts to accelerate the energy transition worldwide. Students could thus learn at an early stage that international cooperation is needed to master the human task of climate protection.

Based on their economic power, Japan and Germany both play an important role in their respective region, Germany in the European Union and Japan in the Association of Southeast Asian Nations (ASEAN), and this also makes them important players in the strive for climate change mitigation. Their ambitious goals of becoming climate-neutral by 2050 (2045) can have an important impact on the nearby countries and by that stimulate mitigation processes throughout the world.

However, both countries' strategies to become climate-neutral differ considerably as Germany largely focus on the expansion of renewable energy sources while Japan keeps relying on nuclear energy. Against the background that Germany eventually decided on the phase-out of nuclear energy because of an event that took place in Japan interconnects both countries in a very particular way. These circumstances suggest that an exchange between students from Germany and Japan on climate protection measures is valuable. Comparing CF might also reveal cultural differences that have an impact on CF (for example, in school nutrition).

One possible way to realise such an exchange could be through the implementation of the Schools4Future project in a number of Japanese schools.

While comparing the respective schools CF assessments, students should also be encouraged to discuss the different narratives of what is defined as "clean energy" or also exchange views about the differing relevance of environmental social movements in both countries.

The assessments at the schools would reveal a number of interesting differences concerning the overall school system. To name just one example, while it is common in Japan to spend the entire day in school (8:45 am to 3:15 pm) and eat a standardised school lunch that is distributed to the whole school community, students in Germany often bring their own lunch, buy something to eat nearby, or even go home for lunch. This kind of difference impacts the overall amount of energy consumption of schools, which is something that students can discuss. This kind of exchange would also allow for the students to encounter different ways of educational systems, increasing their awareness of global diversity and empower them to tackle global problems on a global scale trough cross-national exchange. Such a project could also contribute to the gaining of intercultural competence.

Existing initiatives in Japan could serve as a venue to connect middle school or high school students from a Schools4Future school in Germany with a school that participated either in the fifty/fifty programme and/or the Eco-school programme in Japan.

4. Conclusion

The analysis presented in this chapter shed light on the different approaches to CCE of the Schools4Future project in Germany and the Eco-school programme in Japan. While the latter focuses on measures related to increasing the energy efficiency of school buildings, the Schools4Future project seeks to empower students to take actions themselves by approaching the relevant decision makers (e.g., the school principal, the school authority, local politicians, etc.). In doing so, the Schools4Future approach fosters students' self-efficacy, which potentially increases the likelihood that they will have a more positive attitude toward climate protection and will stay actively involved in the long-term.

The on-site meeting of German students in May 2022 revealed that direct exchange among peers from different schools contributes significantly to the motivation of the students to stay involved. Building on this insight, we argue that a joint project between Germany and Japan would likely raise climate change awareness considerably among students from both countries. It would not only encourage them to continue working towards protecting the climate, but also deepen their understanding of global differences in approaches to climate change mitigation, depending on economical, geographical, and cultural context. The geographical distance between the two countries may potentially even lead to the realisation that the climate crisis is a global challenge that needs to be tackled by all of us together. Cross-national student exchange in the context of CCE could thus become an important trigger for increased efforts among students to contribute to the protection of a global public good – the climate.

References

Albert-Seifried, Sebastian/Nawothnig, Lotte/Tholen, Lena/Seifried, Dieter/Straßen, Amelie/ Vogler, Amelie/Venjakob, Maike/Wagner, Oliver (2022): Secondary School Student Participation in Carbon Footprint Assessment for Schools. Conference Proceedings: European Council for an Energy Efficiency Economy (ECEEE). Hyères, France.

Anderson, Allison (2012): Climate Change Education for Mitigation and Adaptation. In: *Journal of Education for Sustainable Development* 6 (2): 191–206. DOI: 10.1177/ 0973408212475199.

Avenell, Simon (2016): Antinuclear Radicals: Scientific Experts and Antinuclear Activism in Japan. In: *Science, Technology and Society* 21 (1): 88–109. DOI: 10.1177/ 0971721815622742.

Bundesregierung (2023): Der Atomausstieg macht unser Land sicherer. www.bundesregierung. de/breg-de/aktuelles/ausstieg-aus-der-kernkraft-2135796, [Accessed 26 May 2022].

Bandura, Albert (1997): *Self-Efficacy: The Exercise of Control,* New York: W. H. Freeman.

BMWK (Bundesministerium für Wirtschaft und Klimaschutz) (2022): Überblickspapier Osterpaket. www.bmwk.de/Redaktion/DE/Downloads/Energie/0406_ueberblickspapier_ osterpaket.pdf?__blob=publicationFile&v=12, [Accessed 15 April 2022].

BNE Portal (2017): Nationaler Aktionsplan Bildung Für Nachhaltige Entwicklung. www.bne-portal.de/bne/de/nationaler-aktionsplan/nationaler-aktionsplan.html, [Accessed 10 February 2022].

Bundesregierung (2021): Koalitionsvertrag. www.bundesregierung.de/resource/blob/974430/19 90812/04221173eef9a6720059cc353d759a2b/2021-12-10-koav2021-data.pdf?download=1, [Accessed 15 March 2022].

Cantell, Hannel/Tolppanen, Sakari/Aarnio-Linnanvuori, Essi/Lehtonen, Anna (2019): Bicycle Model on Climate Change Education: Presenting and Evaluating a Model. In:

Environmental Education Research 25 (5): 717–31. DOI: 10.1080/13504622.2019.1570487.

Cherp, Aleh/Vinichenko, Vadim/Jewell, Jessica/Suzuki, Masahiro/Antal, Miklós (2017): Comparing Electricity Transitions: A Historical Analysis of Nuclear, Wind and Solar Power in Germany and Japan. In: *Energy Policy* 101 (February): 612–28. DOI: 10.1016/j.enpol.2016.10.044.

City of Hamburg (2022): Energie Hoch4. https://www.energie4.hamburg/, [Accessed 10 October 2022].

Constitutional Court (2021): Entscheidung des Bundesverfassungsgerichts (1BvR 2656/18). https://www.bundesverfassungsgericht.de/SharedDocs/Pressemitteilungen/DE/2021/bvg21-031.html, [Accessed 31 March 2022].

Cordero, Eugene C./Todd, Anne M./Abellera, Diana (2008): Climate Change Education and the Ecological Footprint. In: *Bulletin of the American Meteorological Society* 89 (6): 865–72. DOI: 10.1175/2007BAMS2432.1.

Drucksache 20/4217 (2022): Entwurf eines Neunzehnten Gesetzes zur Änderung des Atomgesetzes (19.AtGÄndG). dserver.bundestag.de/btd/20/042/2004217.pdf, [Accessed 26 May 2023].

Ecoschool (2022): Eco-school: Promotion of environmentally friendly school facilities. www.mext.go.jp/content/20220527-mxt_sisetujo-100001893_01.pdf, [Access 15 January 2022].

Flora, June A./Saphir, Melissa/Lappé, Matt/Roser-Renouf, Connie/Maibach, Edward W./Leiserowitz, Anthony A. (2014): Evaluation of a National High School Entertainment Education Program: The Alliance for Climate Education. In: *Climatic Change* 127 (3–4): 419–34. DOI: 10.1007/s10584-014-1274-1.

FoE (Friends of the Earth) (2014): Fifty/Fifty Japan. www.foejapan.org/climate/fiftyfifty/index.html, [Accessed 14 May 2022].

Gengenbach, Katrin/Trunk, Maria (2012): Vor und nach »Fukushima«: Dynamiken Sozialer Protestbewegungen in Japan seit der Jahrtausendwende. In: *Japan 2012: Politik, Wirtschaft Und Gesellschaft*, edited by David Chiavacci and Iris Wieczorek. Vereinigung für sozialwissenschaftliche Japanforschung e.V. (VSJF).

Hasegawa, Koichi (2021): Participation and Solidarity for the Climate Crisis: Analysis of Fridays for Future Campaigns from a Social Movements Perspective. In: *The Nonprofit Review*. DOI: 10.11433.

Haunss, Sebastian/Sommer, Moritz (2020): *Fridays for Future: Die Jugend Gegen Den Klimawandel: Konturen Der Weltweiten Protestbewegung*. X-Texte zu Kultur und Gesellschaft, Bielefeld: Transcript.

Hennicke, Peter/Welfens, Paul J.J. (2012): *Energiewende nach Fukushima: deutscher Sonderweg oder weltweites Vorbild?* München: oekom.

Hungerford, Harold R./Volk, Trudi L. (1990): Changing Learner Behavior Through Environmental Education. In: *The Journal of Environmental Education* 21 (3): 8–21. DOI: 10.1080/00958964.1990.10753743.

Ikezawa, Tomoko/Sunaga, Noboyuki (2009): Questionnaire Survey on the Actual Conditions of Eco-schools Funded by MEXT. In: *Journal of Environmental Engineering* (Transactions of AIJ) 74 (641): 783–88. DOI: 10.3130/aije.74.783.

Isaka, Yoshiaki/Miyagawa, Ayuko/Tobita, Kunihito/Matsubara, Naoki/Muneta, Yoshifumi (2013):

Research on the effects of installing air-conditioning in public schools: Educational, health and environmental effects through continuous research. In: *Human Beings and The Living Environment* 20 (1): 41-49. DOI: 10.24538.

Kharecha, Pushker A./Sato, Makiko (2019): Implications of Energy and CO2 Emission Changes in Japan and Germany after the Fukushima Accident. In: *Energy Policy* 132 (September): 647–53. DOI: 10.1016/j.enpol.2019.05.057.

Kristof, Kora (2010): *Wege zum Wandel: wie wir gesellschaftliche Veränderungen erfolgreicher gestalten können*, München: Oekom.

Kutani, Ichiro/Hennicke, Peter/Gericke, Naomi/Bunge, Fiona (2021): Energy and Climate Policy in the Post COVID-19 Era Comparative Analyses on Germany and Japan. Wuppertal, Tokyo. gjetc.org/wp-content/uploads/2022/06/GJETC-Study_Energy-policy-Post-Covid_FINAL-210428.pdf, [Accessed 20 May 2022].

Lasen, Michelle/Skamp, Keith/Simoncini, Kym (2017): Teacher Perceptions and Self-Reported Practices of Education for Sustainability in the Early Years of Primary School: An Australian Case Study. In: *International Journal of Early Childhood* 49 (3): 391–410. DOI: 10.1007/s13158-017-0200-x.

METI (Ministry of Economy, Trade and Industry) (2020): Japan's 14 Priority Areas for Carbon Neutrality by 2050 (Report by the Ministry of Economy, Trade and Industry). www.meti.go.jp/english/policy/energy_environment/global_warming/roadmap/report/20201212.html, [Accessed 12 July 2022].

METI (Ministry of Economy, Trade and Industry) (2021): Strategic Energy Plan. www.enecho.meti.go.jp/en/category/others/basic_plan/pdf/6th_outline.pdf, [Accessed 20 October 2021].

MEXT (Ministry of Education, Culture, Sports, Science and Technology) (2022): Eco-school accreditation achievements. www.mext.go.jp/a_menu/shisetu/ecoschool/detail/1289509.htm, [Accessed 25 October 2022].

Mochizuki, Yoko/Bryan, Audrey (2015): Climate Change Education in the Context of Education for Sustainable Development: Rationale and Principles. In: *Journal of Education for Sustainable Development* 9 (1): 4–26. DOI: 10.1177/0973408215569109.

Monroe, Martha C./Plate, Richard R./Oxarart, Annie/Bowers, Alison/Chaves, Willandia A. (2019): Identifying Effective Climate Change Education Strategies: A Systematic Review of the Research. In: *Environmental Education Research* 25 (6): 791–812. DOI: 10.1080/13504622.2017.1360842.

Nawothnig, Lotte (2022). *Paving the Way Toward Climate-Neutral Societies: Empowering Students to Stimulate Transition Processes*. Master Thesis at Christian-Albrechts-University Kiel, Kiel. NYP.

Ninomiya, Yasushi/Sasakawa, Akiko/Schröder, Judith/Thomas, Stefan (2020): Peer-to-Peer (P2P) Electricity Trading and Power Purchasing Agreements (PPAs) Part 2 of the GJETC Study on Digitalization and the Energy Transition. Wuppertal, Tokyo. gjetc.org/wp-content/uploads/2022/07/GJETC_Digitalization-Study-II_P2P-and-PPA.pdf, [Accessed 13 August 2022].

Noda, Hajime (2006): Eco-school: Analysis of environmentally friendly behaviour of pupils attending eco-schools. Conference Proceedings: Japanese LCA Scientific Society. DOI: 10.11539/ilcaj.2006.0.59.0.

Obane, Hideaki/Gericke, Naomi/Nawothnig, Lotte/Bunge, Fiona/Hennicke, Peter (2022): Key Strategies towards Decarbonization of Energy Use and Supply in Japan and Germany: Insights from a Comparison Study on Long-Term Scenario Analyses up to 2050. Wuppertal, Tokyo: German Japanese Energy Transition Council. gjetc.org/wp-content/uploads/2022/06/GJETC_Scenario-study.pdf, [Accessed 10 April 2022].

Okamoto, Yasuhiko/Sato, Masahisa (2012): Implication of FEE's Eco School Programme in UK and Applicability to Japanese Formal Education in Regard to Education for Sustainable Development. In: *Kyoseikagakku* 4 (3): 43–56.

Ouariachi, Tania/Wim, Elving J. L. (2020): Escape Rooms as Tools for Climate Change Education: An Exploration of Initiatives. In: *Environmental Education Research* 26 (8): 1193–1206. DOI:10.1080/13504622.2020.1753659.

Pütz, Hans-Georg/Kuhnen, Sebastian U./Lojewski, Johanna (2011): Identität, Selbstwertgefühl und Selbstwirksamkeit: Der Einfluss von Schulklima und sozialer Herkunft auf Persönlichkeitsmerkmale. In: *Der Übergang Schule – Hochschule*, edited by Philipp Bornkessel and Jupp Asdonk, 139–89, Wiesbaden: VS Verlag für Sozialwissenschaften. DOI: 10.1007/978-3-531-94016-8_5.

Qi, Liyan (2012): Comparative Analysis of Environmental Education in Japan and China: Focus on the Analysis of Environmental Education Models. In: *Comparative Study of Education and Culture* 12: 29–38.

Schafhausen, Franz-Josef (1998): 'Fifty-Fifty' - an Unexpectedly Successful Start. Implementation of Agenda 21 Results in Energy Savings in School Buildings. In: *Sanitaer- und Heizungstechnik* 63 (10): 122–26.

Schneidewind, Uwe (2019): *Die große Transformation: eine Einführung in die Kunst gesellschaftlichen Wandels.* 4. Auflage. Fischer 70259, Frankfurt am Main: Fischer Taschenbuch.

Song, Jing/Suzuki, Yoshihiko (2006): A Investigation of The Green School in China and The Eco-School in Japan. Proceedings of the Symposium on Global Environment 14: 103–8. DOI: 10.2208/proge.14.103.

Takahashi, Keiko/Hijioka, Yasuaki/Takahashi, Kiyoshi/Hanasaki, Naota (2016): Study on Climate Change Education Aimed at Fostering Regional Leaders: Based on a Comparative Analysis between Climate Change Education in Japan and Germany. In: *Japanese Journal of Environmental Education* 26 (2): 2_29-42. DOI: 10.5647/jsoee.26.2_29.

Takahashi, Keiko/Hoffmann, Thomas (2019): Can Systems Thinking Competency Be Improved?: Potential of 'Mystery' Learning Method for Climate Change Education in Japan. In: *Japanese Journal of Environmental Education* 29 (2): 214-23. DOI: 10.5647/jsoee.29.2_14.

Takahashi, Keiko/Utagawa, Manabu (2021): Development and Trial of a CCE Program for Taking Efficient Climate Change Measures at the Regional Level. In: *Japanese Journal of Environmental Education* 30 (3): 3_18-28. DOI: 10.5647/jsoee.30.3_18.

Thomas, Stefan/Schüwer, Dietmar/Vondung, Florin/Wagner, Oliver (2022): Heizen Ohne Öl Und Gas Bis 2035: Ein Sofortprogramm Für Erneuerbare Wärme Und Effiziente Gebäude. Studie im Auftrag von Greenpeace e.V. Wuppertal: Greenpeace. www.greenpeace.de/publikationen/Heizen%20ohne%20%C3%96l%20und%20Gas%20bis%202035.pdf, [Accessed

25 June 2022].

Toyoda, Masakazu/Arima, Jun/Fujii, Yasumasa/Ikaga, Toshiharu/Nomura, Koji/Ogasawara, Junichi/ Takeuchi, Kuzuhiko (2020): *GJETC Report 2018*. Wuppertal: Wuppertal Institut für Klima, Umwelt, Energie. DOI: 10.48506/opus-7915.

UfU (Unabhängiges Institut für Umweltfragen) (2022): Fifty/Fifty. www.fifty-fifty.eu/, [Accessed 25 October 2022].

UN Agenda 2030 (2022): Goal 13. www.globalgoals.org/goals/13-climate-action/, [Accessed 2 August 2022].

Vogler, Amelie (2022): *Schools Transitioning towards More Climate Awareness: A Multi-Level-Analysis of Climate Protection Projects in German Schools*. Master Thesis at Karl-Franzen University Graz, Graz: NYP.

Wagner, Oliver (2021): X Gründe jetzt zu Handeln: Warum Schulen zu klimaneutralen Lernorten werden müssen. In: *Schulen handeln in der Klimakrise: Change School! Guidebook - Leitfaden für Transformative Bildung*, edited by Petra Eickhoff, 65–67, Köln: Zukunftswerkstatt Akademie.

Wagner, Oliver/Tholen, Lena/Nawothnig, Lotte/Albert-Seifried, Sebastian (2021): Making School-Based GHG-Emissions Tangible by Student-Led Carbon Footprint Assessment Program. In: *Energies* 14 (24): 8558. DOI:10.3390/en14248558.

Wagner, Oliver/Venjakob, Maike/Schröder, Judith (2020): The Growing Impact of Decentralised Actors in Power Generation: A Comparative Analysis of the Energy Transition in Germany and Japan. In: *Journal of Sustainable Development of Energy, Water and Environment Systems* 9 (4): 1-23. DOI: 10.13044/j.sdewes.d8.0334.

WBGU (Wissenschaftlicher Beirat der Bundesregierung Globale Umweltveränderungen) (2021): *Planetare Gesundheit: Worüber wir jetzt reden müssen*, Berlin: Wissenschaftli cher Beirat d. Bundesregierung Globale Umweltveränderungen.

Weidner, Helmut (2020): Ups and Downs in Environmental Policy: Japan and Germany in Comparison. In: *The Ecological Modernization Capacity of Japan and Germany*, edited by Lutz Mez, Lila Okamura, and Helmut Weidner, 25–40. Energiepolitik Und Klimaschutz. Energy Policy and Climate Protection, Wiesbaden: Springer Fachmedien Wiesbaden. DOI: 10.1007/978-3-658-27405-4_3.

Chapter 3

A Revolution in Consciousness?
Changes in Environmental Attitudes and Behaviours
in Germany and Japan

Carola Hommerich
Joanna Kitsnik

Uncontrolled economic growth has placed humanity on a collision course with Earth's finite resources, leaving us with the inescapable reality of climate change (Richardson et al. 2023). As the point of possible prevention or reversal has passed, the shared commitment to mitigating its effects becomes increasingly relevant. While clearly necessary, achieving environmental action, however, has proven to be complex, and vested interests have prevented more fundamental changes until now. Overall, actions to address climate change are triggered at two levels: At the systemic level, where institutional and political frameworks for environmental policies are discussed and implemented by governments, consequently setting the stage for what can happen and within which timeframe. At the same time, and maybe even more pivotal, there is the role of the individual, who not only operates within these frameworks, but also helps to create them. While institutional and governmental policies play a crucial role in addressing climate change, both individual actions and in-actions collectively exert a significant influence on the environment as well as on the available policy measures.

The choices we make in our daily lives, such as energy consumption, transportation habits, and consumption patterns, have cumulative effects that can either contribute to environmental degradation or set us on a path towards environmental and social sustainability. While the specific manner of the relationship has been contested, environmental attitudes and environmental concern have been identified as central predictors of such ecological behaviours (Geiger et al. 2018). A 'revolution in consciousness' (Alexander 2015: 113) at the individual level is, thus, crucial to create citizen's active demand for systemic transformation and to enhance their willingness to accept changes to their current lifestyle in order to protect the environment.

To gain a deeper insight into the possible emergence of a 'revolution in consciousness', we examine the shifts in environmental attitudes in Germany and Japan over the past three decades. During this period, the threat of the climate crisis has become increasingly imminent and tangible. We focus on Germany and Japan as examples of two affluent industrialized countries who are not only important players in the global playing field but who also display differing approaches to the climate crisis at the systemic level encompassing politics and the public sphere. Drawing on data from the International Social Survey Programme's (ISSP) Environment module spanning from 1993 to 2020, allows us to explore and describe how environmental problems are perceived, how these perceptions have changed over time, and uncover possible disparities across different age groups.

1. From awareness to action: Environmental attitudes as agents of change

Environmental policies formulated at institutional and political levels often hinge on public compliance and support. The willingness of individuals to adopt, adhere to, or initiate these policies directly impacts their effectiveness. While the relationship is not straightforward, as prominently shown in the psychological literature on the attitude-behaviour-gap, attitudes are decisive for actions, as individual's behaviour 'follows reasonably from their believes, attitudes, and intentions' (Ajzen & Fishbein 2005:174). Henn et al. (2020), for example, show how a change in environmental attitudes also results in an increase in the frequency of pro-environmental behaviour. To achieve this kind of behavioural spillover, they conclude, instead of directly targeting specific behaviours, it is necessary to inspire changes in people's environmental attitudes instead.

Understanding individual-level attitudes as well as identifying the mechanisms or contexts which facilitate their translation into behavioural outcomes, is, thus, essential for mobilizing a collective shift towards environmentally responsible behaviours. At present, the majority of research in this field is grounded in psychology, with a strong focus on how internal factors, like, social values, attitudes, environmental knowledge, and specific personality traits (i.e., altruism, empathy, self-efficacy), may translate into behavioural intentions and – eventually – behaviour itself. In a comprehensive overview of these theories, Kollmuss and Agyemann (2002) develop a sociopsychological model that expands beyond internal factors and incorporates external factors likely to shape pro-environmental behaviour, namely the social, political, economic, and cultural context (**Figure 1**). This leaves room for consideration of how sociodemographic characteristics, national climate policies, or culturally distinct traditions of civic engagement may impact on pro-environmental behaviour in combination with specific social values or personality traits. Within this framework, internal and external conditions are not independent, but enable and restrict each other in complex interrelations. The strongest positive

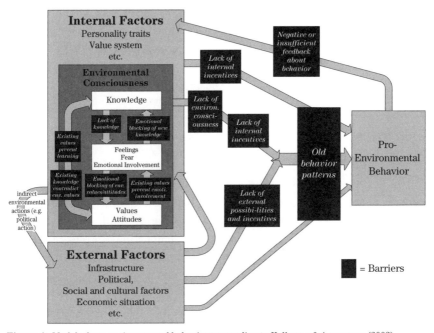

Figure 1: Model of pro-environmental behaviour according to Kollmuss & Agyemann (2002)

effect for pro-environmental behaviour is expected when external and internal factors act synergistically, without restraining hurdles, as, for example, low environmental awareness (internal) or lack of opportunities to act for the environment (external). For our own analysis presented here, we loosely rely on this model to guide us in the interpretation of our data and in identifying factors which encourage or prevent pro-environmental behaviour in Japan and Germany.

While Kollmuss and Agyemann (ibid.) believe that the model itself is applicable across all stages of the life course, they contest that the individual factors as well as the synergies between them may play out in diverging ways at different developmental stages. This coincides with our own interest in whether environmental attitudes and behaviours differ by age groups. Younger generations will be affected by climate change to a much larger extent than older generations, which could result in higher environmental awareness. Not strongly settled within the established social structures of their society, the young may be more likely to protest against the status quo and call for change. At the same time, young people at the outset of their career are also economically more vulnerable and, therefore, might be less willing to make financial sacrifices for the environment.

After a short overview of the differing political landscapes of Japan and Germany, specifically in the context of environmental policy and action, we present our empirical analysis of three decades of data on this topic.

2. Germany and Japan: Differing political landscapes

The affluent lifestyle and consumer-dependent economic systems of the Global North have played a substantial role in exacerbating the contemporary climate crises. Germany and Japan both are strong industrial and export-oriented economies – Japan positioned as the world's third, and Germany as fourth largest economy,[1] and serve as conspicuous illustrations of nations deeply entrenched within this paradigm. However, both countries have also emerged as trailblazers and frontrunners within their geographical sphere – the

---

1   At the time of writing, the International Monetary Fund has projected for Germany to overtake Japan as the third largest economy in 2023 (IMF 2023).

European Union and East Asia, wielding significant geopolitical and economic influence, shaping the global discourse on sustainability and environmental stewardship. However, their road to such roles has been notably different as has their current position regarding climate action. According to the Environmental Performance Index (EPI), which ranks country performance on sustainability issues and gauges at a national scale how close countries are from established environmental policy targets, in 2022, Germany ranked 13th and Japan 26th out of 180 countries (EPI 2022, Wolf et al. 2022). The fact that rankings depend very much on what is being measured and who is being compared, is indicated by a somewhat different placement – especially of Japan – in the Climate Change Performance Index (CCPI 2024, Burck et al. 2024), which compares 67 countries who altogether are responsible for more than 90% of global greenhouse gas emissions. Here, Germany ranks 14th, whereas Japan ranks 58th. Even though the Japanese government has announced to aim for carbon neutrality by 2050 and a 46% emissions reduction by 2030 compared to 2013 levels, the country has been criticised for the absence of a clear plan for achieving these goals and the lack of concrete policies in place for meeting these targets (ibid.). In the following section, we give a short overview of environmental policy and climate protection efforts in Germany and Japan, painting the backdrop against which environmental attitudes develop and – potentially – change.

Germany has been actively shaping the international climate policy landscape since the late 1980s, a stark contrast to its earlier status as a laggard in the emergence of 'modern' environmental policies during the 1960s. During that era, nations like the United States, Japan, Sweden, and, to some extent, Great Britain, spearheaded the establishment of innovative environmental institutions, procedures, instruments, standards, and technologies (Weidner & Mez 2008). At present, Germany holds a prominent leadership position not only within Europe but also globally, particularly excelling in the realms of renewable energy and climate change policy. Moreover, when formulating and implementing environmental policy Germany negotiates with the multiple levels of government within the European Union (e.g., the Commission, Council, and Parliament), its own federated states, in addition to various other political and civil stakeholders, and business interests.

Structural change in Germany has been a long-term process that led to the establishment of a systematic environmental policy starting in the late 1960s. In

Germany, environmental advocates have been notably political in their approach, with the clear goal of entering the political system to actively shape environmental policies from 'within the system'. To this end, members of West Germany's anti-nuclear, pro-peace and environmental movement formed the Green Party in 1980. After a merger with the East German Alliance 90 in 1993, the Green Party, under its new name of Bündnis 90/Die Grünen, quickly entered governmental institutions from the local to the national level (Weidner 2020: 33), all the while keeping a strong base of citizen support. In 1998, when a coalition of Social Democrats and the Green Party came into power at the national level, government policy explicitly shifted to an approach driven by ecological modernization (Jänicke 2020:17). Even after the red-green coalition lost to the Christian-Democrats in 2005, who stayed in power until 2021 led by Angela Merkel, environmental topics have remained central to policy making processes, not least due to the active role of Bündnis 90/Die Grünen as active opposition in parliament, as well as mounting international obligations to make changes. External events such as the nuclear disasters of Chernobyl and Fukushima were leveraged to accelerate the phase-out of nuclear energy and initiate the 'Energiewende' (energy transition), with a transition to renewable energy (Weidner 2020). This has recently been paired with the long-term goal of phasing out fossil fuels, starting with exiting coal by 2030 (BMF 2020).

Japan, in contrast, briefly stood out on the global scale during the 1970s as a successful example of an effective response to extensive industrial pollution issues without compromising economic growth. As a result of the fast government-driven industrialization of the late Meiji-period, which was continued by the developmental state of the post-war era, Japan faced an unprecedented surge in environmental pollution paired with visible health effects for the local population. What became known as Japan's 'four pollution diseases' (*yondai kougaibyou*) caused strong public awareness of industrial pollution (for a detailed discussion, cf. Matanle 2020). Increasing public pressure eventually caused the Japanese government to take responsibility by introducing rigid anti-pollution measures, victim compensation, monitoring and regulation of industrial activities, as well as by the establishment of the Environmental Agency[2] in 1971 (ibid.). Nevertheless, these early efforts in

---

2   In 2001, this was turned into the Ministry of the Environment.

environmental policy were primarily instigated by public pressure related to specific incidents and did neither signify a fundamental paradigm shift nor trigger significant structural change (Mori 2012, Weidner 2020). Japan's 'iron triangle' comprising government, bureaucracy and big business quickly turned the focus back to an exclusive emphasis of economic growth and technological development (Johnson 1982), resulting in stagnation in Japan's environmental policy efforts. With local governments leading the responses to industry-generated pollution, the addressed issues became localized, and environmental movements transitioned from nationwide legal actions and campaigns to advocating for local solutions. This shift not only led to decreased public attention but also brought about a reorientation of environmental groups to focus on more local matters (Mori 2012). Environmental activism continued beyond the early 1970s, but numerous protest movements disbanded once their concerns were addressed. By the 1980s, the environmental movement saw a decline in size and political influence, accompanied by a decrease in pollution cases reaching the courts. It was only in the late 1980s and early 1990s that a few small national environmental groups emerged, with no independent environmental think tanks during this period (Schreurs 2005). Except for a short surge in anti-nuclear demonstrations immediately after the nuclear disaster at Fukushima Daiichi nuclear power plant in 2011 (cf. Wiemann 2018), active environmentalism has mostly disappeared from Japan's public and political arena. While especially young activists from rich industrialized nations around the world are joining forces in mobilizing a global environmental movement, Japan's youth is largely absent from this development, and participation by Japanese youth in Greta Thunberg's Fridays for Future movement remains low (Hasegawa 2021). Obstacles which hinder the progress of environmental policies in sectors where business interests strongly oppose them remain (Mori 2012), as for example in agriculture and fisheries (e.g., overfishing and whaling), the energy sector (e.g., the construction of new coal-fired power plants, or the release of radioactive waste water from Fukushima Daiichi nuclear power plant into the Pacific Ocean), or the construction of the largest US military base Henoko in Okinawa.

Overall, this stands in contrast to Germany, where environmental interests have become integrated into political institutions and all spheres of society (Weidner 2020), with the Green Party being the third largest parliamentary group since the 2021 federal election and part of the federal government. At the same time, an active environmental movement functions as external corrective, with large environmental groups with a focus on the climate crisis, like Fridays for Future Germany, as well as the more radical Letzte Generation, or Extinction Rebellion. Especially Fridays for Future Germany has developed a large following of young activists and has become a strong and visible non-parliamentarian voice who criticizes the federal government's climate policies as insufficient and pushes for more ambitious climate action (Marquardt 2020). This goes as far as successfully taking the federal government to court in 2021 (Kotzé 2022), with the groundbreaking decision of the German Constitutional Court declaring the Federal Climate Protection Act as partly unconstitutional and ordering the German legislature to correct and significantly tighten climate laws.

With their similarly large economic affluence and global power, but differing political landscapes and approaches to climate change, Japan and Germany present compelling case studies for assessing how populations perceive, respond to, and mobilize in the face of environmental crises.

3. Research questions and analytical approach

Against the backdrop outlined above, we aim to understand how individuals within these two societies perceive environmental problems, as well as whether and how individual-level attitudes toward environmental issues, the willingness to act in favour of the environment, and actual behaviour have changed over the past three decades as the climate crisis has become an increasingly prominent and tangible topic. To this end, we examine repeated cross-sectional survey data spanning three decades (1993-2020) and assess the strength of environmental attitudes and willingness to take action among the populations of Japan and Germany, while focusing on change over time. Given the growing prominence of environmental issues – particularly global warming and the climate crisis – in media and political discussions, we anticipate a rising awareness of environmental problems over time in both countries. We refrain from establishing explicit hypotheses concerning potential differences between the countries, as our research is, in essence, exploratory in nature.

The second objective of our analysis is to investigate possible differences in how the climate crisis is perceived among certain demographic segments of the population. We specifically focus on a comparison of different age groups due to the projected impacts of global warming in the future. As younger age groups will be experiencing the strongest impact on their quality of life due to climate change, especially at our last data point in 2020, we expect them to be more invested in this topic than older age groups, and ready to make changes to their current lifestyle to mitigate possible hurdles in the future. This assumption is opposite to results of previous studies of ecological behaviour across the life course, which points to a positive relationship between ecological behaviour and age (Otto & Kaiser 2014). However, it is in line with recent findings from research, which takes the urgency of the climate crisis and its effect on younger generations into account (Meyer, Shamon & Vögele 2022, Milfont et al. 2021).

For our analysis, we utilize data for Japan and Germany from the International Social Survey Programme's (ISSP) Environment module[3]. This dataset spans three decades and encompasses four distinct data collection waves: 1993 (Japan N = 1305, Germany N = 2106), 2000 (Japan N = 1180, Germany = 1501), 2010 (Japan N = 1307, Germany N = 1407), and 2020 (Japan N = 1491, Germany = 1702). To ensure the accuracy and representativeness of the German data, weights were applied to account for the oversampling of East German respondents during data collection.

Our descriptive and exploratory approach allows for us to uncover patterns and trends within the dataset while providing a comprehensive summary of the key findings. To evaluate the statistical significance of the observed differences between countries or age groups and across time, we employ two-way analysis of variance (ANOVA).

4. Environmental attitudes and behaviour in Germany and Japan

For the analysis presented in this chapter, we decided to concentrate on four topical areas. First, we look at respondents' general salience of and concern about environmental issues. Next, we inspect whether respondents felt economic growth to be part of the solution for environmental problems. Then,

---

3　https://www.gesis.org/en/issp/modules/issp-modules-by-topic/environment

in trying to understand to what extent attitudes cohere with behavioural intentions, we analyse how willing respondents were to make sacrifices to protect the environment, and whether they actually engage in pro-environmental behaviour. Finally, we compare how they evaluate the individual power to make changes and their preferences regarding environmental policy interventions.

4.1 Salience of environmental issues

To measure the extent to which respondents felt environmental issues to be of central concern among several topics, the ISSP survey includes a question that asks respondents to choose the issue they think is most important for their country among the following topics: Health care, education, crime, the environment, immigration, the economy, terrorism, poverty. Within the four waves of the ISSP Environment survey, this question was only included since 2010, leaving us with only two timepoints to compare. **Figures 2** and **3** depict the top five priorities selected by respondents in Germany and Japan, respectively. German respondents attached less importance overall to the economy, education and poverty in 2020 compared to 2010. The percentage of respondents considering the environment as the most important issue for Germany, however, increased from 6.5% in 2010 to 21.1% in 2020. In Japan, the percentage of respondents viewing the environment as the most pressing issue also increased from 4.1% in 2010 to 10.3% in 2020, although this share remained lower than in Germany. Despite a decline from 57% in 2010 to 39.9% in 2020, the highest percentage of Japanese respondents still considers the economy to be the most important issue in both years. The stark surge in the importance attached to health care in 2020 observed in both countries can most likely be attributed to the impact of the COVID-19 pandemic.

As outlined above, our analysis had a second objective, which was to identify possible differences based on age. To achieve this, we categorized respondents into distinct age groups. We identified two younger age groups – encompassing 18-24-year-olds, likely still engaged in education or recently entering the workforce, and 25-34-year-olds, often in the early stages of their career and family formation. Additionally, we grouped 35-64-year-olds into a middle-aged category, representing the majority of the working population and individuals likely engaged in family care work. Lastly, respondents aged 65 and

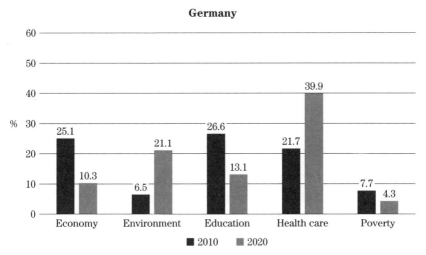

Figure 2: Most important issue for Germany in 2010 and 2020

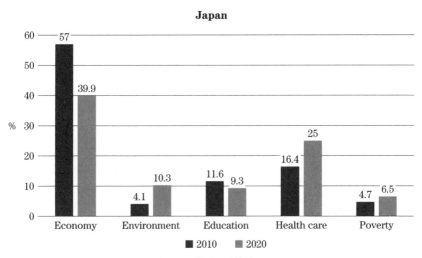

Figure 3: Most important issue for Japan in 2010 and 2020

older were categorized as elderly, as they are typically in or approaching retirement.

Examining the perceived importance of key issues across age groups revealed distinct trends in the two countries. In Germany, there is a noticeable

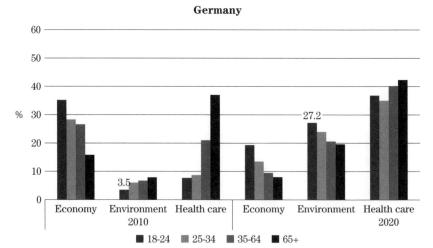

Figure 4: Most important issue for Germany in 2010 and 2020 by age groups

decline in the significance attributed to the economy across all age groups, accompanied by a heightened emphasis on the environment (**Figure 4**). Particularly noteworthy is the youngest age group's concern for the environment in 2020, where 27.2% identified it as the most pressing issue – a substantial increase from 3.5% in 2010. Conversely, in Japan the importance assigned to the economy, though somewhat reduced, remains substantial across all age groups in 2020, with a comparatively modest rise in the significance given to the environment (**Figure 5**). In 2020, 6.3% of individuals aged 18-24 regarded the environment as the most critical issue – a marginal change from their counterparts in 2010 (6.4%). Among older age groups, slightly larger proportions than in 2010 considered the environment as the most important issue in 2020, with the largest percentage found among those 65 and older (11.5%).

General concern about environmental issues increased slightly in both countries between 2010 and 2020[4], although differences between the two time points were small. Notably, in Germany, the youngest and oldest group were more concerned in 2020, compared to their peers in 2010 (**Figure 6**), with

---

4   Respondents evaluated their concern about environmental issues on a 5-point-scale, ranging from 1 = not concerned at all, to 5 = very concerned.

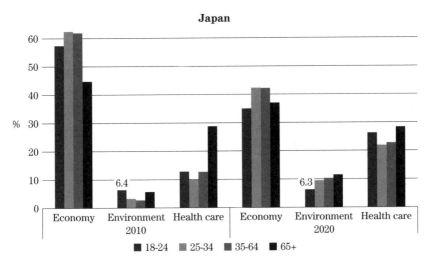

Figure 5: Most important issue for Japan in 2010 and 2020 by age groups

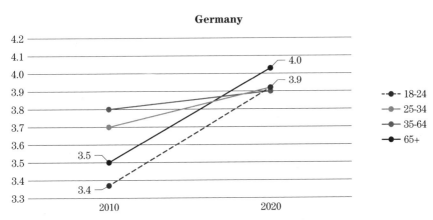

Figure 6: Concern about environmental issues (means), in Germany, by age groups
Note: 1 = not concerned at all, 5 = very concerned; Interaction between year and age group significant, p < .001; Main effects for year and age group significant, p < .005.

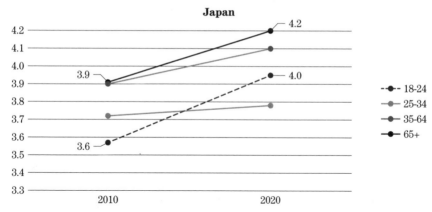

Figure 7: Concern about environmental issues (means), in Japan, by age groups
Note: 1 = not concerned at all, 5 = very concerned; Interaction between year and age group not significant; Main effects for year and age group significant, p < .001.

minimal variation between age groups in 2020 (overall mean for Germany = 4.0). Meanwhile, in Japan, the 18-24-year-olds displayed the biggest increase in concern compared to their peers in 2010 (**Figure 7**). The oldest age group, however, demonstrated the highest level of concern, with a mean of 4.2. Overall, mean values for concern in 2020 were slightly more dispersed around the overall mean of 4.1 in Japan, compared to Germany, indicating greater variation in public sentiment on this issue in the Japanese population.

4.2 Prioritizing economic growth over environmental impact

To understand how the interrelation of economic growth and environmental protection was evaluated, respondents were asked whether they agreed with the statement 'In order to protect the environment, Germany/Japan needs economic growth'. Agreement with this statement is interpreted as prioritization of economic growth over environmental protection. In Japan, support for the belief that economic growth is a prerequisite for environmental protection has remained strong over the past three decades (**Figure 8**). This attitude is also reflected in the large share of Japanese respondents who named the economy as the most important issue for Japan, both in 2010 and 2020, as described above. In Germany, however, we can observe some changes over time, with overall less strong agreement with the idea that environmental protection can

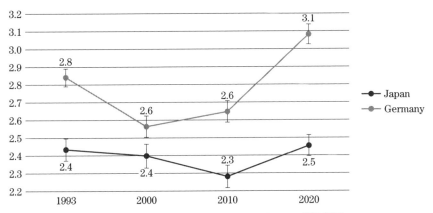

Figure 8: Environmental protection needs economic growth (means, 1993-2020)
Note: 1 = strongly agree, 5 = strongly disagree. Interaction between year and country significant, p < .001. Main effects for year and country significant, p < .001.

only be achieved via economic growth. In 2020, the mean score for this statement was for the first time larger than 3.0 (neutral), crossing over into the realm of responses that indicate disagreement with this growth-dependent mindset. The general trend held true across all age groups in Germany; however, it was notably the younger age groups that expressed the highest level of scepticism toward the notion that environmental protection can only be achieved through increased economic growth (**Figure 9**).

In contrast, in Japan, all age groups maintained their support for the necessity of economic growth (**Figure 10**). This trend is particularly noteworthy among the 18-24-year-olds. Unlike Germany, Japan's youngest age group has displayed a growing inclination towards supporting economic growth since 2000. Despite the persistent backing of economic growth as prerequisite for environmental protection in Japan, this support does not stem from a belief in the ability of technological advancement to mitigate the effects of climate change. When asked to evaluate the statement 'Modern science will solve our environmental problems with little change to our lives,' Japanese respondents consistently disagreed with the statement across all four survey waves (**Figure 11**). German respondents also tended to disagree, although to a lesser extend with disagreement slightly intensifying in 2020.

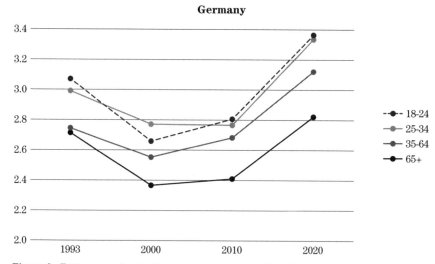

Figure 9: Environmental protection needs economic growth, in Germany, by age groups (means, 1993-2020)

Note: 1 = strongly agree, 5 = strongly disagree. Interaction between year and age group not significant. Main effects for year and age group significant, p < .001.

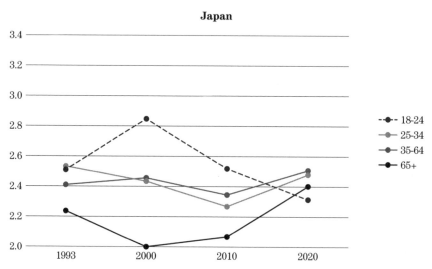

Figure 10: Environmental protection needs economic growth, in Japan, by age groups (means, 1993-2020)

Note: 1 = strongly agree, 5 = strongly disagree. Interaction between year and age group significant, p < .001. Main effects for year and age group significant, p < .001.

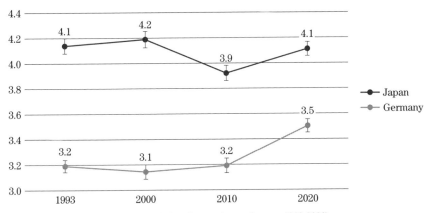

Figure 11: Modern science as remedy for climate change (means, 1993-2020)
Note: 1 = strongly agree, 5 = strongly disagree. Interaction between year and country significant, p < .001. Main effects for year and country significant, p < .001.

4.3 Willingness to make sacrifices

As indicated by research on the attitude-behaviour gap, intentions and concern do not directly translate into action (Farjam et al. 2019). Much scholarship in recent years has tried to identify the specific factors that contribute to closing the gap between intention and action, specifically in the context of climate change mitigation efforts. One aspect that has been analysed as a possible bridge between environmental awareness and pro-environmental behaviour, is individuals' willingness to act (Meyer et al. 2022). This kind of behavioural intention is measured in the ISSP Environment Module with several items, one of which asks respondents whether they would be willing to accept cuts to their standard of living to protect the environment. Responses in both countries tended to hover around the neutral midpoint, with slight change throughout the three decades under investigation, indicating the avoidance of clear-cut statements (**Figure 12**). German respondents were slightly more willing to accept a reduction in their living standard in favour of the environment in 1993 and again in 2020. Japanese respondents, on the other hand, became slightly more unwilling to do so in both 2010 and 2020. In Germany, in 2020, it was specifically the youngest age group who was most willing to accept cuts to their living standard (**Figure 13**). In contrast to Japan, where the two youngest age groups have grown least willing to accept cuts to

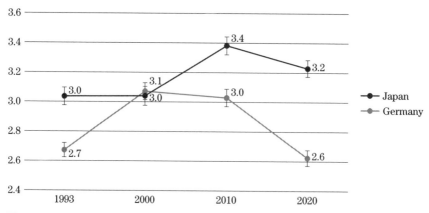

Figure 12: Willingness to accept cuts to standard of living (means, 1993-2020)
Note: 1 = strongly agree, 5 = strongly disagree. Interaction between year and country significant, p <
.001. Main effects for year and country significant, p < .001.

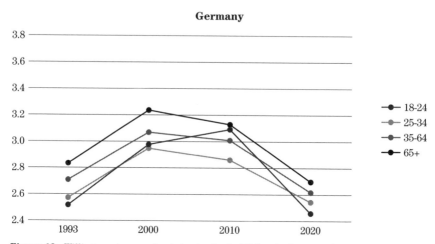

Figure 13: Willingness to accept cuts to standard of living, in Germany, by age groups (means,
1993-2020)
Note: 1 = strongly agree, 5 = strongly disagree. Interaction between year and age group not
significant. Main effects for year and age group significant, p < .001.

their standard of living in the most recent survey waves (**Figure 14**).

The second item capturing behavioural intention was the willingness to pay
higher prices or higher taxes to protect the environment. This continuously

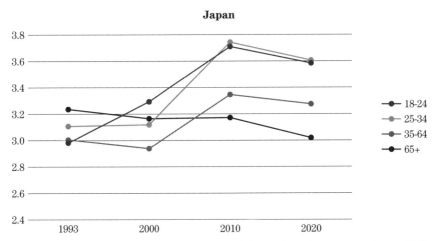

Figure 14: Willingness to accept cuts to standard of living, in Japan, by age groups (means, 1993-2020)

Note: 1 = strongly agree, 5 = strongly disagree. Interaction between year and age group significant, p < .001. Main effects for year and age group significant, p < .001.

decreased in both countries over the past three decades. In Germany, this trend spanned across all age groups, while in Japan it applied mainly to the two younger age groups. Hence, it appears more straightforward to express a general willingness to accept reductions in one's living standard than to endorse specific proposals on how this could be achieved, such as paying higher prices or taxes. This is in line with Farjam et al. (2019), who find that individuals are more likely to undertake low-cost actions to reduce the cognitive dissonance between their attitudes and their behaviour – in this case, merely considering hypothetical behaviour – but are likely to avoid high-cost behaviour, despite the greater impact the latter would have for the environment.

4.4 Pro-environmental behaviour

Actual pro-environmental behaviour is assessed in the ISSP Environment module for the action in both private and public sphere. For the former it was measured by asking respondents how often they made an effort to sort glass, tins, plastic, newspapers, etc., for recycling. Both countries have implemented systems for household waste recycling, with Germany initiating its program in the 1980s and Japan in the 1990s. These systems have undergone continuous refinement since their inception and the extra effort involved in recycling household waste is small, while non-participation is negatively sanctioned[5]. Therefore, it does not come as a surprise, that overall participation rates were high in both countries in 1993 and have increased further over time. Overall, answers range between respondents stating to 'always' or 'often' engage in recycling (**Figure 15**), with recycling efforts being slightly stronger in Germany than in Japan. Differences between age groups were small in both countries, with the older age groups being more disciplined in their recycling behaviour.

However, when it comes to action in the public sphere in the form of political activism, such as actively demanding concrete political measures to protect the environment and counter climate change, country differences were more explicit. When asked whether they had taken part in a protest or demonstration about an environmental issue in the past five years, German respondents stated higher incidences of participation compared to Japanese

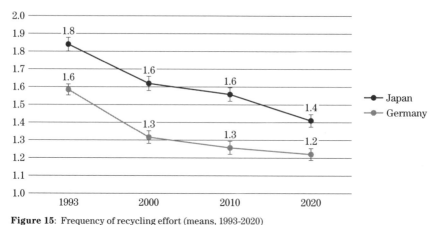

Figure 15: Frequency of recycling effort (means, 1993-2020)
Note: 1 = always, 2 = often, 3 = sometimes, 4 = never[6]. Interaction between year and country significant, $p < .005$. Main effects for year and country significant, $p < .001$.

---

5 In Germany, not participating in recycling will lead to higher monetary costs for waste disposal. In Japan, some types of wastes are collected only on specific days, with non-compliance meaning that the consumer would not be able to dispose of their waste.

6 As both countries have recycling systems in place, the answer option 'not 5vailable' was set as missing.

respondents at all four time points (**Figure 16**). In Japan, participation in environmental protests was low for all age groups and has decreased over the course of the past three decades, with close to no protest participation at all in 2020 (1993 = 2.7%, 2000 = 2.1%, 2010 = 1.4%, 2020 = 0.2%). Differentiating by age groups showed that this was a general trend within the population. Given the historically low participation in public protests in Japan following the student protests of the 1960s up until the Fukushima nuclear catastrophe in 2011, this observation is not surprising. It is striking, however, that the short uprising of large-scale demonstrations against nuclear power in the wake of the nuclear meltdown at the Fukushima Daiichi Nuclear Power Plant in 2011 (cf. Wiemann 2018, among others), has quickly died down, with next to no participation in environmental protests being reported from Japanese respondents in Japan in 2020. This result seems to question the 're-emergence from invisibility' of Japan's civil society (Chiavacci & Obinger 2018) that was proclaimed by several scholars in the late 2010s – at least, when it comes to street protest.

For Germany, after a steady decrease from peak levels of participation in 1993 (8.5%), 2000 (6.1%), to 4.5% in 2010, participation increased again in 2020, when 6.7% of respondents stated to have participated in an environmental protest in the past five years. Here, differences between age groups were

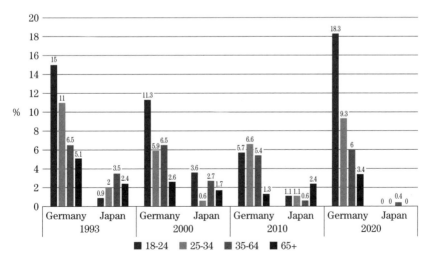

Figure 16: Participation in environmental protest or demonstration in past five years, by country and age group (1993-2020)

significant. Except for 2010, the youngest age group of the 18-24-year-olds proved to be most politically active (**Figure 16**). This peaked in 2020, when 18.3% of the youngest age group stated to have participated in some kind of environmental protest. This clearly reflects the strong presence and membership of Germany's environmental youth movement, especially Fridays for Future (Marquardt 2020).

4.5 Environmental efficacy

Similar differences emerged when comparing the extent to which individual action was believed to have meaningful impact. This measure of self-efficacy evaluates whether respondents believe to be capable of taking the necessary action to achieve the desired outcome (Bandura 1977). Asked whether they felt it to be too difficult to do much about the environment as an individual, average responses in Japan stayed close to the neutral mid-point, with a very slight tendency towards disagreement (**Figure 17**). German attitudes toward this question exhibited slight changes over time. Responses moved closer to the neutral mid-point from 1993 (mean = 3.5) to 2010 (mean = 3.1) before showing a return to somewhat stronger disagreement in 2020 (mean = 3.6). This suggests an increasing sense of self-efficacy among Germans regarding environmental issues.

In Germany, the oldest age group consistently expressed the least conviction that individuals can positively impact the environment at all time

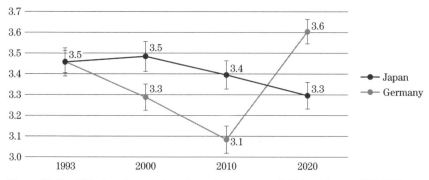

Figure 17: Too difficult to do much about the environment as an individual (means, 1993-2020)
Note: 1 = strongly agree, 5 = strongly disagree. Interaction between year and country significant, p < .001. Main effects for year significant, p < .001. Main effect for country not significant.

points (**Figure 18**). Conversely, in Japan, the younger and middle-aged groups have shown a declining belief in the meaningful positive impact of individual actions on the environment, particularly noticeable in **Figure 19**. Interestingly, the over 64-year-olds, who initially tended to dismiss the relevance of individual action, have gradually shifted their perspective. By 2020, they have caught up with other age groups in supporting the idea that every action can make a difference.

This difference in the perceived individual empowerment, especially in recent years, was further underpinned by a stronger and unchanged agreement of Japanese respondents that there was no point in doing something for the environment unless others did the same. Attitudes in Germany, however, pointed to a stronger positive recognition of their individual agency. This reflects findings of cross-cultural research investigating possible differences in the importance of self-efficacy in individualistic as opposed to collective cultures. In an extensive review of this body of literature, Klassen (2004) concludes that self-efficacy beliefs tend to be lower in collectivist settings of East Asian societies than in individualistic settings of Western societies. However, this does not mean that efficacy beliefs do not play a role in the

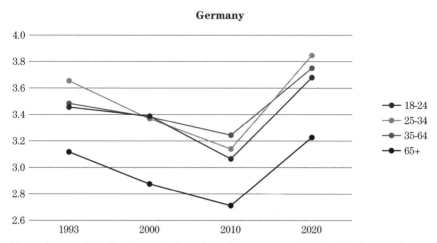

Figure 18: Too difficult to do much about the environment as an individual, in Germany, by age groups (means, 1993-2020)
Note: 1 = strongly agree, 5 = strongly disagree. Interaction between year and age group not significant. Main effects for year and age group significant, $p < .001$.

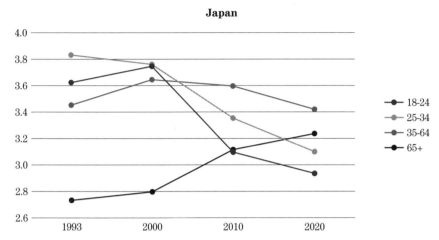

Figure 19: Too difficult to do much about the environment as an individual, in Japan, by age groups (means, 1993-2020)
Note: 1 = strongly agree, 5 = strongly disagree. Interaction between year and age group significant, p < .001. Main effects for year and age group significant, p < .001.

motivation of behaviour in collectivist societies. Self-efficacy is a robust predictor of behavioural performance in both Western and non-Western cultural contexts. In our data, the stark difference in levels of self-efficacy between age groups in Japan points to the fact that other factors besides the cultural context also play a role in determining whether individuals feel in control of achieving desired outcomes. The growing sense among the young Japanese that their actions lack significance may also reflect the broader disillusionment, stemming from the perceived inability to make an impact as a sociodemographic minority in a hyper-aged society.

4.6 Environmental policy

Lastly, we explore the preferences of Japanese and German respondents regarding the most effective political interventions for encouraging businesses, industries, as well as private citizens to protect the environment. In both 2010 and 2020, participants were presented with three strategies to choose from, ranging from the most stringent and punitive to guiding and informing, as well as incentivizing. Either assigning heavy fines for businesses or individuals that damage the environment, providing more information and education about the advantages of protecting the environment, or using the tax system to reward businesses or individuals who protect the environment. In 2010 and 2020 in Japan, respondents highly endorsed the strategy of 'providing more information' for companies to become more active in protecting the environment (**Figures 20**), albeit to a somewhat lesser extent in 2020. Overall, in 2020, support for tax breaks for businesses who protect the environment were most strongly endorsed by Japanese respondents (45.4%), followed by the laxer strategy of 'providing more information' (34.4%), showing a robust preference for a positive incentive structure or soft guidelines, over strict regulations and penalties. German respondents, on the other hand, were less inclined to believe that the core issue might be the lack of information about environmental problems and preferred more punitive measures˘. In both 2010 and 2020, they showed stronger preference of heavy fines and tax breaks as a strategy to promote environmental

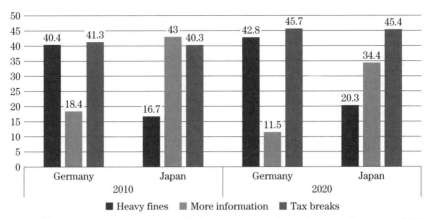

Figure 20: Best way to get business and industry to protect the environment, by country (2010, 2020)

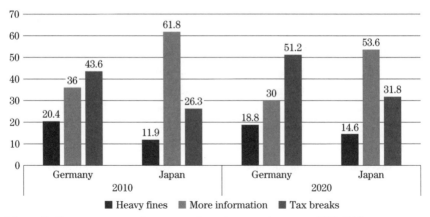

Figure 21: Best way to get people to protect the environment, by country (2010, 2020)

protection by business and industry.

For policy interventions directed at environmentally friendly behaviour at the individual level, the largest share of German respondents favoured a positive incentive approach through providing tax breaks for pro-environmental behaviour both in 2010 and – even more so – in 2020 (**Figure 21**). Japanese respondents still felt that more information and guidance will encourage environmental protection, with highest shares endorsing this strategy in both survey years. Given the existing high awareness and concern about environmental issues in Japan, insufficient knowledge should not pose a hurdle to pro-environmental behaviour. It is more likely that the respondents' views encapsulate the general preference for the least punitive and least responsibility-assigning option.

5. Conclusion

Over the last three decades, there has been a notable rise in awareness and concern about environmental issues, albeit this increase having been more pronounced in Germany than in Japan. In Japan, while environmental concerns are high, respondents continued to place more emphasis on the economy and endorsed further economic growth. In line with findings from previous research, the heightened awareness does not translate directly into a willingness to take action, let alone lead to meaningful pro-environmental behaviour. Here, we witness clear country differences, particularly between the age groups. In Germany, the youngest age group exhibits the highest level of environmental consciousness paired with a noteworthy readiness to make personal sacrifices. This age group also exhibited an overall increase in the belief that individuals can make a significant impact even on their own. Moreover, a substantial portion of the younger demographic in Germany actively participates in pro-environmental protests, highlighting a growing commitment to environmental causes in the society. Interestingly, there is a discernible shift in attitude, particularly among younger Germans, towards a more critical stance on the idea of economic growth as a prerequisite for environmental protection, leading to an increase in street protests. This stands in contrast to Japan, where the oldest age group displays the highest awareness and the strongest willingness to make personal sacrifices for environmental causes. The youngest age group in Japan, however, is the least willing to make sacrifices and holds the belief that individual actions have minimal impact. At the same time, trust in a growth-driven approach to addressing environmental problems remains robust in Japan, again most pronounced among the young.

While both Germany and Japan exhibit similarly high levels of concern about environmental problems, the subsequent behavioural intentions and actual behaviours diverge between the two countries. These results suggest that understanding pro-environmental behaviour requires consideration not only of attitudes but also of the political, cultural, and economic context where these attitudes are fostered. These factors influence whether and how attitudes translate into behavioural intentions and, ultimately, actual behaviour (cf., **Figure 1** above).

Circling back to our initial question about the specific context, in which a 'revolution of consciousness' (Alexander 2015) – and with it changes in behaviour – is likely to occur, our two countries of comparison give us some valuable hints. In Germany, over time, we have started to see positive spillover effects of attitudes into ecological behaviour. This is likely to be due to specific institutional characteristics of the German case. Structural change to promote environmental protection has been achieved from within the political system with BÜNDNIS 90/DIE GRÜNEN having developed into one of the three largest parties in the German party system. At the same time, Germany sports a strong environmental movement which functions as external control. The combination of both has led to a continuous presence of environmental topics in public and political discourse. Active discussion and implementation of climate change mitigation policies at government level, as well as citizen-led initiatives which successfully advocate for specific policies or policy changes, as, for example through the 2021 ruling of the German Constitutional Court, likely create an atmosphere of a shared public arena, in which everyone is called on to participate and take action. As witnessed in the data, particularly young Germans in 2020 seem to be highly motivated to speak up and join in the fight to tackle climate change.

In Japan, on the other hand, while environmental problems are acknowledged and concern is high, the responsibility to handle them does not seem to be perceived to lie with the individual. Instead, trust in the developmental mantra of economic growth as the solution to everything continues to be deeply ingrained in individual values, also throughout the last three decades of economic stagnation. This mirrors government policy, which advocates 'green growth' and mainly relies on the economy and the 'visible hand' of the market to take care of these problems, while merely preparing soft guidelines and recommendations about climate change mitigation measures. While no noteworthy environmental movement is visible in Japan that could critically question the current strategy, topics concerning climate change are present in public discourse. They manifest either in form of a PR focus on the United Nations' Sustainable Development Goals (SDGs), visible in somewhat uncritical media reports on business efforts in finding 'green' solutions aiming to enable life to continue as usual with little room for suggestions of far-reaching systemic changes.

For us, a most concerning trend lies in the environmental attitudes of Japan's youth, which we feel deserve further close monitoring. While the life prospects of young people in economically developed societies, including Germany and Japan, have become increasingly precarious over the past three decades, a distinct difference emerges. Despite both groups facing challenges in navigating the socio-economic contexts shaping their life chances, Japanese youth, unlike their German counterparts, fail to perceive themselves as the catalysts for meaningful changes at the individual level. This lack of self-recognition impedes their ability to bridge the gap between environmental attitudes and pro-environmental actions and activism.

Overall, changing individual behaviours is pivotal for a comprehensive response to climate change, as individual-level actions can initiate a cascade of changes, from influencing peer groups to fostering community-level initiatives or triggering changes in government policy. With our comparative analysis of Germany and Japan, we hope to have contributed to the development of a better understanding of what triggers pro-environmental behaviour. While the mechanisms behind behavioural decisions are complex, understanding why and how individuals adopt eco-friendly environmentally sustainable behaviours or resist them is essential for designing effective interventions that promote sustainable choices and climate change policies.

References

Alexander, Samuel (2015): *Prosperous Descent. Crisis as Opportunity in an Age of Limits*, Melbourne: Simplicity.

Ajzen, Icek/Fishbein, Martin (2005): The Influence of Attitudes on Behavior. In: D. Albarracín/ Johnson, B. T./Zanna, M. P. (eds.): *The Handbook of Attitudes*, Lawrence Erlbaum Associates Publishers, 173–221.

Bandura, Albert (1977): Self-efficacy: Towards a unifying theory of behavioral change. *Psychological Review* 4(2): 191–215. DOI: 10.1037/0033-295X.84.2.191.

Bundesministerium der Finanzen (BMF) (2020): Klimaschutzprogramm 2030 und Kohleaustieg. BMF-Monatsbericht, Mai 2020. www.bundesfinanzministerium.de/Monatsberichte/ 2020/05/monatsbericht-05-2020.html, [Accessed 28 November 2023].

Burck, Jan/Uhlich, Thea/Bals, Christoph/Höhne, Niklas/Nascimento, Leonardo (2024) Climate Change Performance Index 2024 Results: Monitoring Climate Mitigation Efforts of 63 Countries plus the EU – covering more than 90% of the Global Greenhouse Gas Emissions. Germanwatch, NewClimate Institute, Climate Action Network, ccpi.org/, [Accessed 28 November 2023].

Chiavacci, David/Obinger, Julia (2018): Towards a New Protest Cycle in Contemporary Japan? The Resurgence of Social Movements and Confrontational Political Activism in Historical Perspective. In: D. Chiavacci/Obinger, J. (eds.): *Social Movements and Political Activism in Contemporary Japan: Re-Emerging from Invisibility*, London: Routledge, 1-23.

Farjam, Mike/Nikolaychuk, Olexandr/Bravo, Giangiacomo (2019): Experimental evidence of an environmental attitude-behavior gap in high-cost situations. Ecological Economics 166: 1-12. sciencedirect.com/science/article/abs/pii/S0921800919303969. DOI: 10.1016/j. ecolecon.2019.106434.

Geiger, Sonia Maria/Dombois, Claudia/Funke, Joachim (2018): The Role of Environmental Knowledge and Attitude: Predictors for Ecological Behavior Across Cultures? An Analysis of Argentinean and German Students. *Umweltpsychologie* 22 (1): 69-87.

Hasegawa, Koichi (2021): *Kikō kiki wo meguru sanka to rentai – Fridays for Future no shakai undōronteki bunseki* (Participation and Solidarity for the Climate Crisis: Analysis of Fridays for Future Campaigns from a Social Movements Perspective). *The Nonprofit Review* 20(2): 69-78. DOI: 10.11433/janpora.NPR-SI-20-00004.

Henn, Laura/Otto, Siegmar/Kaiser, Florian G. (2020): Positive spillover: The result of attitude change. *Journal of Environmental Psychology* 69:101429. DOI: 10.1016/j.jenvp.2020.101429.

International Monetary Fund (IMF) (2023): *World Economic Outlook: Navigating Global Divergences*. Washington, D.C., October. www.imf.org/en/Publications/WEO/Issues/2023/10/10/world-economic-outlook-october-2023, [Accessed 28 November 2023].

Jänicke, Martin (2020): Ecological Modernization: a Paradise of Feasibility but no General Solution. In Mez, Lutz/Okamura, Lila/Weidner, Helmut (eds.): *The Ecological Modernization of Japan and Germany. Comparing Nuclear Energy, Renewables, Automobility and Rare Earth Policy*, Wiesbaden: Springer, 13-24.

Johnson, Chalmers (1982): *MITI and the Japanese Miracle: The Growth of Industrial Policy: 1925-1975*, Stanford: Stanford University Press.

Klassen, Robert M. (2004): Optimism and realism: A review of self-efficacy from a cross-cultural perspective. *International Journal of Psychology* 39(3): 205-240.

Kollmuss, Anja/Agyeman, Julian (2002): Mind the Gap: Why do people act environmentally and what are the barriers to pro-environmental behavior? *Environmental Education Research*, 8: 3, 239-260. DOI: 10.1080/13504620220145401.

Kotzé, Louis J. (2021): Neubauer et al. versus Germany: Planetary Climate Litigation for the Anthropocene? *German Law Journal* 22: 1423-1444.

Marquart, Jens (2020): Fridays for Future`s Disruptive Potential: An Inconvenient Youth Between Moderate and Radical Ideas. *Frontiers in Communication* 5:48. DOI: 10.3389/fcomm.2020.00048.

Matanle, Peter (2020): Japan and the Environment: Industrial Pollution, Biodiversity Loss, and Climate Change. In Takeda, H./Williams, M. (eds.): *Routledge Handbook of Contemporary Japan*, London: Routledge, 291-303.

Meyer, Frauke/Shamon, Hawal/Vögele, Stefan (2022): Dynamics and Heterogeneity of Environmental Attitude, Willingness and Behavior in Germany from 1993 to 2021. *Sustainability* 14:16207. DOI: 10.3390/su142316207.

Milfont, Taciano L./Zubielevitch, Elena/Milojev, Petar/Sibley, Chris G. (2021): Ten-year Panel Data Confirming Generation Gap but Climate Beliefs Increase at Similar Rates Across Ages. *Nature Communications* 2. DOI: 10.1038/s41467-021-24245-y.

Mori, Akihisa (2012): Development and environmental policy under neo-corporatism: Slow progress toward pluralistic decision-making in Japan. In Mori, Akihisa (ed.): *Democratization, Decentralization, and Environmental Governance in Asia*. Kyoto: Kyoto University Press, 26-51.

Otto, Siegmar/Kaiser, Florian G. (2014): Ecological Behavior across the Lifespan: Why Environmentalism Increases as People Grow Older. *Journal of Environmental Psychology* 40: 331-338. DOI: 10.1016/j.jenvp.2014.08.004.

Richardson, Katherine et al. (2023): Earth Beyond Six of Nine Planetary Boundaries. *Science*

Advances 9(37) eadh2458. DOI: 10.1126/sciadv.adh2458.

Schreurs, Miranda A. (2005): Environmental policy-making in the advanced industrialized countries: Japan, the European Union and the United States of America compared. In: H. Imura/M. Schreurs (eds.): Environmental policy in Japan. Cheltenham: Edward Eldgar, 315-341.

Weidner, Helmut (2020): Ups and Downs in Environmental Policy: Japan and Germany in Comparison. In Mez, Lutz/Okamura, Lila/Weidner, Helmut (eds.): *The Ecological Modernization of Japan and Germany. Comparing Nuclear Energy, Renewables, Automobility and Rare Earth Policy*, Wiesbaden: Springer, 25-40.

Weidner, Helmut/Mez, Lutz (2008): German Climate Change Policy: A Success Story with Some Flaws. *The Journal of Environment & Development* 17(4): 356-378.

Wiemann, Anna (2018): *Networks of Mobilization Processes: The Case of the Japanese Anti-Nuclear Movement after Fukushima*, München: Iudicium.

Wolf, M. J./Emerson, J. W./Esty, D. C./de Sherbinin, A./Wendling, Z. A., et al. (2022): 2022 Environmental Performance Index, New Haven, CT: Yale Center for Environmental Law & Policy. epi.yale.edu, [Accessed 28 November 2023].

Sustainable and Resilient: Regional and Urban Development

Chapter 4

Sustainability and Adaptation in Planning: Community Resilience Against Accelerating Environmental Change

Christian Dimmer
Mark Kammerbauer

1. Introduction

Urban and regional planning can be both the context and an instrument to create and foster resilience on the scale of the city, district, or neighborhood, against the background of growing and increasingly compounded climate-related and socio-economic uncertainty and risk. How can planning help communities cope with and adapt to the related societal and spatial challenges? Why is resilience relevant to sustainable planning in the context of adaptation to accelerating environmental risk and how can it be 'built' into formal planning processes?

To answer these questions, this chapter contrasts sustainability in planning in Germany and Japan in the context of environmental risk and disaster. Unlike most planning scenarios in advanced, developed societies, post-disaster reconstruction holds at least the promise to transform the built environment swiftly and profoundly. We argue that sustainability has the potential to support the adaptation and transformation of the built environmental with the aim of becoming resilient against disaster. The unquestioned growth paradigms of the past led to an expansion of settlements into risk-prone locations such as floodplains, paralleled by an optimism that environmental risks could be adequately managed. This modernist approach increased vulnerability and still prevails today, despite sustainability goals later grafted onto it. We claim that planning concepts oriented on resilience can help to overcome this situation. To illustrate our theoretical reflections, we present two short case studies from recovery and reconstruction efforts in Deggendorf, Germany after the 2013 Danube floods and Onagawa, Japan after the 2011 Great East Japan Earthquake and *tsunami*. Both cases demonstrate exceptional degrees of destruction in their respective contexts—the main selection criterion. Hence, rapid environmental and social change due to disaster in both communities is at the root of our deliberation. While the cases differ in their cultural and institutional context, they permit a discussion on how notions of resilience can contribute to a sustainable form of recovery and reconstruction and why or why not this played a role in these communities.

For this purpose, we consider community resilience as 'the [shared] capability to anticipate risk, limit impact, and bounce back rapidly through survival, adaptability, evolution, and growth in the face of turbulent change' (Plodinec 2013: 10). One way of cultivating such forms of collective resilience is through more intensive, purposeful participation in formal and informal place-based governance measures that are established early on, are open-ended, well moderated, integrated and reflect a broad political consensus. The resulting creation of social capital, problem-solving skills and notions of self-realization supports local communities and reinforces trust between residents and local political decision-makers. Effective and sustainable implementation of related planning aims, however, requires a change in the local political and planning *culture*—from a static towards a dynamic understanding of planning and governance, with regards to institutional dimensions of planning. Adaptation efforts oriented towards environmental risk are dependent on how planning institutions develop and implement plans and projects and to which degree residents and communities adhere to them and accept them as being in the community's best interest, instead of being seen as imposed 'from those above'. Our empirical research in Japan and Germany indicates that the development of resilient planning aims should follow sustainability criteria to ensure continuous adaptation to an environment undergoing increasing and increasingly rapid change, while also considering contextual, socio-economic conditions more thoroughly.

This chapter first revisits concepts of planning, sustainability and resilience in order to propose analytical criteria for the evaluation of post-disaster urban planning interventions. We suggest that regenerative sustainability and community resilience are two important ideas that can help to understand whether reconstruction plans and projects can prepare communities impacted by disaster for unanticipated future shocks that are becoming more frequent and severe due to environmental and socio-demographic changes (cf. Pörtner, Roberts et al. 2022: 662). Next, we look at urban planning as one institutionalized mechanism to effect spatial change and how current, highly bureaucratized, and institutionalized formal urban and regional planning—hereafter, simply planning—constitutes a mechanism that is theoretically well-suited to transition communities towards more resilience and sustainability, but often fails to deliver on these imperatives (cf. Pörtner, Roberts et al. 2022: 910). The two case studies are not intended as systematic comparison, but to highlight how urban planning *can* act in post-disaster situations, when potentially a window of opportunity opens for far-reaching socio-spatial transformation. The examples further illustrate that important factors obstruct such transitions, despite a strong stated will of important stakeholders to make post-disaster communities more resilient and sustainable. Our discussion is based on contrasting both case studies in terms of extent of physical destruction caused by the disaster, demographic trends pre- and post-disaster, impact of institutional assistance, the degree of participatory planning and the role social capital played in recovery planning. We conclude with five theses of how an alternative place governance could bypass institutional and other organizational challenges that stand in the way of creating more resilient and sustainable communities.

2. What is wrong with institutionalized planning?

Accelerating environmental change, political polarization and the development of new technologies have given rise to informal and citizen-based place-making initiatives beyond formal and institutional planning (Ermacora & Bullivant 2016: 33). Even formal planning is undergoing processes of change, although many experts fail to recognize this (Streich 2018: XIII). In the past innovative approaches were developed that offer important impulses for formal planning today. For example, in response to top-down urban renewal and slum clearance in the USA in the 1950s and 1960s, more participatory, inclusive forms of planning developed, seeking to give voice to hitherto marginalized demographics and create capacities for local self-government (e.g., Jacobs 1961;

Davidoff 1965; Arnstein 1969).

It is helpful to examine the underlying ontological assumptions of planning (what *is* planning?) in order to appreciate why progressive planning ideas, embracing the idea of change as normal, conflicted with a modernistic, more static orthodox idea of planning. For example, since the Enlightenment in Europe and the subsequent rise of modernism, the world has been increasingly conceived as something that could and should be planned and rearranged following principles of efficiency—i.e., achieving a stated goal by using the least amount of resources. Thus, planning developed into an activity that contributed to increasing stability of the socio-economic order and made ever more space available for the expansion of modern industrial societies. The so-called 'civilized world'—in opposition to 'uncivilized' nature—became something that moved towards an ideal condition of ever greater *rationality, order,* and *efficiency* in support of the prevailing (capitalist) economic *system*. Nature was either internalized or transformed into a 'second nature' to serve the industrial expansion as resource base. The term *master planning* reflects the intent and the self-attributed ability of planners of controlling environmental change and, by extension, future itself. The world became a space in which the future appeared to be something that planners could predictably plan. A rather static, expert-centric idea of planning emerged, with planning instruments and complex processes increasingly incapable of responding to sudden, unanticipated change. Progressive local governments and planning theorists across Japan experimented during the late 1960s and 70s with adaptable, flexible forms of planning—so-called rolling planning—more responsive to change and more participatory and democratically legitimized (Rix 1975: 535-6).

3. 'Tame' planning versus 'Wicked Problems'

A second ontological assumption regarding planning is the assumed nature of problems proper. Modernist scientists, professionals and planners saw the world populated with so-called 'tame problems' that 'appeared to be definable, understandable and consensual' (Rittel & Webber 1973: 156). Planners were 'hired to eliminate those conditions that predominant opinion judged undesirable' (ibid.), inefficient and irrational. Supposedly simple problems called for rather simple and bold solutions. Robert Moses, self-proclaimed 'master-builder' of New York City, displaced tens of thousands of residents and bulldozed previously lively neighborhoods to build expressways and promote automobility. He famously declared that:

'(w)e wouldn't have any economy without the automobile. ... I believe this is a great industry that has to go on and that has to turn out cars, trucks and buses. Then there have to be places for [their circulation]. There have to be modern roads, modern arteries. Somebody has to build all of that and in order to get things done ... done properly, people (who are in the way of infrastructure construction) need to be inconvenienced' (in Burns 2001: 50:11-36).

This is a very top-down understanding of planning, centered on experts, who supposedly know better than ordinary people what is good for them.

Jane Jacobs showed as early as 1961 in *Death and Life of Great American Cities* how measures, meant to solve simple traffic or housing problems, led to disastrous socio-economic outcomes. Formerly healthy neighborhoods such as the Bronx turned into social hotspots for decades to come. In 1965, psychoanalyst Alexander Mitscherlich published his bestseller *Die Unwirtlichkeit unserer Städte (The Inhospitality of our Cities)* in Germany, in which he criticized inhumane modernist planning centering on inflexible principles of resource efficiency while failing to meet fundamental human needs, thus leading to the weakening of communities and the rise of mental health issues. He advocated for a more collaborative, human-centered way of making cities. Swiss sociologist Lucius Burckhardt pioneered the interdisciplinary analysis of man-made environments (Fezer & Schmitz 2012). From the late 1950s onward, he pointed out that environmental, political, social processes are just as important for making livable cities than visual and technical ones—where complex, dynamic, emergent entities evade modernist planning principles. Thus, over 60 years ago, in different places of the early developed world urbanists found modernist planning sorely lacking the ability to make cities lively and, yes, sustainable, and resilient, although they did not use these terms. Worse, urbanists such as Jane Jacobs denounced orthodox planning as an ideology-driven activity, destroying self-organized, adaptable communities (1961).

Rittel and Webber suggest that most real-world policy and planning problems are 'wicked problems' —opposed to the 'tame problems' that most planners sought to tackle. They recognize socio-spatial processes

'as the links tying open systems into large and interconnected networks of systems, such that outputs from one become inputs to others. ... it has become less apparent where problem centers lie, and less apparent where and how we should intervene even if we do happen to know what aims we seek' (Rittel & Webber 1973: 159).

Every planning intervention creates 'waves of repercussions generated by a problem-solving action directed to any one node in the network' (ibid.), so that one local problem is inducing problems of greater severity at some other node. For wicked problems there is no definitive formulation as society and space develop dynamically. Aside from defining where the root problem lies, it is even more challenging to determine whether the problem has been solved or not. In our case, can we ever know that a land-use plan has tackled climate change, or that a post-disaster recovery plan has succeeded? What this suggests is that more modest, incremental, open-ended, and flexible strategies are needed, as well as the realization that spatial and socio-economic properties are closely connected. Moreover, planning takes place in increasingly pluralistic democratic societies and top-down interventions no longer enjoy the same legitimacy they once did (Selle 2011; Ermacora & Bullivant 2016; Streich 2018). Most importantly, research suggests that social capital strengthens communities and makes them more resilient to shocks (Jacobs 1961; Aldrich 2012, 2019; Aldrich and Meyer 2015). Social networks can foster a more collaborative local society, better suited to developing creative problem-solving strategies that can help communities to cope with unanticipated shocks and promote perpetual adaptation to a rapidly changing world.

As early as 1973, Rittel and Webber recognized that '(t)he professionalized cognitive and occupational styles [of planning] ... refined in the first half of this [20th] century, based in Newtonian mechanistic physics, are not readily adapted to contemporary conceptions of interacting open systems and to contemporary concerns with equity' (1973: 156). They stress that 'societies of the Western world are becoming increasingly heterogeneous, ... increasingly differentiated, comprising thousands of minority groups, each joined around common interests, common value systems, and shared stylistic preferences that differ from those of other groups' (ibid. 167).

Yet, 45 years later eminent planning theorist Bernd Streich soberly notes that 'the domain of urban planning has essentially remained what it has been from the start: a service institution achieving, at best, a sound balance between public and private interests, executed by experts—who still habitually claim to know the right way—in a statist [paternalist] manner' (2018: 138).

4. Proliferation of alternative place-making practices and 'urban activities'

As shown above, visions of a more human-centered, collaborative, and adaptive type of planning that acknowledges the complexity and interconnectedness of the human and non-human environment have long been around. In recent years, new informal, 'subversive' forms (Streich 2018: pp.13) of placemaking and 'co-creating urban futures' (Ermacora & Bullivant 2016: 94) gain momentum that reflect ontological perspectives of more bottom-up driven change. The Great East Japan Earthquake of 2011 was depicted as a catalyst that catapulted nascent grassroots place-making trends into the planning mainstream (Dimmer 2014; 2016). Today, the frequent use of the phrase 'change is the new normal' illustrates this, while institutional planning still seems fixated on the ontology of stability. Along with others, we argue for alternative forms of planning, better able to address increasing climate-related, socio-economic, and other types of change and to make communities resilient against short-term stressors. Theoretical planning discussions on the role of sustainability, resilience and adaptation should, therefore, be tested as to how planning performs in the context of change. Alternative planning practices can either complement institutional planning through informal place-making processes or be integrated into conventional planning through mainstreaming (Wamsler 2014). New forms of planning should encourage social learning that supports an incremental, iterative, and community-driven approach to change, based on participation.

5. Planning for sustainability, resilience, and adaptation

Sustainability in the context of planning refers to solutions to problems that modernist planning contributed to while retaining aspects of modernism it attempts to overcome. The UN Sustainable Development Agenda (UN 2022) defines sustainable development aims as 'building an inclusive, sustainable and resilient future for people and planet', to be based on three central elements, 'economic growth, social inclusion and environmental protection' (ibid.). The argument can be made, however, that the growth paradigm is contributive to current unsustainable conditions (Sachs 1992). The Sendai Framework for Disaster Risk Reduction establishes a link between the United Nations sustainable development agenda by calling for cities to be inclusive and safe, resilient, *and* sustainable (UNISDR 2015). Against the background of climate change and increasing environmental risk, planning for resilient cities and communities emerges as *the* central task of urban planning. It also refers to questions on why resilience is relevant to sustainable planning in the context of environmental risk.

Resilient cities are supposed to be capable of absorbing or coping with rapid change, stress, or shock in various forms. Planners in all relevant domains—either urban or regional planning or planning and preparedness within disaster management—bear a shared responsibility to foster such cities. At the same time, institutionalized planning practice encounters tremendous difficulty in meeting this challenge. Available financial and human resources, governance cultures and the capacities of residents and communities to cope with uncertainties are significant obstacles to resilient urban planning goals (Kammerbauer 2019). Resilience can be integrated within sustainable planning efforts in the context of the relevant planning domains. In other words, resilience must be sustainable, *even if* sustainability is not dependent on resilience (Sieverts 2013). The rationale behind this statement is that resilience is oriented at forms of stability or robustness that, in the manner of urban planning and design, are supposed to enable or support the adaptability of the built environment. Sustainability, however, is oriented towards the bigger picture: Preserving our living environment in which cities are embedded. Yet, for a sustained transition towards more sustainable futures, resilience against short-term shocks is essential (Kammerbauer 2021).

In cities, many opportunities exist to achieve resilience through adaptive measures. This includes experimental design approaches that allow testing, observation, and evaluation (Sieverts 2013). Possible steps include combining functions, such as in the case of protective structures that also permit use for recreational purposes. The required incremental planning approaches for implementation and transformation on the level of buildings comprise interdisciplinary fields of action. Inter- or transdisciplinarity are on the minds of many academic actors, yet have not been established in everyday planning practice to effective degrees. Related strategies such as the managed retreat of settlement space at risk of rising sea levels or floods can comprise different structural ('hard') and non-structural ('soft') measures. This includes instruments such as buyback options for residential properties or approaches such as rewilding, as well as changes to legal frameworks or building codes (Kammerbauer 2021). Subsumed under the term adaptation, these strategies, instruments, and approaches are of decisive relevance to planning as preparation for different forms of short-term stress. Vulnerable actors, however, lack the access to required resources to cope with stress (Wisner 2016). Planning aimed at sustainability and resilience can serve to reduce the risk they are exposed to and, hence, their vulnerability.

In the case of an environmental disaster, earlier notions of resilience as 'bouncing back' to the status quo ante have been superseded by ideas of 'bouncing forward', which implies that adaptation targets drive post-disaster recovery and reconstruction (Kuhlicke, Kabisch & Rink 2020). Resilience is important for policymaking in relation to disaster risk management on the one hand and urban planning and development on the other. It is understood as a planning goal to achieve adaptation to future environmental risk in urban space. Rather than trying to create 'fail-safe' urban systems, urban resilience should aim at 'safe-to-fail'-strategies in the context of sustainable development (ibid.). The difference is that an ontology of fail-safe implies total safety from harm, with the danger that citizens blindly trust specific urban infrastructures and remain oblivious to their own active disaster preparedness activities. The failure of *tsunami* seawalls in Japan surprised many citizens in 2011 in Japan, who often did not know how to properly respond (Aldrich 2019). The same is true for breached floodwalls in the case of riverine flood disasters. On the other hand, safe-to-fail strategies assume multiple lines of defense while actively engaging citizens in the design of preparedness measures and subsequent social practices that keep disaster awareness and readiness high.

Significant differences exist between planning in the context of disaster management and everyday development planning under perceived normal circumstances. Scholars point out that after disasters less time is available, more is at stake, more resources are needed, and public interest is, at least initially, high (Blanco, Olshansky, Chang et al. 2009). In developed industrial nations, disaster management is embedded in governance configurations that determine how institutions act when disaster impacts communities, either through coordination and cooperation, funding, or other support measures. In the case of Germany, member of the EU, disaster management is a responsibility of the individual states (*Länder*) that can draw upon support from the federal government. At the same time, EU water directives have led to a shift of risk management and related planning and preparedness responsibilities to private individuals, while voluntary add-on insurance coverage against natural hazards is considered relatively low (Kammerbauer 2019). Repeated floods in Germany have led to significant damages and related federal funding for individual homeowners, despite popular calls for terminating such post-disaster assistance or providing mandatory flood insurance. How and whether local institutions can support residents in their efforts in reconstructing impacted homes is a key issue of recovery planning and governance. Mainstreaming adaptive planning approaches into everyday planning is, thus, considered an important measure to support sustainable and resilient planning aims (UNISDR 2015: 22; Wamsler 2014).

In the context of water-related planning, experimentation can enable reducing tensions between involved actors and stakeholders and support employing resilience to achieve sustainable transformation within urbanization processes (Olsson, Galaz & Boonstra 2014). Recently, calls for 'restorative' or 'regenerative sustainability' are getting louder, based on the assumption that given the damage that has been already done to the environment it is no longer sufficient to be *passively* 'less bad' (Brown et al. 2018). Instead, steps need to be urgently taken to *actively* regenerate the environment and settlement space. Thus, strategies and actions oriented on regenerative forms of sustainability can address positive socio-ecological change in the context of environmental risk (ibid). Such change can be planned for by using resilience as a guiding image or formulating resilience as a planning goal. Sustainability is generally considered an approach to limiting the impact of human activity on the environment. Aligned with long-term adaptation aims, related building strategies can encompass a continuum of preservation, restoration and reconstruction, re-use and revitalization measures while perpetuating cultural narratives under consideration of ecological and social concerns. Against this background, reconstruction is defined as 'returning a place nearly as possible to a known earlier state (...) distinguished by the introduction of [new aspects] into the fabric' (Brown et al. 2018: 20). On the other hand, the currently prevailing reconstruction paradigm 'building back better' (UNISDR 2015) aims at more far-reaching reconfiguration based on an earlier state. Despite the difference between the two, the role of planning and design is to create buildings and human habitats that are location-specific catalysts for positive socio-ecological change under the engagement of the affected community while enabling continuous learning. Regenerative sustainability, in this context, supports the continuous evolution of interrelated social, economic, and ecological systems.

As Manzini (2013) states, adaptive capacity plays an important role in the design of resilient systems. Distributed systems that are closely integrated in their natural environment have the capacity to avoid collapse based on their diversity, even if components fail. Such distributed systems reflect trends related to ongoing global developments, comprising a shift from systemic hierarchies to networks and localized systems of production and consumption. Outcomes of this shift are a renewed interest in traditional craftsmanship, lean manufacturing and production methods, developments of DIY (do it yourself) culture and point-of-use production (Manzini 2013; Dimmer 2016: 212-4). The increase in networking activity leads to a corresponding increase of exposure in societal terms, and as a result, the greater the 'surface', the greater the degree of social interaction in local terms. Here, proximity is a quality, derived 'from the direct experience of the place where a product comes from and of the people who produce it' (ibid.). This can serve to promote community resilience against uncertainties, defined as the 'collective ability (...) to deal with stressors and efficiently resume the rhythms of daily life through cooperation following shocks' (Aldrich & Meyer 2015: 255). Informal place-making endeavors play an important role in activating social capital, raising the awareness and interest of local citizens in their built environment, giving voice to marginalized groups, and facilitating cooperation beyond official, bureaucratized planning processes (Dimmer 2014; 2016). This can be brought into relation with 'building back better' as the 'existence, development and engagement of community resources by community members to thrive in an environment characterized by change, uncertainty, unpredictability and surprise' (Magis 2010: 401). Thus, resilient planning approaches defined by sustainable qualities, i.e., 'small, local, open, connected' (Manzini 2013), can inspire innovative planning processes based on the collaboration of community members within the socio-ecological context. In sum, these sustainable qualities can contribute to the planning efforts of communities aimed at the reduction of risk and vulnerability and, hence, resilience.

6. Social capital and public participation

Citizen participation was introduced in many countries of the Global North in the late 1960s, but it is often carried out in a ritualistic, tokenistic way, with many elements of plans decided well ahead of the actual participation (Arnstein 1969; Streich 2018). It is often conducted simply to increase acceptance of measures, reduce potential for conflict, or because it is en vogue—as in the case of large-scale infrastructure projects—and allows decision-makers to appear as responsive to citizens' concerns. Planning theorist Klaus Selle goes as far as calling this 'participainment' (2011). In Japan, *machizukuri*, or 'town making' evolved since the late 1960s as a bottom-up counter-discourse to the above-discussed top-down, expert-centered planning that is in Japan referred to as *toshikeikaku*. *Machizukuri* 'puts greater emphasis on public participation, the decentralization of planning power, respect of local individuality, 'soft' welfare, identity-oriented aspects of planning, and incremental advancement without disrupting communities' (Dimmer 2016: 214-5). Similar to Germany, citizen participation is required in official urban planning in Japan since the late 1960s. In practice, however, this seldom went beyond merely informing citizens about the government's plans (Sorensen 2001: pp.219). *Machizukuri*, in contrast, often seeks deeper citizen participation, starting from exploring initial ideas. One outcome of intensive participation and cooperation in place-governance is the creation of social capital.

Many recent empirical studies show that disaster casualties are lower if social capital in a community is stronger. To the same token post-disaster recovery and reconstruction is faster and more far-reaching (Aldrich 2012, 2018; Aldrich & Meyer 2015). Thus, the existence of 'soft' social capital is seen at least as decisive for disaster mitigation and recovery as 'hard' infrastructure (e.g., levees). It is fair to assume that if social capital facilitates a speedier recovery, it can also help with adaptation.

Robert Putnam defines social capital as 'features of social organization such as networks, norms, and social trust that facilitate coordination and cooperation for mutual benefit' (1995: 67); reciprocal social relations between individuals that, in turn, create the potential for collective action.

For our analysis, we differentiate between three types of social capital. *Bonding social* capital are 'connections between individuals who are emotionally close, such as friends or family, and result in tight bonds to a particular group' (Aldrich & Meyer 2015: 258). In place-making workshops or during a neighborhood festival *within* one community, bonding social capital can be established. *Bridging social* capital comprises 'individuals loosely connected that span social groups, such as class or race' (ibid.). It is created through involvement in social organizations such as civil society associations or political institutions. If local residents share their experience from a development or reconstruction project with residents of *other neighborhoods*, bridging social capital is created. Lastly, *linking social capital*, 'connects regular citizens with those in power' (ibid.: 259). When local citizens seek the support of their parliamentary representative or of a university planning professor, linking social capital is invoked.

We suggest that citizen participation should be purposefully designed to create or strengthen social capital and, by extension, community resilience and local capacity for problem-solving. In this manner, interactive and cyclical planning processes can facilitate and reinforce continuous social learning processes, capacity for cooperation and mutual trust. This can, in return, serve to prepare local communities for ongoing change and unexpected developments. Conceived this way, citizen participation is clearly more than Selle's dismissive 'particitainment' (2011). From the point of view of institutional planning, such understandings can impact whether and how planning suggestions find acceptance within informal processes with emphasis on participation and who is included in the related discussions. It is important to note that this requires a reversal of planners' mindsets. Many expert planners see citizen participation as necessary *means* to achieve the *end* of successfully implementing a plan. A new generation of participatory place-makers and community designers sees planning projects more as *means* to activate citizens and catalyze the creation of social capital, with the latter being the *end*. A complete special issue of the influential Japanese art magazine *Bijutsu Techo* was dedicated in January 2015 to 'architects who are no longer interested to build' and called these place-makers 'relational architects' (Dimmer 2016: 216).

7. Case Study I: 2013 Danube floods in Deggendorf, Germany

In May and June of 2013 continuous and excessive rainfall led to floods in central Europe. High water levels were measured along the Danube and Isar rivers in Germany's southeastern state of Bavaria. Two levees were breached and the flood protection system failed in two locations near the villages of Winzer and Fischerdorf. The adjacent settlement space was submerged in floodwaters up to two meters in height. In parts of the city of Deggendorf that were impacted by the flood, specifically the Natternberg and Fischerdorf neighborhoods, where the use of heating oil was common, oil tanks were dislodged, pipes were ruptured and oil contaminated the floodwaters. It took 11 days until all flooding was removed from the area. This time was sufficient for oil to permeate building materials, yet unevenly and randomly. In Deggendorf, altogether 1000 residential units were impacted (Kaltenbach & Kammerbauer 2014).

Following the response phase, publicly sworn-in expert surveyors were contracted by the municipality to survey damaged and contaminated structures. More buildings than had been hoped were contaminated to degrees that required demolishing them. This also applied to homes owned by residents who had already repaired and rebuilt these buildings quickly after floodwaters had receded. At the same time, questions regarding funding recovery and reconstruction efforts emerged, since many residents did not own flood insurance and those who did had no guarantee that insurance companies would accept expert surveys on the contamination of buildings. For uninsured homeowners, immediate assistance was provided based on dedicated federal recovery and reconstruction legislation paired with special funding which was jointly facilitated by the German federal government and the state government of Bavaria (BMI 2013), covering 80 percent of expenditure for repair, replacement or reconstruction efforts. Applications for governmental recovery funding had to be submitted within an original timeframe of 3 years, while the awareness grew over time that this process would last until 2018 (Kammerbauer & Wamsler 2018). Alterations of existing structures were permitted, for instance, redistributing functions and areas within buildings for mitigation purposes. These exceptional procedures required for the recovery and reconstruction of an impacted community took place within the standard land-use planning and permit context. The use of heating oil remained optional until 2017 and the levee system was improved in the years to follow to nominally ensure regional flood protection (Kammerbauer & Wamsler 2018).

The Deggendorf case paints a heterogeneous picture of the post-flood recovery and reconstruction efforts and questions whether 'building back better', a sustainable form of recovery that includes measures for risk reduction, was actually achieved. Survey data (Kammerbauer & Wamsler 2018) indicate that many uninsured homeowners received governmental rebuilding funding. However, almost half of all respondents encountered difficulties in completing funding applications, with nearly a fifth stating to have experienced great difficulty. Individual access to resources determined who was able to quickly rebuild, and correspondingly, those who initially lacked resources (or had to wait until they were made available, either based on governmental rebuilding funding or insurance payouts) witnessed delays. In sum, more than half of all respondents experienced oil contamination, while one quarter of respondents demolished their homes. Some rebuilt on site, few on new, slightly elevated reserve plots that were available in limited numbers to the local planning department. Those homeowners who improved their homes were able to minimize individual risk. However, this was done based mainly on individual initiative and not on community-wide, participatory planning. Vulnerable residents—renters, seniors, disabled residents, migrants—experienced particular difficulties.

There are positive and negative outcomes of this recovery process. Based on social capital, vulnerable residents found support from civil society actors who provided assistance, either with information or by helping them complete applications. This did not apply to all pre-flood residents, especially renters, of which many left the area, due to lacking resouces. While, in this case, housing tenure emerges as one critical demarcation line between those who can stay and rebuild and those who can't, delays in rebuilding related to various reasons led to undue stress among those who attempted to recover on site. Individual initiatives took place in absence of a coherent sustainable planning process to achieve community resilience (Kammerbauer & Wamsler 2018).

8. Case Study II: 2011 Tsunami in Onagawa, Japan

In Japan, disaster preparedness has long been one of the central drivers for urban planning and redevelopment. Every new major disaster has led to stricter disaster precautions in national legislation to minimize damage and casualties. However, it is problematic if planning for disaster risk mitigation and engineered resilience take a center stage over long-term sustainability and adaptation-to-climate-change thinking. Such one-sided focus can contribute to a silo mentality, and, as a result, the spectrum of possible solutions is narrowed, with an emphasis on large-scale disaster prevention infrastructure projects, such as *tsunami* protection structures. Instead, a holistic view on sustainability and strategic foresight should focus on other long-term challenges as well such as demographic decline, depopulation, disintegration of communities, lack of economic opportunity and environmental regeneration (Dimmer 2018). *Machizukuri* and reconstruction expert Michio Ubaura states that 'the sole focus on disaster risk and coastal protection creates cities that are uncomfortable to live in and not sustainable. By the time the next large *tsunami* strikes, few people will be still living in these inhospitable places' (Ubaura 2013).

Accordingly, in the impacted communities, participation in planning could be undertaken in a more extensive manner, both in terms of quantity and scope of participants, as well as the topical issues under discussion. Increasing the widths of streets, the creation of evacuation parks and other means comprise only the beginning of a future-oriented planning approach under the auspices of disaster management. The trigger (or incentive) for planning—i.e., the reduction of disaster risk—can be embedded in a comprehensive future dialogue. Such endeavors can also serve to discuss wider measures that can strengthen the local economy, address demographic change, propose solutions to vacant buildings (*akiya*), reinforce tourism and the protection of local built heritage. In many places along the *tsunami*-stricken coast of the Tohoku region, this kind of intensive, broad future dialogue was not carried out for complicated reasons and planners mostly focused on disaster risk reduction (Dimmer 2018). Under great time pressure, the reconstruction process was undertaken, for the most part, by external technical experts with an narrow focus on the reduction of future disaster risk and a predominant concern for their own sectoral project. A holistic integration of the partial reconstruction projects was often lacking. Thus, residential developments were planned on higher ground, safe from future *tsunamis* and the low-lying areas were declared suitable only for commercial, non-residential land uses. Up to 14.5-meter-tall protective seawalls were erected along hundreds of kilometers of pristine coastal landscapes. Often, the rebuilding process was limited to a succession of separate ad-hoc measures that lacked overall coordination and were planned and implemented by different contractors and organizations and financed by separate government authorities (Sue 2017). While 'building back better' as adaptation to future disasters was, in part, achieved, other central challenges related to demographic change which affect peripheral communities that experience population decline, aging and shrinkage as well as economic dependency on fishery were rarely considered. Truly sustainable development in the ecological, social, and economic sense was, thus, not widely tackled (Dimmer 2018).

Onagawa in Miyagi prefecture presents a different approach. The town that was largely destroyed by the *tsunami* of March 11, 2011 had already been shrinking for a long time. The peak population of 18.080 in 1965 had declined to 10.051 in 2010, and the community was suffering from a lack of economic opportunity for the younger generations, who – as a result – had migrated out, with a disproportionately large share of elderly remaining (Onagawa Town 2016: 3). The *tsunami* left 827 persons dead or missing, and as of 2020 only 6319 people resided in town (ibid.).

The Onagawa case is an exception to reconstruction planning in Japan inasmuch as it represents a comprehensive form of post-disaster rebuilding with a broad spectrum of structural issues being addressed in the reconstruction process, going beyond mere rebuilding. A broad future dialogue was carried out that equally addressed all three dimensions of sustainability goals: social, economic, and ecological (Onagawa 2016). As early as April of 2011—months before formal recovery and reconstruction planning had begun—initial visions for rebuilding were discussed within a non-governmental Recovery Coordination Association (FRK, *Fukkō Renraku Kyōgikai*). It constituted an ad-hoc institution that included actors from the chamber of industry and commerce, the tourism promotion association, the fishery association and the fishermen's union. The committee had been formed shortly before the disaster to tackle the regeneration of the aging town (Yamazaki et al. 2013; Aoki 2018). The older members of the council emphasized the need to listen to young residents and entrepreneurs, since the overall concern was the future of the community itself. In November 2011, Yoshiaki Suda, only 39 years of age at the time, became the mayor of Onagawa. He purposely expanded the participation process further to create more legitimacy for the plans. Coordinators for different partial projects and neighborhoods were appointed, as well as an overall coordinator who supervised the integration of the otherwise disconnected projects (Sue 2017). Takahiro Aoyama, head of FRK, captured the complex reconstruction challenges as follows:

'Stay, return, and come to live in Onagawa—these are the three main themes of our municipal rebuilding plan... People need to come to live in Onagawa—here we mean young people, outsiders and 'fools' - and without these people Onagawa won't be rebuilt. However much (sic!) old-timers ... cannot help but be influenced by the old Onagawa. We need the 'fools' who can overturn our plan and create something totally new' (cited in Yamazaki et al. 2013: 1).

Soon, a consensus was formed that building a protective seawall against future *tsunamis* would not be sufficient to ensure that the community would thrive in the future and adapt to new challenges. In dozens of other coastal communities, groups of citizens resisted the erection of seawalls as they worried about lost tourism revenues because of the spoiled landscape, among other reasons. Often, the whole reconstruction process was stalled because it was not clear which parts of the communities will be protected from future *tsunamis* and which not. This led to deep rifts between people willing to rebuild quickly and those asking for better future options, thus damaging the social fabric. Only in a handful places such as Onagawa a consensus was reached to find alternative ways of coping with future *tsunamis*. The community abstained from building a tall *tsunami* protection barrier and chose to preserve the scenic landscape, which is a main resource for tourism. Instead, the whole town center was elevated and zoned for exclusive commercial use, while all housing was relocated to higher ground.

Simultaneously, while the official recovery projects were underway, external entrepreneurs were invited to or found their way into Onagawa. They contributed to the diversification of the local economy that had hitherto mostly relied on fishing. Renowned architect Shigeru Ban who had designed widely recognised, high-quality emergency shelter structures for the community shortly after the *tsunami* disaster, created the railway station as a striking landmark that signals the entrance to the town and contains a thermal spa. From the station, a pedestrian axis, lined with carefully arranged timber shopping pavilions, leads to a park near the harbor that serves as a place of remembrance for the victims of the *tsunami*. The *Qatar Friendship Fund*, which was set up by the State of Qatar to support the victims of the 2011 disaster, sponsored the construction of a fish refrigeration facility and a combined elementary and middle school because the town had demonstrated a commitment to an ambitious, holistic reconstruction project.

Even after the initial recovery phase, the future dialogue continues. The non-profit organization '*Asuenokibou*' (hope for tomorrow), founded by social entrepreneur Yosuke Komatsu, helped to promote a view of Onagawa as a future lab, where the intensive dialogue between residents, municipal authority and local as well as non-local social enterprises allows prototyping new socio-economic models for adaptation to demographic change. Onagawa hopes to offer valid future strategies for rural communities across the world that are equally impacted by demographic change. An example of this can be seen in the town's effort in creating a connection with social innovators in Detroit, Michigan, a post-industrial city which is similarly challenged by depopulation and economic decline —thus creating bridging social capital.

9. Discussion

There are obvious similarities and dissimilarities between the two cases from Germany and Japan (see **Table 1**). Since case studies can be selected according to their exceptional character, they cannot be expected to completely match up, given the cultural differences between them. Rather than a systematic comparison, the two case studies illustrate different aspects of our initial theoretical discussion. What unites them is the exceptional degree of destruction experienced due to the respective disaster impact and the need for sustainable and resilient planning for the recovery and reconstruction of the two communities. Our assumption is that a pro-growth paradigm has contributed to an increase of vulnerability in the past – in both case studies. It seems that in both instances a modernist planning bias resting on the idea that risk could be conclusively managed still informs solutions that have been implemented. Environments historically subject to risk are, thus, transformed into spheres of protection that disregard vulnerability, brushing it off as a mere statistical probability of individual hardship. However, as the selected cases show, there is no absolute protection against floods that impact vulnerable residents to differing degrees. In Deggendorf, individuals decided whether to rebuild or leave based on joint federal and state funding, insurance payouts or their individual resources. Participative, collective, adaptive future-oriented planning, however, was absent. Rebuilding was implicitly handled as an everyday, "normal" process, driven by governmental spending, yet without facilitating a sustainable planning process for long-term community resilience. The state government merely repaired and improved the existing floodwall system as part of the status quo. Some vulnerable citizens left, while others received help through bonding and bridging social capital. One important distinguishing factor in this regard was housing tenure. On the other hand, the case of Onagawa shows that although the national government provided comprehensive reconstruction subsidies, many survivors chose to leave the city because of a lack of socio-economic opportunities and uncertainty about the reconstruction process. However, here, the local government used the reconstruction process for developing a broad, transformative agenda to increase the economic and social sustainability of the community, while simultaneously strengthening the resilience against future shocks.

Evaluating the recovery in the two communities described here poses an intriguing challenge. Can they be considered a 'failure' or a 'success'? Here we remind the reader of the preceding discussion of wicked problems that are hard to delineate, with the root causes of problems being discussed differently (or

Table 1: Comparison of social and spatial aspects in Deggendorf and Onagawa

Aspect	Deggendorf	Onagawa
Extent of destruction by disaster in the built environment	Extensive floodwater damage and oil contamination, 1,000 houses impacted	827 people dead or missing, out of 10,000 residents, Nearly 3,000 buildings fully destroyed (66% of housing stock); loss of economic base
Demographic trend pre- and post-disaster	Individual departure of vulnerable residents after the flood, in particular renters	Population decline from 18,080 (1965) to 10,051 (2010). As result of *tsunami* casualty and lack of housing decline to 6,319 (2020).
Impact of institutional assistance (individual or community)	Individual applications for state recovery funding for uninsured homeowners, or possible insurance payouts if homeowners were insured against floods, while insurance coverage was (and is) low	State subsidies for individual housing reconstruction, public housing, infrastructure, disaster prevention measures (landfills, relocation of all housing to *tsunami*-safe, higher ground)
Degree of participatory planning	None: replacement of status quo, very few individual rebuilding efforts on new adjacent sites (higher ground), individual flood mitigation and adaptation	Intensive degree of participation. Debates about economic and social renewal had already broadly started before the disaster, participation in many different arenas (formal + informal)
Role of social capital	Bonding and linking social capital: individual impacted citizens/members of institutions helped vulnerable homeowners in application processes; Bridging social capital: consultation by publicly sworn-in expert surveyors	Bonding: Strong local identity and sense of shared challenge; bridging: construction of selfhelp network between similar communities; Linking: Lobbying of mayor and social entrepreneurs from Onagawa in Tokyo; *Qatar Friendship Fund* finances fishery store house and unified elementary and junior high school
Proposed risk management solutions	Improvement of state flood protection system and floodwalls, use of oil heaters no longer permitted	Disaster risk reduction: Landfill and relocation to higher ground for *tsunami* protection; Community resilience: Comprehensive regeneration plan for economic diversification and strengthening of community cohesion

not at all) among different disciplines (cf. Wisner 2016). What might look like a failure initially might be interpreted as a success by later observers. Acknowledging these limitations, we apply the classification of disaster recovery by Davis and Alexander (2016: 44-46) who suggest four possible outcomes: a) no recovery, b) insufficient or erratic recovery, c) replacement recovery as restoration of the status quo ante and d) recovery as development that leads to sustainability and resilience. From this point of view, the recovery in Deggendorf can be, at best, described as replacement of existing structures, whereas the Onagawa case gestures at farther-reaching adaptation. Why is this so?

In Germany, the concept of hazard governance is intended to enable local communities to cope with the impact of disaster based on funding, resources and capacities jointly provided by federal and state levels of government. This conventional approach to disaster management tends to work well in the response phase, but encounters problems in the recovery phase (Kammerbauer 2019). 'Flood protection' remains the overarching aim, while alternatives such as 'living with the water' as potential design task are not collectively explored. The focus on large-scale measures such as flood protection megastructures that are intended to enforce 'normal' everyday planning (*Bauleitplanung*) are precisely the big, regional 'modernities' that are opposed to small, local, informal, distributed systems that can enable capacity building and contribute to community resilience (Manzini 2013).

Currently, disaster reduction planning in Japan is a central part of overall urban planning. Whereas Japanese cities are designed to be resilient in the event of disasters such as earthquakes, *tsunamis* or floods, this is currently only weakly connected to other sustainability agendas such as dealing with demographic change, food or energy security, etc. Onagawa presents itself as a promising model, but as only 12 years have passed since the disaster, it is not possible yet to conclusively evaluate whether the reconstruction project was, in fact, a success.

Environmental risk and disaster lead to rapid socio-spatial processes of change. A regenerative type of sustainability can address change through planning by defining resilience as a guiding image or planning aim (Brown et al. 2018). This would enable a community to 'be resilient' in the case of disaster impact and use the reconstruction process to reorient overall future urban development with regenerative sustainability and resilience in mind. In its recovery and reconstruction, a community can 'bounce forward' to adapt to a changing environment in terms of resilience oriented on the ecology (Gunderson 2000). Ecological resilience thinking can, thus, enable actors to cope with environmental risk within complex socio-ecological systems to maintain, adapt and improve related (socio-spatial) system characteristics. Restorative and regenerative concepts can, in this way, become part of the adaptation strategy. This offers the opportunity to enable continuous learning and feedback to integrate a diverse set of social (community) and spatial (ecology) characteristics (Brown et al. 2018).

10. Conclusion

It is necessary to embed resilient planning aims within sustainability approaches to planning to include vulnerable residents in the planning process for the recovery of their communities after disaster. This, however, requires a cultural shift from a static towards a dynamic notion of the world, and, by extension, planning. A shift in mindsets is needed, from large-scale institutional planning of megastructures oriented on establishing a static, fixed, modernist type of 'normality' to an emergent, open-ended 'normality' in which perpetual citizen engagement and capacity building through future-oriented planning initiatives promote ongoing adaptation to new situations. Creating and fostering social capital plays a central role in this regard, especially in terms of its potential to encourage and cultivate iterative processes of learning and self-organization, also within institutions. As a result, concepts such as adaptation, resilience and regenerative sustainability can contribute to incremental planning, planning advocacy or participatory placemaking—all aimed at actually and comprehensively 'building resilience' (Aldrich 2012). Given the auspices, 'building back better' appears as an unattainable ideal that real-life situations can never do justice to. The case studies illustrate this to varying degrees— Onagawa being more successful than Deggendorf in this regard. The deliberation on social capital and its relevance for post-disaster recovery and reconstruction shows how important it is to view social and spatial aspects in an integrated, holistic, and future-oriented manner.

Built structures at best symbolize how communities can deal with a disaster. The disaster is actually overcome when the social vulnerability of residents and the risk they are exposed to are reduced (UNISDR 2015) and when capacities are built to enable them to shape their own future through collective action and active self-government (Jacobs 1961). Carefully cultivated participation in planning processes can create social capital for this purpose. As a result, knowledge-based planning and preparedness are indispensable and can be supported by research on the social and spatial aspects of planning for recovery after environmental disasters across geographical regions. To conclude on the relevance of resilience to sustainable planning in the context of environmental risk and how it can be 'built' into related planning and design processes, we propose 5 theses on how institutional planning in the context of post-disaster recovery can better address the adaptation needs of impacted populations. Regenerative sustainability, community and ecological resilience, inclusion and public participation through place-making are key to achieving adaptation to an increasingly changing environment. Our 5 theses suggest:

1. Establish a planning context not only for *passive* sustainability in the sense of 'being less bad', but for *active*, regenerative sustainability. The notion of 'maintaining' the current status quo and the access to resources for future generations is inadequate to address ongoing climate change and rapid environmental disaster. Regenerative sustainability creates room for thought on adequate ecologically resilient planning and design approaches. Actively regenerative sustainability can also reduce disaster risks.

2. Within frameworks of regenerative sustainability as a planning goal, community resilience should be embedded in relation to local adaptation needs. Regenerative sustainability allows the flexibility required to achieve resilience to experiment with adaptive solutions to ongoing climate change and unanticipated environmental disasters within a community.

3. Within a regenerative sustainability planning context and by proposing adaptive solutions aimed at creating and fostering community resilience, inclusion and broad as well as intensive co-creation of plans and projects is key. All stakeholders from government institutions, the market and civil society need to share information and resources to jointly develop holistic approaches that reflect local needs. Capacities must be built, especially

when dealing with post-disaster recovery for communities that were ill-prepared to cope with disaster impacts. The more intensive the future dialogue, the more scenarios are debated—even unlikely ones—the greater becomes the community's resilience.

4. All the above requires active citizen participation in planning for post-disaster recovery and ongoing place governance after reconstruction is achieved. It must be more than 'particitainment' with merely formalistic, proforma citizen involvement that allows municipalities to claim adherence to sustainability criteria while not really being inclusive and consequential. Public participation is required to develop adaptive solutions that qualify as 'building back better' according to local needs. Only if stakeholders can be sure that they have an equal say in the making of their common future, can controversial issues be tackled and community members feel invested in and committed to the plans. However, it should also be noted that while participative forms of urban development hold greater potential in terms of sustainability and resilience, they are also based on the assumption that residents are willing to participate. This is not always the case. Thus, both top-down as well as bottom-up approaches need to be combined according to the specific local situation.

5. Participatory placemaking is an emergent domain oriented on shaping the built environment while aiming at regenerating local environments close to the spaces of everyday life and mostly outside of the domain of formal, official urban planning. It thus has the potential to activate a greater number of citizens and engage them—also playfully—in local future dialogues, beyond the limited circle of people directly affected by reconstruction projects. Such an empowered citizenry can play a more active role in recovery planning after disasters, while simultaneously using this 'window of opportunity' for co-creating resilient future strategies that seek to tackle climate change, resource depletion, loss of habitat or demographic change, to name just a few policy issues.

Our two case studies show that modernist, growth-oriented planning paradigms may have created an assumed level playing field for spatial production. However, what they also created are environments of increasing vulnerability against the background of failures of protective structures and increasing climate risks. It is not enough to provide funding and hope everyone will be able to cope with the effects of climate disasters. Instead, it is of paramount importance to facilitate and engage in participative planning approaches that inclusively help communities to achieve sustainable and resilient results that enable them to adapt to a changing environment. This is indispensable to 'build' resilience into sustainable planning processes.

References

Aldrich, D. P. (2012): *Building Resilience: Social Capital in Post-Disaster Recovery.* University of Chicago Press.

Aldrich, D. P. (2019): *Black Wave: How Networks and Governance Shaped Japan's 3/11 Disasters.* University of Chicago Press.

Aldrich, D. P./Meyer M. A. (2015): Social Capital and Community Resilience. In: *American Behavioural Scientist.* Vol. 59 (2): 254-269.

Aoki, N. (2018): Sequencing and Combining Participation in Urban Planning: The Case of tsunami-ravaged Onagawa Town, Japan. In: *Cities* (72): 226-236

Arnstein, S. (1969): A Ladder Of Citizen Participation. In: *J. of the Am. Planning Association* (35): 216-224.

Blanco, H./Marina Alberti/Robert Olshansky/Stephanie Chang/Stephen M. Wheeler/John Randolph/James B. London/Susan Parnell/Edgar Pieterse/Vanessa Watson (2009): Shaken, Shrinking, Hot, Impoverished and Informal: Emerging Research Agendas in Planning. In: *Progress in Planning* (72): 195–250.

BMI. (Bundesministerium des Innern und für Heimat) (2013): *Bericht zur Flutkatastrophe 2013: Katastrophenhilfe, Entschädigung, Wiederaufbau. Bundesministerium des Innern.*

Brown, M./Haselsteiner, E./Apró, D./Kopeva, D./Luca, E./Pulkkinen, K./Vula Rizvanolli, B. (eds.) (2018): *Sustainability, Restorative to Regenerative*, COST Action CA16114 RESTORE, Working Group One Report: Restorative Sustainability.

Burns, R. (2001): The City and the World (1945-2000). PBS Home Video.

Davidoff, P. (1965): Advocacy and Pluralism in Planning. In: *Journal of the American Institute of Planners* (31): 331-338.

Davis, I./Alexander, D. (2016): Recovery from Disaster. Oxford.

Dimmer, C. (2014): Evolving Place Governance Innovation and Pluralising Reconstruction Practices in Post-disaster Japan. In: *Planning Theory & Practice* (15): 260-265.

Dimmer, C. (2016): Place-making before and after. 3.11: The Emergence of Social Design in Post-Growth Japan. In: *Review of Japanese Culture and Society* (28): 198-226.

Dimmer, C. (2018): Japan After March 11th 2011: Between Swift Reconstruction and Sustainable Restructuring. In: W. Yan and W. Galloway (eds.) *Rethinking Resilience: Adaptation and Transformation in a Time of Change.* Springer, 23-40.

Ermacora, T./Bullivant, L. (2016): *Recoded City: Co-Creating Urban Futures.* London:

Routledge.

Fezer, J./Schmitz, M. (eds.). (2012): *Lucius Burckhardt Writings. Rethinking Man-made Environments: Politics, Landscape & Design.* 1st ed. Ambra Verlag, Vienna.

Gunderson, L. H. (2000): Ecological Resilience—In Theory and Application. In: *Annual Review of Ecology and Systematics* (31): 425-439.

Jacobs, J. (1961): Death and Life of Great American Cities. New York: Vintage Books.

Kaltenbach, F./Kammerbauer, M. (2014): Housing Rehabilitation after Oil Contamination in Floodplains – Anticipating the 'Flood Adaptive Home'. In: DETAIL International Edition 4/2014.

Kammerbauer, M./Wamsler, C. (2018): Risikomanagement ohne Risikominderung? Soziale Verwundbarkeit im Wiederaufbau nach Hochwasser in Süddeutschland. In: *Raumforschung und Raumordnung* 76, 485-496.

Kammerbauer, M. (2019): Natural Hazards Governance in Germany. In: *Oxford Research Encyclopedia of Natural Hazard Science*, B. Gerber, C. Wamsler (eds.), New York: Oxford University Press.

Kammerbauer, M. (2021): Resilience – Time is of the Essence. In: *TOPOS* 116.

Kuhlicke, C./Kabisch, S./Rink, D. (2020): Urban Resilience and Urban Sustainability. In: M. Burayidi, A. Allen, J. Twigg, C. Wamsler (eds.), *The Routledge Handbook of Urban Resilience*, 17-25.

Magis, K. (2010): Community Resilience: An Indicator of Social Sustainability. In: *Society & Natural Resources* (23): 401-416. DOI: 10.1080/08941920903305674

Manzini, E. (2013): Small, Local, Open and Connected. Resilient Systems and Sustainable Qualities [WWW Document]. Design Observer. URL designobserver.com/feature/small-local-open-and-connected-resilient-systems-and-sustainable-qualities/37670, [Accessed 31 August 2022].

Mitscherlich, A. (1965): *Die Unwirtlichkeit unserer Städte (The Inhospitality of our Cities)*, Suhrkamp.

Olsson, P./Galaz, V./Boonstra, W. J. (2014): Sustainability Transformations: a Resilience Perspective. In: *Ecology and Society* 19(4): 1.

Onagawa Town (2016): Start! Onagawa - *Onagawa-chō: machi, hito, shigoto Sōsei Sōgō Senryaku* (Start Onagawa: Comprehensive strategy for the Creation of Community, People and Work), July 2016, www.town.onagawa.miyagi.jp/pdf/sogokeikaku/machi_hito_shigoto_01.pdf, [Accessed 31 August 2022].

Plodinec, M. J. (2013): *Definitions of Community Resilience: An Analysis.* Washington, DC.: Community and Regional Resilience Institute.

Pörtner, H.-O./Roberts, D. C. (eds.). (2022): *Climate Change 2022: Impacts, Adaptation and Vulnerability.* Contribution of Working Group II to the Sixth Assessment Report of the Intergovernmental Panel on Climate Change.

Putnam, R. D. (1995): Bowling Alone: America's Declining Social Capital. In: *Journal of Democracy* (6): 65-78.

Rittel, H. W. J./Webber, M. M. (1973): Dilemmas in a General Theory of Planning. In: *Policy Sciences* (4): 155-169.

Rix, A.G. (1975): Tokyo's Governor Minobe and Progressive Local Politics in Japan. In: *Asian*

Survey (15): 530-542.

Sachs, W. (1992): *The Development Dictionary: A Guide to Knowledge as Power.* Zed Books.

Selle, K. (2011): »Particitainment« oder: Beteiligen wir uns zu Tode? In: *PND* 111. www. planung-neu-denken.de/images/stories/pnd/dokumente/3_2011/selle_particitainment.pdf.

Sieverts, T. (2013): Am Beginn einer Stadtentwicklungsepoche der Resilienz? Folgen für Architektur, Städtebau und Politik. In: *Informationen zur Raumentwicklung* (4): 315.

Streich, B. (2018): *Subversive Urban Planning.* Springer VS.

Sue, Y. (2017): Coordinating Post-Desaster Community Redevelopment - Grounded in the Experience Coordinating Onagawa's Post-Disaster Reconstruction, *Journal of JSCE*, Vol. 5, 335-345

Ubaura, M. (2013): *Kyodai bōchōtei wa kajō bōeika? Mazu, machizukuri kara kangaeyo* (Are Giant Seawalls Excessive Disaster Prevention? Let's First Start from Machizukuri), *Asahi Shinbun* (22 December 2013), Miyagi Morning Edition.

UN (2022): Sustainable Development Agenda.

UNISDR (2015): *Sendai Framework for Disaster Risk Reduction 2015–2030.* Geneva: United Nations Office for Disaster Risk Reduction.

Wamsler, C. (2014): *Cities, Disaster Risk and Adaptation.* London: Routledge.

Wisner, B. (2016): Vulnerability as Concept, Model, Metric, and Tool. In: B. Gerber et al. (eds.): *Natural Hazard Science.* Oxford: Oxford Research Encyclopedias.

Yamazaki, M./Yoshimine, F./Yanagisawa, H. (2013): *Rebuilding the Tsunami-strickenn Onagawa Town*, ETIC, www.etic.or.jp/recoveryleaders/en/wp-content/uploads/Rebuilding-Onagawa.pdf, [Accessed 30 April 2023].

Chapter 5

Sustainable and Resilient Societies? Comparing Notions of the 'Smart City' in Germany and Japan

Andrea Hamm
Yuya Shibuya
Christoph Raetzsch

1. Introduction

Sustainable development (Brundtland Commission, 1987) will depend on tangible outcomes of policy initiatives that aim to bring together civil society actors, businesses, academia and municipal legislators around a shared common vision of development (cf. Martinez-Fernandez et al. 2016; Cavallini et al. 2016). We address the smart city as a specific innovation space in the direction of sustainable development, as well as an ambiguous concept that is interpreted differently in Japan versus Germany. Smart city discourses often merge enthusiasm for technology, social control, acceleration of innovation, surveillance, sustainable development, resilience, prosperity and efficient resource consumption (cf. de Waal & Dignum 2017; Heitlinger et al. 2019; Hollands 2008; Kitchin 2015; Spiliotopoulou & Roseland 2020; Albino et al. 2015). These conflicting claims complicate efforts to pin down the smart city to one unifying paradigm (cf. Greenfield 2013; Shelton & Lodato 2019). It can be argued that the initial, industry-led claims about the efficiency of smart solutions, promises of cross-sectoral collaboration and more resilient urban habitats have both hollowed out *and* widened the concepts of the smart city. Given the broadening and often conflicting claims about the benefits of smart city approaches (see Lara et al., 2016 for a comprehensive systematisation), it appears pertinent to look for actual manifestations of local smart city approaches rather than pursue the broader (often generalizing and overly academic) critiques that have initially informed the field. In this chapter, we provide such an approach through a small case study of two quite different smart city initiatives in Japan and Germany. In both cases, the broader concept of the 'smart city' generates diverse actions that are geared towards specific local settings and problems, and which implicate sustainable development to varying degrees (cf. Baykurt & Raetzsch 2020; Bibri & Krogstie 2017). The aim of this chapter is to present these different settings and approaches and inform a wider debate about the value of understanding the smart city as an analytic frame and a practical development in Japan and Germany, which lead to different visions of how the city of the future is shaped in the present as it adapts to ecological, economic and social challenges of sustainability transitions (cf. Köhler et al. 2019).

The practical making of smart cities is still in its infancy, and there are significant socio-geographical differences in how the paradigm of the smart city is interpreted in Japan versus in Germany (cf. Angelidou 2017; Huovila et al. 2019). In this ethnographic study, we explored two projects in Kashiwanoha[1] (Japan) and Cologne[2] (Germany) to better understand how the broader concept of smart cities was interpreted in practice. Our German-Japanese team of researchers visited the two sites in November 2018 (Japan) and February 2019 (Germany), including on-the-ground tours and conversations with local actors. Both cities can be seen to transform themselves in a strong top-down manner, that is, they are highly shaped by larger businesses and authorities (cf. Breuer et al. 2014). We conducted a smart city scenario analysis with both cases. We developed the methodology of a scenario analysis ourselves and adopted core categories from De Waal & Dignum (2017). Our findings suggest that more efficient energy consumption and storage are prioritised in both cases. However, we also found several differences. For instance, the Japanese smart city prioritises reducing commuting by public transport, improving public health, fostering start-up innovations and providing disaster supplies. The German smart city, however, focuses especially on mobility apps and monitoring, increasing automotive e-mobility, raising public awareness of sustainability

---

1   https://kashiwanoha-smartcity.com/en/
2   https://www.smartcity-cologne.de/

transitions and conducting local experiments. Further differences are evident in the ways in which citizen participation is envisioned (or is absent) and how research collaborations form part of the smart city initiatives. Finally, we have observed that efforts to increase resilience and sustainability transitions sometimes appear to be contradictory.

In this chapter, we discuss these differences and similarities by considering geolocational, historical and economic aspects. Finally, we provide approaches on how the two countries' interpretations of the 'smart city' concept can inform each other and which questions could be addressed by future research.

2. Research design

The goal of this research was to better understand how the concept of the smart city is interpreted in practice in Japan and Germany. To do so, we operationalised smart cities in Germany and Japan by selecting two existing smart city projects as case studies, one in each country. We selected the two smart city locations on the basis of initial online research. The smart city locations in Germany and Japan were purposefully selected (Patton, 2015) because both projects had existed for more than five years in 2018/2019 and, moreover, prominently incorporated elements of sustainability transitions from the beginning:

- *Case 1: Smart City Cologne* applies the testbed *Klimastrasse* (engl. climate street) since 2013/14; field work conducted in November 2018
- *Case 2: Kashiwanoha Smart City* has the objective of 'eco-friendly urban development' since 2001; field work conducted in February 2019

Though both cases fulfilled the selection criteria of existing for a longer time and placing an emphasis on sustainability transition, they are rather diverse in terms of cultural and historical context (see more details on the cases' backgrounds in the fourth section).

We developed a case study design which was applied in both cases. The methods contained on-the-ground tours, conversations with local actors and analysis of online materials. We collected a diverse data set, including diary and photo data from site-visits, data from online sources and materials.

3. Smart city scenario analysis

To analyse the data collected according to the recent state of research on smart cities, we used a smart city scenario analysis scheme that we derived from related work. De Waal & Dignum (2017) conducted a smart city discourse analysis and provided useful insights relating, in particular, to the social sustainability of smart cities and addressing issues such as privacy, innovation and legitimisation. Based on the three major scenarios depicted in De Waal's and Dignum's 'smart city' discourse analysis, we developed the following smart city scenario analysis scheme (see **Table 1**).

The scheme differentiates between three types of scenarios related to three main actors driving smart city initiatives. In the Control Room scenario, government actors address the principal fields of public governance and infrastructure through smart city solutions. In the Creative City scenario, it is largely enterprises and businesses driving technological innovation to enhance the development of new products and services (e.g. through incubators or seed funding for start-ups). In the Smart Citizen scenario, citizens are principal actors in the development of new services and technologies that aim to support and enhance civic culture, resilience and cohesion. While these scenarios can overlap and are not mutually exclusive, the most common convergence is often found between the interests of business actors and government officials (local or national). This dominant overlap between government and business has brought forth the critical view of smart cities as a "narrative according to which the smart city appears inevitable, the only reasonable response to an impending urban crisis" (Sadowski & Bendor 2018: 542).

De Waal & Dignum describe numerous risks and chances depicted in the 'smart city' discourse they analysed, which can be found in **Table 1**. In our case analyses, we took these risks and chances as items and examined whether we could 'observe' or 'not observe' them in our field trips and data (see **Tables 2** and **3**).

Table 1: Smart city scenario analysis schemes

Scenario type	Description	Main actor	Chances	Risks
Control Room scenario	Relates to the management of the city: basic infrastructures, consumption, public services	Government	▪ Optimisation of urban processes ▪ Energy and mobility efficiency ▪ Reduced resource consumption	▪ Black-box applications ▪ Manifestation of power structures ▪ Nudging ▪ Privacy infractions ▪ Paternalism
Creative City scenario	Envisages smart cities as hubs for (technological) innovation	Economy	▪ Increasing local economy ▪ Attracting highly educated people, fostering a start-up culture ▪ Citizens as co-creators in the innovation process ▪ Modern administration and regulation	▪ Polarisation ▪ Social fragmentation ▪ Growing inequality ▪ Disciplinary strategies
Smart Citizen scenario	Describes how civil society uses technology to mobilise for collective interests	Citizens	▪ Making the local government more cost-effective ▪ More responsive and transparent local government	▪ Governments outsource responsibility ▪ Citizenship understood as efficiency ▪ Problem of legitimisation

Table 1 shows the analytic categories and items, which we developed from the smart city scenarios presented by De Waal and Dignum (2017).

4. Background of the Cases

Cologne is a city of about 1 million inhabitants (in 2023) in the Western part of Germany. The first records of the city indicate that it was founded in the year 50 AD. Cologne is characterised by a long history of trade, production and growth resulting from its prime location next to the Rhine River, a main shipping route in Europe. In the Second World War, the city was heavily damaged and was reconstructed in post-World War II urban development with priority given to automobile traffic. The result of this post-war reconstruction in Cologne is that today, the city must struggle with conflicting structural demands and system legacies. For instance, public space used to be constructed for car mobility does not meet today's demands of more sustainable, energy efficient and less-polluting urban habitats for growing numbers of residents. Integrating (digital or 'smart') solutions in legacy systems and buildings to respond to such demands creates multiple constraints for designers and developers as well as urban planners.

The area of Kashiwanoha is located about 25 km from Tokyo, counting only 4,000 inhabitants (in 2019). Following World War II, it was used as a U.S. Air Force communications base, and it even offered golf courses. In 1979, the base was returned to Japan and the area started to be redeveloped. In 2000, the extension of the small city started by building new residential areas. Kashiwanoha was characterised by free spaces for innovative buildings and infrastructure. New technologies and the latest building designs could be made use of in the construction phases. Currently, Kashiwanoha Smart City anticipates attracting 26,000 new residents and 15,000 working commuters by 2030.[3]

The two cases are contrasting examples of interpretations of the smart city concept. Cologne is the centre of a whole metropolitan region and it innovates within a dense historical network and between layers of legacy systems. Whereas Kashiwanoha can be regarded as a small experimental urban space, a greenfield, or brownfield site of innovation, where the smart city concept can be implemented almost from scratch without needing to pay heed to existing infrastructures. The purpose of selecting these examples from Japan and Germany is to show that despite the structural differences, there is an overarching emphasis on innovation in the fields of energy efficiency and ecological improvements. At the same time, however, it is harder to transfer specific innovations such as disaster management and civic experimentation between two cultures and political systems.

---

3   https://www.kashiwanoha-smartcity.com/en/initiatives/ (last access: Sept 8, 2022)

5. Case 1: Smart City Cologne

Smart City Cologne is an initiative by the City of Cologne, together with the local energy provider RheinEnergie. Many smart city projects under this initiative are related to energy infrastructure, provision and the reduction of consumption.

During the smart city scenario analysis, we found tendencies toward the Control Room and the Smart Citizen scenarios (see **Table 2**). We could not trace many characteristics of the Creative City scenario. The details of the analysis shown in **Table 2** are provided below.

Table 2: Scenario analysis of *Smart City Cologne*

Cologne	Chances		Risks	
	observed	not observed	observed	not observed
Control Room	▪ Optimisation of urban processes ▪ Energy and mobility efficiency ▪ Reduced resource consumption	-	▪ Black-box applications ▪ Manifestation of power structures ▪ Nudging	▪ Privacy infractions ▪ Paternalism
Creative City	-	▪ Increasing local economy ▪ Attracting highly educated people, fostering a start-up culture ▪ Citizens as co-creators in the innovation process ▪ Modern administration and regulation	-	▪ Polarisation ▪ Social fragmentation ▪ Growing inequality ▪ Disciplinary strategies
Smart Citizen	▪ Making the local government more cost-effective	▪ More responsive and transparent local government	▪ Governments outsource responsibility	▪ Citizenship understood as efficiency ▪ Problem of legitimisation

Table 2 shows prevailing Control Room and Smart Citizen scenarios in the *Smart City Cologne*.

The *Control Room scenario* describes the optimisation of urban processes. In Cologne, we observed such processes being mainly in the mobility and energy sectors, attempting to increase efficiency in both. Such increased efficiency would often lead to decreased resource consumption, for example, through an LED installation project to make public lighting less energy-consuming. The energy provider RheinEnergie further invested in the installation of several charging stations for electric cars and bicycles (see **Figure 1**). *Smart City Cologne* promotes itself and aims to attract citizens to try and continuously use the technologies. All projects related to the initiative were collected on an online platform of the same name. Smart city innovations are advertised as such and become more visible to citizens on the streets (e.g., on large poster walls, see **Figure 2**). We learned that there is a certain degree of control executed by the platform provider when new projects want to become part of the network. An expert team from RheinEnergie would decide whether a project will be displayed on their platform or not. According to one manager we interviewed, the platform is managed in a relatively inclusive way. Potentially, any project can be allowed to become part of the smart city initiative if it fulfils one criterion: to contribute to one or more of the goals of *Smart City Cologne*. Such inclusive platform management then also leads to the support of smart city projects that are less digital. In Cologne, 'smart' does not necessarily need to mean 'digital'. For instance, the project *HonigConnection*[4] (engl. honey connection) seeks to create habitats for bees in the city, contributing to a healthy biosphere through analogue means, such as beehives.

Smart City Cologne also includes an experimental space called *Klimastraße* (engl. climate street), which bundles multiple projects in a local street and has been selected as an operational area for smart city applications that can serve the Cologne population. Technologies and applications in this street include solar-powered charging stations for electronic devices such as smart phones that can be used by passers-by as well as homeless people, free Wi-Fi hubs attached to public lights (see examples in **Figure 3**), diverse implementations and tests of Smart Home and Smart Meters in local shops, and measurements and improvements of building insulation.

To improve public parking space usage, camera-supported monitoring of

---

4   https://www.honigconnection.com/ (last access: Sept 4, 2023)

Figure 1 shows charging stations for electric cars and bicycles attached to existing infrastructure, i.e., city lights.

Figure 2 shows an info wall presenting how public lights came to be equipped with LED technology. The poster highlights the reduced energy consumption of LEDs.

Figure 3 shows experimental installations in the Climate Street in Cologne. Left: A person charges a device in the public space. Upper right: Shows the public solar-powered charging station. Lower right: Information about free public Wi-Fi.

Figure 4 shows an installed camera device and the monitored parking space.

parking spaces has been installed and can be connected to smartphone apps for drivers to guide them to free spaces (see **Figure 4**). This parking app is configured to protect the privacy of drivers because camera data are analysed in the camera device itself and not transferred to a data server. Car drivers only receive information about available parking slots and where they are located. Additionally, LED displays in public spaces (attached to 27 public lights) lead drivers to free slots without the need for a smartphone app.

Regarding the smart citizen scenario, we learned about a form of civic engagement called *Klimastraßenfest* (climate street festival), which celebrates the street community and promotes ongoing smart city experiments. The annual climate street festival was created to raise awareness of energy consumption and foster energy-saving measures in the district. A small group of engaged citizens created the event, and this group has been responsible for making this event happen since it began, in 2013 (before the pandemic).

To sum up the first case study, on *Smart City Cologne,* Cologne is an historic city with a heterogeneous society. The city management aims to provide inclusive applications for its citizens. *Smart City Cologne* focuses on improving existing issues in the city management, such as how parking can be found much more quickly. We observed an awareness of the need for sustainability transitions, which are addressed by conducting local experiments directly in the city. Such an experimental approach includes various local projects. The managing company RheinEnergie provides access to basic infrastructures and an online platform for exchange and public visibility.

In the German case, we can diagnose a 'soft' Control Room scenario as well as a 'soft' Smart Citizen scenario. Cologne seeks to improve city management, which is the main benefit of a Control Room scenario, while trying to avoid several risks of this scenario through better integration of citizens. For instance, we did not observe activities or projects that related to privacy concerns and issues of paternalism. We learned about the central, powerful position of the local energy provider RheinEnergie, which controls access to the smart city platform. RheinEnergie is also using 'black-box' applications to conduct calculations on activities in the city without the awareness of the public. At the same time, several infrastructural changes in the city seek to decrease energy consumption, particularly in the experimental area of *climate street* as an open and collaborative testbed. This experimental space as well as the citizen activities structured around it feed into a Smart Citizen scenario, where the primary benefits are increases in public responsiveness to civic needs, transparency about innovation and enhanced cost-effectiveness of energy expenditure.

We believe that the Cologne smart city approach would be useful for future scenarios since the smart city platform, which is managed by the local energy provider, provides a stable backbone and promotes diverse projects. Still, this stability comes with a slight trade-off in terms of openness, as the platform provider decides who can be part of the platform. Ultimately, it is our view that such platform control and management needs to be checked by other stakeholder groups, such as designated NGOs or the city administration, to guarantee that platform power is executed in a way that reflects the demands of the city and its residents.

6. Case 2: Smart City Kashiwanoha [5]

Kashiwanoha Smart City is a newly built city which counted only a small population of 4,000 residents in 2019. The social structure is observed to be homogeneous, comprised by well-educated and well-situated people who voluntarily moved there. The smart city in Kashiwanoha was initially planned by the real estate company Mitsui Fudosan. They developed a multi-stakeholder approach including private, public and academic actors, that is, the local railway company, the citizen council, a university and the local government. The original objectives foregrounded eco-friendly urban development, longer and healthy life expectancy for its citizens, and the creation of new industries. After the Great East Japan Earthquake and Tsunami in 2011, the multi-stakeholder group added 'resilience' as another focus topic.

Applying the scenario analysis scheme to the Kashiwanoha case (see **Table 3**), we mainly see characteristics of the Control Room scenario and the Creative City scenario owing to the specific constellation of actors brought together under the initiative.

The goal of eco-friendly urban development is planned and conducted in a top-down manner and strongly relates to the *Control Room scenario*. This goal is operationalised primarily with regard to energy management and consumption as well as the construction of built infrastructure. The Kashiwanoha Smart Center is responsible for the operation, management and control of energy for the entire city. By sharing electrical interchange devices between districts, the city achieves a peak power reduction of approximately 26 percent[6]. The local energy building is equipped with one of the largest lithium-

---

5   We cannot provide photos of this case study as it was not allowed to take photos during the on-the-ground tour in *Kashiwanoha Smart City*.

6   https://www.mitsuifudosan.co.jp/english/corporate/news/2014/0424_01/ (last access: Feb 7, 2023)

Table 3: Scenario analysis of the *Kashiwanoha Smart City*

Kashiwano ha	Chances		Risks	
	observed	not observed	observed	not observed
Control Room	• Optimsation of urban processes • Energy and mobility efficiency • Reduced resource consumption	-	• Privacy infractions • Black-box applications • Manifestation of power structures • Nudging • Paternalism	-
Creative City	• Increasing local economy • Attracting highly educated people • Fostering a start-up culture • Citizens as co-creators in the innovation process	• Modern administration and regulation	• Polarisation • Social fragmentation • Growing inequality	• Disciplinary strategies
Smart Citizen	-	• More responsive, transparent and cost-effective local government	-	• Governments outsource responsibility • Citizenship understood as efficiency • Problem of legitimisation

Table 3 shows prevailing Control Room and Creative City scenarios for *Kashiwanoha Smart City*.

ion storage battery systems in Japan, as well as an emergency gas generator. It also generates solar power. This equipment can uphold local energy provision for a limited time during disaster events such as earthquakes or general energy blackouts. Kashiwanoha also plans to heavily decrease CO_2 emissions, although enhanced urban development drives up CO_2 emissions in Kashiwa city. For instance, in 2014, the city managed to decrease CO_2 emission from 14 kilotons (Kt) to 11 Kt by 21 percent compared to the estimated CO_2 emissions without the energy management and plans, and in 2030, it further reduced the increased CO_2 emission predictions from 53 Kt to 21 Kt, that is, by 60 percent[7]. As new residential and facility buildings were constructed, the city could reduce CO_2 emissions by making use of the latest architectural and design solutions that fit the goal of highly efficient energy consumption. The building infrastructure in *Kashiwanoha Smart City* uses climate-neutral materials and energies, such as natural ventilation systems instead of air conditioning in one of the central buildings, wood for building insulation and a large number of solar panels that produce decentralised energy with lower emissions. Non-climate-neutral infrastructure is optimised for higher energy efficiency, for example, by using LED lights for buildings and outer areas. Where possible, trees are planted to provide shade in the humid and hot summer months and to equip rooftops with greenery to foster natural climate regulation. Such building designs and approaches to built infrastructure demonstrate multiple aspects of the Control Room scenario, as building designers anticipate people's daily life beforehand and seek to provide facilities with the lowest possible energy consumption.

In addition, due to the specific geographic challenges of a high-risk zone for earthquakes in Japan, Kashiwanoha emphasises disaster prevention and management measures as an important part of its smart city approach. These measures can also be subsumed under a *Control Room scenario*, as they are intended to keep the city functioning in times of disasters. Resilience, therefore, became an important goal in the smart city initiative, especially after the Great East Japan Earthquake and Tsunami in 2011 violently showed the vulnerability of the Japanese public infrastructure. In the case of a disaster, outside areas in the *Kashiwanoha Smart City* serve as emergency evacuation sites for the community. For instance, the independent energy supply in Kashiwanoha provides stable public lighting. Seating arrangements in the public park areas can be transformed into emergency BBQ sites to ensure food supply. The building infrastructure also provides facilities for storing emergency goods in case of disaster, such as emergency blankets, tents, water and canned foods, which are stored in the local hotel building for public use in emergency

---

7   See: https://www.kashiwanoha-smartcity.com/en/initiatives/ Tab: 'Working on the environment' (last access: Sept 12, 2022). https://www.jraia.or.jp/webmagazine/detail.html?n=259&g=666 (last access: Feb 7, 2023).

situations.

We further observed the characteristics of the *Creative City scenario* in *Kashiwanoha Smart City*. The fostering of new industries and the emergence of business innovations are important goals of *Kashiwanoha Smart City*. The central business building houses the Kashiwanoha Open Innovation Lab (KOIL), which provides co-working areas for start-ups, a workshop room for prototyping with 3D printers, and event space for meetings and conferences. The facilities also include larger office spaces for small and medium-sized companies. *Kashiwanoha Smart City* has engaged TX Entrepreneur Partners (TEP), an organisation that supports start-up businesses through collaborations with universities, research institutes, government organisations, private businesses and individual experts active along the Tsukuba Express railway line linking Tsukuba to central Tokyo. For instance, large IT companies offer regular networking meetings. In the IoT Business Co-Creation Lab, private businesses, governmental organisations and research institutions are working jointly to develop new products and services with the help of the local Internet of Things (IoT) communication environment, that is, partly automated sensor systems and applications. Centred in the Kashiwanoha Campus, it is intended to spread IoT applications to neighbouring areas and to create IoT-related business opportunities and collaborations. Innovation Field Kashiwanoha provides a verification test platform for all innovation projects taking place in KOIL. The public facilities in Kashiwanoha are situated within a 3 km radius of each other and therefore provide a useful environment for testing and verifying new applications and solutions in the fields of AI/IoT and life sciences/medicine.

Regarding goals and objectives of tech-related start-ups and businesses, there is a risk of bias arising from the fact that employees living and working in Kashiwanoha form a homogenous, tech-savvy and predominately male group (see, e.g., Ahmadi et al., 2018). Such development could potentially lead to further risks in the Creative City scenario, such as polarisation and growing inequalities, since people with lower socio-economic and educational status might not have the same access to Kashiwanoha laboratory and residential spaces.

Regarding *Kashiwanoha Smart City's* goal for improving public health, we can observe a mixture of the Creative City and Control Room scenarios. Health centres offer preventive medicine by encouraging healthy lifestyles in collaboration with researchers from The University of Tokyo and several businesses. For instance, the LOCABO ('low carb') campaign promotes healthier eating by promoting and selling food that contains the same number of calories but with a lower count of carbohydrates. Such diets seek to prevent high blood sugar or significant oscillations in blood sugar. Further, in the outside areas of the city, the urban design provides park areas covered with grass where citizens can gather and relax to improve their well-being. Outside infrastructures are designed to implement 'a city that makes you want to walk'. Outside areas also provide venues for live performances. To our understanding, these measures to improve public health are designed to do several things. On the one hand, characteristics of the Control Room scenario can be seen, as the public health goal, which collects information on the health of residents, seems to be a reaction to an aging society. On the other hand, however, there are several characteristics of the Creative City scenario, such as the maintaining of employee productivity through a range of offers (e.g., sports clubs, medical check stations and food health information points) and efforts to keep businesses interested in promoting a healthy population.

With regard to the applications around public health, we see a risk of social fragmentation between residents who participate in health improvement offers and those who do not. Further, we are concerned about the privacy management of health-related applications containing highly private data. We also see risk regarding nudging and paternalism, for example, with regard to isolated programmes that aim to foster healthy eating behaviour; although, differences in eating behaviour are often a matter of socio-economic inequalities, levels of education and income.

To sum up our second case study, we found that the smart city initiative places its focus on (1) attracting new inhabitants and creating new businesses with them, (2) eco-friendly design of selected buildings and applications and (3) fostering a healthy population. Moreover, disaster response and coping with emergency situations are important for city management in earthquake-prone regions.

In summary, we find a strong Control Room scenario and a modest Creative City scenario for the Japanese case in *Kashiwanoha Smart City*. We see a large variety of changes to reduce environmental effects and improve the management efficiency of Kashiwanoha. At the same time, we see several risks that have been mentioned in the Control Room scenario, that is, collection of private data, nudging (manipulating residents' behaviour with psychological measures), paternalism (deciding what is best for the residents without asking them, e.g., concerning public health), and the use of black-box applications. Regarding the Creative City scenario, we observe a strong intention to foster technology-driven start-ups and to strengthen the regional economy. Modern working spaces welcoming co-creation and experimentation attract tech workers and young entrepreneurs to choose Kashiwanoha as their place for working and living.

We believe that the Kashiwa 'smart city' approach is useful in terms of relieving crowded metropolitan areas and offering attractive spaces for innovative start-ups and companies as well as for employees and their families. The newly built infrastructure allows the design of low energy consumption in many areas of life and work, which can hardly be achieved within pre-existing built infrastructures. Nevertheless, we conclude from our observations that smart cities designed in such a way tend to be less accessible for some groups of society, such as people of lower socio-economic and educational status.

7. Discussion: Comparing notions of the 'smart city' in Germany and Japan

In both cases, we find that the use and application of various technologies are central to the smart city's development. In Germany, innovative technologies are installed in small-scale experimental spaces. The open platform infrastructure is managed by corporate actors, while inviting participation from citizens and companies. In Japan, we find a corporate-controlled environment of innovation towards three goals, that is, environmental improvement, public health and new businesses. Both cases show characteristics of a Control Room scenario which is strongly connected to the goal of improved energy and resource management, which reduces the overall energy consumption and CO_2 emissions of urban space and living.

With regard to the notion of a sustainable society, energy efficiency is a shared primary goal in smart city initiatives and primarily highlights an environmental understanding of sustainability. In Kashiwanoha, the ability to construct new buildings, including novel climate-neutral technology such as natural air ventilation, is a benefit when it comes to sustainability goals. At the same time, the construction of new buildings greatly increases CO_2 emissions. Building a new city means that energy and resource consumption first increases heavily before it can be reduced. Energy savings through design and technological assistance show effects of reduced emissions only in the long run. In Cologne, the legacies of the built infrastructure currently only allow for modest modifications of energy consumption, principally in the domains of mobility, lighting and heating (e.g., through building insulation). Existing building designs hamper large reductions of CO_2 emissions. For example, cooling and heating technologies cannot easily be exchanged in existing buildings without significant investment. Enhancing the energy consumption of mobility in different modes is a secondary objective in *Smart City Cologne*. Due to improved traffic management with digital means, fuels and resources might be saved individually, yet it is also clear that widening the modal share of non-motorised traffic is a challenge in an existing urban fabric that is optimised for automobile transportation.

The dominance of the Control Room scenario shows that large organisations, companies and city governments are required to set smart city initiatives in motion, especially when energy and resource consumption of central infrastructure assets such as power grids, traffic systems, public buildings and urban space are concerned. To reduce the energy and material consumption in a city to a significant degree, it is essential to monitor and verify ongoing efforts, as well as to put political and economic clout behind efforts to innovate legacy systems. The installation of energy-efficient applications in Cologne is still in a kind of experimental phase, while in Kashiwanoha, newly constructed buildings and infrastructures respect environmental sustainability from the design phase onwards, for example, by improving insulation, adding solar power panels and using natural ventilation mechanisms. However, legacy buildings and urban structures, as well as diverse ownership structures for buildings in Cologne, limit the scope of the Control Room scenario. Large-scale innovation in terms of mobility solutions and energy consumption needs a complimentary citizen-led approach to translate sustainability demands into everyday actions which are open to experimentation. In Kashiwanoha, the situation is quite different, as smart city buildings belong to the real estate company, which is likewise the manager of the Smart City strategy. In such a focused and exclusive setting, it is much easier to decide on the design and infrastructure of facilities while fostering citizen involvement beyond the entrepreneurial spirit.

Control Room approaches also come with several risks regarding data management, of which there is higher awareness in Germany than in Japan. In the German case, parking monitoring cameras are deliberately equipped with a system that seeks to protect the privacy of car owners to a high degree. In the Japanese case, we learned about tracking applications for health data analysis but could not receive further information regarding privacy concerns or data security management.

With regard to the notion of resilient societies, we see diverse measures of disaster prevention and management in the Japanese case, and scarcely any of them in the German case. The particular geographic location of Japan leads to frequent disaster events, such as earthquakes, tsunamis and typhoons. Japan has a long tradition of living with these events and their consequences, such as blackouts, destruction of housing, and shortness of food and beverage supplies. The Japanese case in Kashiwanoha shows well-established action plans in case of disaster, as well as multiple storage capacities.

In Germany the notion of the 'smart city' is much less connected to disaster prevention measures, although cataclysmic events (such as the floods in the nearby Ahr valley 2021), heavy storms and droughts are becoming increasingly common in Germany as a result of climate change. We argue that the notion of resilient societies adopting mechanisms to react to disasters may need to be taken more seriously in Germany in the near future. The likelihood of disasters in Germany and Japan may be different, but the effects for residents are often similar: evacuation and the need for shelters, disrupted supplies of food and beverages, and blackouts of energy and other resources, such as water and gas. While the smart city is often perceived to relate to the efficiency of public expenditure, energy and resource consumption, or mobility, it is evident from this small study that a local emphasis on different needs can form part of an overall innovation effort. The fostering of entrepreneurial culture and exchange can likewise feed into new modes of mobility and civic engagement. The smart city can also be a healthy city, a safe city and a carbon-neutral city. Moreover, it is not limited to only one approach.

8. Summary

The cases of Cologne and Kashiwanoha show a dominant top-down manner of shaping future development, implementing a Control Room Smart City scenario (De Waal & Dignum, 2017) that is tied to larger businesses and authorities (Breuer, Walravens, & Ballon, 2014). More efficient energy consumption is prioritised in both cases, and 'smart' elements are not necessarily digital. We also revealed several differences between the two cases: (1) Cologne shows stronger connections to the Smart Citizen scenario, and (2) Kashiwanoha's approach relates more to the scenario of creative cities while also highlighting resilience to natural disasters and their effects. The inherited infrastructures also differ significantly between the cities. The Japanese city has more liberty in experimenting with new materials, energy-efficient building facilities and construction techniques. While in the much larger city of Cologne, any innovation in central infrastructure systems, such as mobility or energy supply, necessarily disrupts established legacy systems, and said legacy systems often impede any significant progress towards achieving sustainability transitions.

While our case studies can only offer a glimpse into dominant approaches to interpreting the smart city paradigm from the perspective of sustainability transition, we can draw some preliminary conclusions and map out a few challenges for future studies of Japan and Germany in relation to the subject of the smart city.

(1) *Resilience and Responsiveness*: Both countries share common demographic as well as economic challenges, such as an aging population, rural depletion (United Nations 2021) and a paradigmatic transition from manufacturing and automobile industries to service-oriented and digital services. In both countries, resilience will be strongly linked to enhancing the digitalisation of public services and governance. The lack of reliable digital service infrastructures represents a significant challenge for future resilience and the development and maintenance of civic, political and cultural cohesion. Responsiveness to natural disasters, which are becoming more widespread in the wake of climate change and resource depletion, offers another field of mutual collaboration. As in Kawashinoha's example, smart city strategies only work successfully when they are implemented across domains (e.g., mobility,

energy and housing). Such cross-domain approaches are beneficial when infrastructure assets are disrupted or need to be replaced by short-term responses. Planning for disruption and responding pre-emptively to such dangers can be a crucial element in city-wide innovation efforts that help to win and sustain support from city administration, citizens, businesses and local communities.

(2) *Smart City vs. Smart Regions*: The discourse around smart cities is heavily focused on the urban as a prime site of future challenges due to the complexities of demands it raises for urban sustainability and the growing populations of urban centres around the world. However, cities are not isolated geographic or economic units. In the time of the COVID-19 pandemic, many residents fled densely populated urban centres to seek regional alternatives (UN Habitat Report 2021). The city is both a marketplace and meeting point of diverse flows of goods, people, services and relations, many of which extend to and implicate the wider regions they are located in. Building durable and resilient infrastructures between cities and their regions, nurturing the exchange of innovative resources and enabling contacts can also be a way to counter trends of diminishing populations in rural areas (see for Germany, Kaczorowski & Swarat, 2018). Regional development in both Germany and Japan is closely tied to the structures of political decision-making and the strong role of communities and local traditions that are challenged by increasing demands for efficiency and entrepreneurial intervention, a clash between old and new paradigms of economic value generation, personal well-being and civic engagement.

(3) *Citizen Participation vs. Citizen Ownership*: A final suggestion for future research concerns the pivotal role of citizens in the definition and governance of sustainability transitions and the contested role that technology has in these transitions. Both cases show timid examples of allowing citizens to participate in these transitions, while leadership roles of corporations and local governments set the frame for such engagement. It is indeed challenging for a city government or energy corporation to directly approach citizens in leadership roles to experiment with new approaches to challenges of sustainability (see, e.g., Hamm 2020, Shibuya et al. 2021). However, the demands of resilience and civic cohesion also require shaping institutionalised pathways for experimentation, where development and co-creation are embedded in

structured procedures for multiple stakeholders (Brynskov et al., 2018). The emerging claim of 'digital civics' (Vlachokyriakos et al., 2016; Boehner & DiSalvo, 2018) makes a case in point about the connection between digital technologies and the needs of local populations to co-create the infrastructures that govern their daily lives. It is a difference in kind whether citizens are invited for user testing, participating in a top-down design process, or whether they are invited to own the solutions that are part of their daily interactions with urban spaces. Nowadays, questions of design are also questions about democratic and inclusive participation (DiSalvo, 2022).

Conflicting concepts of smart cities, especially with regard to sustainability and resilience, arise from different geographical, economic and historical-cultural contexts. We believe that different smart city implementations, such as those in Germany and Japan, can learn from each other and better meet their demands if they are further developed in exchanges between the cities. As an instrument for such an exchange, we developed a smart city scenario analysis, which was applied in this study to two cases to shed light on the opportunities and risks of smart city developments. We would like to encourage researchers to use this analysis tool to conduct further comparisons and exchanges between smart city implementations worldwide.

Acknowledgements

This work was partly funded by the Federal Ministry of Education and Research of Germany (BMBF) under grant no. 16DII131 ('Deutsches Internet-Institut').

References

Ahmadi, Michael/Weibert, Anne/Ogonowski, Corinna/Aal, Konstantin/Gäckle, Kristian/ Marsden, Nicola/Wulf, Volker (2018): Challenges and Lessons Learned by Applying Living Labs in Gender and IT Contexts. In: *Proceedings of the 4th Conference on Gender & IT*, GenderIT '18, New York, NY, USA: Association for Computing Machinery, 239–49. DOI: 10.1145/3196839.3196878.

Albino, Vito/Berardi, Umberto/Dangelico, Rosa Maria (2015): Smart Cities: Definitions, Dimensions, Performance, and Initiatives. In: *Journal of Urban Technology* 22 (1): 3–21. DOI: 10.1080/10630732.2014.942092.

Angelidou, Margarita (2017): The Role of Smart City Characteristics in the Plans of Fifteen

Cities. *Journal of Urban Technology* 24 (4): 3–28. DOI: 10.1080/10630732.2017.1348880.

Baykurt, Burcu/Raetzsch, Christoph (2020): What smartness does in the smart city: From visions to policy. In: *Convergence* 26 (4): 775–789. DOI: 10.1177/1354856520913405.

Bibri, Simon Elias/Krogstie, John (2017): Smart sustainable cities of the future: An extensive interdisciplinary literature review. In: *Sustainable Cities and Society* 31: 183–212. DOI: 10.1016/j.scs.2017.02.016.

Boehner, Kristen/DiSalvo, Carl (2016): Data, Design and Civics: An Exploratory Study of Civic Tech. In: *Proceedings of the 2016 CHI Conference on Human Factors in Computing Systems*, 2970–2981. DOI: 10.1145/2858036.2858326.

Breuer, Jonas/Walravens, Nils/Ballon, Pieter (2014): Beyond Defining the Smart City. Meeting Top-Down and Bottom-Up Approaches in the Middle. In: *Tema. Journal of Land Use, Mobility and Environment.*

Brundtland Commission (1987): Our Common Future, Chapter 2: Towards Sustainable Development. www.un-documents.net/ocf-02.htm#I.

Brynskov, Martin/Heijnen, Adriënne/Balestrini, Mara/Raetzsch, Christoph (2018): Experimentation At Scale: Challenges for Making Urban Informatics Work. In: *Smart and Sustainable Built Environment* 7 (1): 150-163. DOI: 10.1108/SASBE-10-2017-0054.

Cavallini, Simona/Soldi, Rosella/Friedl, Julia/Volpe, Margherita (2016): *Using the Quadruple Helix Approach to Accelerate the Transfer of Research and Innovation Results to Regional Growth.* Brussels: EU Committee of the Regions.

De Waal, Martijn/Dignum, Marloes (2017): The citizen in the smart city. How the smart city could transform citizenship. In: *It - Information Technology* 59 (6): 263-273. DOI: 10.1515/itit-2017-0012.

DiSalvo, Carl (2022): *Design as Democratic Inquiry: Putting Experimental Civics Into Practice.* Cambridge MA.: MIT Press.

Greenfield, Adam (2013): *Against the smart city: A pamphlet.* Do projects.

Hamm, Andrea (2020): Particles Matter: A Case Study on How Civic IoT Can Contribute to Sustainable Communities. In: *Proceedings of the 7th International Conference on ICT for Sustainability*, 305–313. DOI: 10.1145/3401335.3401815.

Heitlinger, Sara/Bryan-Kinns, Nick/Comber, Rob (2019): The Right to the Sustainable Smart City. In: *Proceedings of the 2019 CHI Conference on Human Factors in Computing Systems*, 1–13. DOI: 10.1145/3290605.3300517.

Hollands, Robert G. (2008): Will the real smart city please stand up? In: *City* 12 (3): 303–320. DOI: 10.1080/13604810802479126.

Huovila, Aapo/Bosch, Peter/Airaksinen, Miimu (2019): Comparative analysis of standardized indicators for Smart sustainable cities: What indicators and standards to use and when? In: *Cities* 89: 141–153. DOI: 10.1016/j.cities.2019.01.029.

Kaczorowski, Willi/Swarat, Gerald (2018): *Smartes Land – Von Der Smart City Zu Digitalen Region. Impulse Für Die Digitalisierung Ländlicher Regionen.* Glückstadt: Innovators Club – Deutschlandforum/ Werner Hülsbusch. [Smart Country - From Smart City to Digital Region. Impulses for the Digitization of Rural Regions. Glückstadt: Innovators Club - Deutschlandforum/ Werner Hülsbusch].

Köhler, Jonathan/Geels, Frank W./Kern, Florian/Markard, Jochen/Onsongo, Elsie/Wieczorek,

Anna/Alkemade, Floortje/Avelino, Flor/Bergek, Anna/Boons, Frank/Fünfschilling, Lea/ Hess, David/Holtz, Georg/Hyysalo, Sampsa/Jenkins, Kirsten/Kivimaa, Paula/Martiskainen, Mari/McMeekin, Andrew/Mühlemeier, Marie Susan/Nykvist, Bjorn/Pel, Bonno/Raven, Rob/ Rohracher, Harald/Sandén, Björn/Schot, Johan/Sovacool, Benjamin/Turnheim, Bruno/ Welch, Dan/Wells, Peter (2019): An Agenda for Sustainability Transitions Research: State of the Art and Future Directions. In: *Environmental Innovation and Societal Transitions* (31): 1-32. DOI: 10.1016/j.eist.2019.01.004.

Kitchin, Rob (2015): Making sense of smart cities: Addressing present shortcomings. In: *Cambridge Journal of Regions, Economy and Society* 8 (1): 131–136. DOI: 10.1093/cjres/ rsu027.

Lara, Alexander Prado/Moreira Da Costa, Eduardo/Furlani, Thiago Zilinscki/Yigitcanlar, Tan (2016): Smartness That Matters: Towards a Comprehensive and Human-Centred Characterisation of Smart Cities. In: *Journal of Open Innovation: Technology, Market, and Complexity* 2 (8): 1-13. DOI: 10.1186/s40852-016-0034-z.

Martinez-Fernandez, Christina/Weyman, Tamara/Fol, Sylvie/Audirac, Ivonne/Cunningham-Sabot, Emmanuèle/Wiechmann, Thorsten/Yahagi, Hiroshi (2016): Shrinking cities in Australia, Japan, Europe and the USA: From a global process to local policy responses. *Progress in Planning* 105: 1–48. DOI: 10.1016/j.progress.2014.10.001.

Newman, Nic/Fletcher, Richard/Robertson, Craig T./Eddy, Kirsten/Nielsen, Rasmus Kleis (2022): *Reuters Institute Digital News Report 2022.* 164.

Patton, M. Q. (2015): Sampling, Qualitative (Purposeful). In: *The Blackwell Encyclopedia of Sociology.* John Wiley & Sons, Ltd. DOI: 10.1002/9781405165518.wbeoss012.pub2.

Sadowski, Jathan/Bendor, Roy (2019): Selling Smartness: Corporate Narratives and the Smart City as a Sociotechnical Imaginary. In: *Science, Technology, & Human Values* 44 (3): 540–563. DOI: 10.1177/0162243918806061.

Shelton, Taylor/Lodato, Thomas (2019): Actually existing smart citizens. In: *City: Analysis of Urban Change, Theory, Action* 23 (1): 35–52. DOI: 10.1080/13604813.2019.1575115.

Shibuya, Yuya/Hamm, Andrea/Raetzsch, Christoph (2021): From Data to Discourse: How Communicating Civic Data Can Provide a Participatory Structure for Sustainable Cities and Communities. In: *Proceedings of the 27nd International Sustainable Development Research Society '21*, Östersund: Mid Sweden University.

Spiliotopoulou, Maria/Roseland, Mark (2020): Urban Sustainability: From Theory Influences to Practical Agendas. In: *Sustainability* 12 (18): 7245. DOI: 10.3390/su12187245.

UN Habitat Report (2021): *Cities and Pandemics: Towards a More Just, Green and Healthy Future, United Nations Human Settlements Program*, United Nations.

United Nations Department of Economic and Social Affairs (2021): *World Social Report 2021: Reconsidering Rural Development*, United Nations.

Villi, Mikko/Aharoni, Tali/Tenenboim-Weinblatt, Keren/Boczkowski, Pablo J./Hayashi, Kaori/ Mitchelstein, Eugenia/Tanaka, Akira/Kligler-Vilenchik, Neta (2021): Taking a Break From News: A Five-Nation Study of News Avoidance in the Digital Era. In: *Digital Journalism* 10 (1): 1-17. DOI: 10.1080/21670811.2021.1904266.

Vlachokyriakos, Vasili/Crivellaro, Clara/Le Dantec, Christopher A./Gordon, Eric/Wright, Pete/ Olivier, Patrick (2016): Digital Civics: Citizen Empowerment With and Through

Technology. In: *Proceedings of the 2016 CHI Conference Extended Abstracts on Human Factors in Computing Systems*, 1096–1099. DOI: 10.1145/2851581.2886436.

Inclusive Societies: Leave No One Behind

Chapter 6

The Urban Poor Under the COVID-19 Pandemic: The Case of Tokyo

Masato Kimura

1. Introduction

The outbreak of the COVID-19 pandemic in early 2020 has challenged the world in many ways. Beyond issues of medical and sociotechnical responses to an unknown pathogen, the impact of the disease has highlighted existing social disparities, both internationally and domestically. In Japan, the socioeconomic impacts were the most conspicuous among precarious and unemployed workers. What changes have taken place in the lives of the urban poor in Tokyo, and what challenges have been identified in their lives as well as in government and private sector support activities?

To answer this question, I will take up the case of Shibuya Ward, Tokyo, where I have engaged in support activities and fieldwork for homeless people since 1996, and describe their situation during the pandemic based on my participatory observations, interviews, and questionnaire surveys. The analysis reveals that the 'stay home' policy of the Tokyo Metropolitan Government (TMG) practically meant a 'stay homeless' policy for people in need who did not have a home as a place of dignified living, and in this sense, there was much room for improvement.

The issue of urban poverty is directly linked to two of the three guiding principles of the sustainable development goals (SDGs), 'human rights-based approach' and 'leave no one behind'. Poverty is severe in developing countries, as absolute poverty can be life-threatening, while in developed countries, the existence of relative poverty is emphasised. However, even in urban societies, many impoverished people face difficulties in their daily lives without social support and improving their circumstances contributes to both goals. In economically developed cities, the urban poor without jobs, homes, or the right to vote are 'forgotten people' who are hardly represented politically and not easily understood by members of the same society. They are often left helpless because existing private and public welfare agencies tend to expect work ethics and sufficient job opportunities. Although their presence is visible in overt ways on the streets, they often remain forgotten, being neglected as if they are not there. Understanding urban poverty as an issue and seeking ways to solve it will be an essential stepping stone to achieving a sustainable society here and now, rather than seeing it as a distant problem elsewhere.

2. COVID-19 outbreak and the state of homeless people in Japan

First, we briefly examine the trends in the disease, especially the initial outbreak of the infection in Japan, and also the general situation of homelessness. Although the number of infected persons has often determined the number of COVID-19 cases, the Japanese government has not actively utilised polymerase chain reaction (PCR) testing to investigate the infection status, including asymptomatic patients. The published number of infected patients represents only the number of patients who had subjective symptoms, were treated in hospitals, and were reported to public health centres, making international comparisons unfeasible. Therefore, we aimed to confirm domestic trends based on the number of deaths rather than the number of patients (**Figure 1**). The number of deaths due to COVID-19 indicates that the pandemic in the country had its first wave in April 2020 and the eighth wave in January 2023.

The first case of infection in Japan was confirmed in a passenger on board the luxury liner Diamond Princess, known as 'Paradise at Sea', which called at the port of Yokohama on 3 February 2020. The number of infected people on board increased to 712, including 13 deaths (MHLW 2020a). The disease then spread nationwide from asymptomatic infected passengers to the first peak of cases on 11 April when 644 people were confirmed to be affected.

As of 29 February, then Prime Minister Shinzo Abe requested the closure of all elementary, junior high, and high schools from 2 March to the end of spring

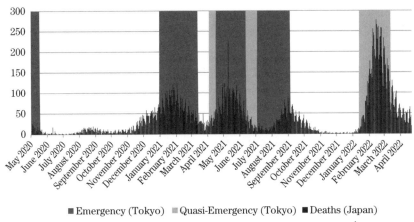

■ Emergency (Tokyo)   ■ Quasi-Emergency (Tokyo)   ■ Deaths (Japan)

Figure 1: Number of Deaths (daily) due to COVID-19 in Japan (Based on MHLW 2023)[1]

vacations in early April, although it lacked legal backing and binding force, and declared a state of emergency on 4 April.

Amid the first wave of infections, Tokyo Governor Yuriko Koike presented a so-called stay home policy at the press conference on 23 April, before the Golden holiday Week of May. The policy called on citizens to 'voluntarily refrain' from 'nonessential and non-urgent' outings and stay home. This policy was promoted as a core guideline for new ways of living to overcome the pandemic. It was subsequently adopted throughout the country in both public and private sectors. While this was only a request and did not involve any legally binding force or penalty, most people complied and refrained from going out and shopping store operations by the end of the first emergency declaration in May 2020.

These measures have had a profound economic impact, particularly on those in precarious employment. From spring onwards, I have met people in the parks who had lost their jobs and homes because of these economic austerities.

Before analysing the impact of these policies, let us briefly look at some

---

1   The Ministry of Health, Labour and Welfare (MHLW) began to publish data only on 9 May 2020. According to NHK Web (2020), however, the peak fatalities in the first wave was 31 on 2 May. **Figure 1** indicates the number of deaths due to COVID-19 per day for all of Japan, but 13 deaths on the cruise ship Diamond Princess were excluded. Since the timing of (quasi-) emergency declarations varied by region, **Figure 1** shows the case of Tokyo, the region this chapter focuses on.

data outlining the state of street poverty, especially those who did not have a duly place to return to, which they could call 'home'.

According to an official survey conducted by the TMG in August 2022, 693 people were confirmed to be living on the streets of Tokyo (TMG 2020a). Tokyo's population was estimated at 14.0 million as of December 2022, and the homeless population seems quite small for a large city of this size.[2] However, it is essential to note that the term 'homeless' under Japanese law refers only to rough sleepers, that is, those sleeping and living on the streets, and does not include those living in shelters or other unstable living conditions.[3]

It is also relevant that official surveys are visual counts performed during the daytime. However, homeless people are not easily visible during the day because many of them do not have fixed huts or tents and live outside only at night, after stores have closed, by laying out simple cardboard boxes in parks or under shuttered eaves.[4]

An alternative night survey conducted by the private research organization Advocacy and Research Centre for Homelessness (ARCH 2020) estimated the number of homeless people at night as of January 2020 as 1,540, which was 2.1 times higher than the TMG's survey results of the same period (618 people).[5]

2　The Department of Homeless Services of New York City reported that the federal Homeless Outreach Population Estimate street homeless survey conducted in 2020 found that 3,857 individuals were experiencing unsheltered homelessness on the streets at night (New York City 2022: 5). Berlin city has done the first homeless census ('*Zeit für Solidarität*' project) in January 2020 and found 1,976 unsheltered persons on the street (City of Berlin 2020). Both cities are much smaller in terms of overall population than Tokyo, so the comparatively low official count of homeless seems somewhat surprising and questionable.

3　See the definition of Japanese Act on Special Measures concerning Assistance in Self-Support of Homeless defines only those rough sleepers outside as homeless, which I have described as 'exclusion by definition' (Kimura 2013: 84). Both the European Typology of Homelessness and Housing Exclusion and the United States (42 U.S. Code § 11302) consider a variety of 'housing poor' including those living in shelters, welfare facilities, or in the homes of acquaintances as 'homeless' and recognize the need for support.

4　A comparison of the results of the national survey of the living conditions of homeless people conducted in 2003 and 2021 shows that the tent and hut dwellers decreased from 54.4 (valid %, N=2,037) to 31.0 (N=1,134). The proportion of respondents who said their place to sleep was a 'park' similarly decreased from 48.9% (N=1,819) to 27.4% (N=911), while the precarious dwellers without a fixed place to sleep increased from 12.3 (N=2,163) to 20.5% (N=1,148) (MHLW 2003, 2022). These changes have led to isolation among people without homes in Tokyo, and communal soup kitchens have provided them with limited opportunities for interaction and exchange of information (see Kimura 2013: 91ff.; Kimura 2019: 147ff.).

Hence, official definitions and surveys have underestimated the homeless population. These structural problems are common to poverty control and public health. Because the Japanese government has remained cautious about using PCR tests and actively identifying asymptomatic infected people, the number of homeless people has also remained implicit, thereby masking and trivialising the problem itself.

3. Homelessness during COVID-19[6]

In this section, I describe homeless people and their support situation in the early stages of an infection explosion, based on active research methods. Since 1996, I have engaged in fieldwork and support activities for the needy homeless on the streets of Shibuya. With a population of approximately 230,000 (as of 2020), Shibuya Ward is known as the centre of young people's fashion culture. According to a national survey, 71 homeless people (rough sleepers) existed under daylight (as of January 2020), and 144 people stayed at night according to the alternative survey conducted by the private organisation mentioned above (ARCH 2020).

During the COVID-19 pandemic, 120.2 people in need, on average, per week (January 2020–January 2023) received support from soup kitchens that our organisation, *Nojiren* (Shibuya Free Association for the Right to Housing and Existence of the Homeless), ran every Saturday. We also provided livelihood counselling, nightly patrols, and assistance with welfare applications. The discussion below is based on data obtained from activities and surveys conducted in this area.

Active research is a method in which a researcher is involved in social issues with people in coming up with solutions to various problems faced by a changing society and verifying the effectiveness of these solutions. I depict the urgent situation during the COVID-19 outbreak based on my field notes of first-person monograph accounts, supplemented by objective data, as appropriate.

---

5   Nighttime (8:00 pm to 9:30 pm) patrol in Shibuya Ward done by *Nojiren* also found 118 people on the street (survey conducted on 11 January 2020), while only 71 people were found on the TMG official record in the same month (TMG 2020a).

6   Parts of this analysis have been published in Japanese (see Kimura 2020a, 2021, 2023).

3.1 Social distancing and its consequences

At the end of February 2020, when the Prime Minister requested the closure of schools across the country, I noticed something unusual in our weekend soup kitchen activities in *Mitake* Park, Shibuya. The number of people gathering for hot meals increased from approximately 80 to 120 at regular times and to 160 on weekends. One of the participants complained of his dire situation and hunger, saying that he had not eaten for three days (interview taken the week after that, on 7 March 2020).

Until the month before, 29 aid groups were running soup kitchens in the eastern central area of Tokyo within Shibuya's walking distance, almost every day. The homeless members informed us that other groups had suddenly refrained from their activities on weekdays to avoid crowding and infection risks associated with the preparation and distribution of food. For the following weeks, we collected information to reveal that 15 of the 29 groups, predominantly Christian churches were forced to suspend or reduce their activities.[7]

The number of meals distributed remained high for the next three months, primarily until the first state of emergency ended at the end of May 2020, when several other groups resumed their activities (See **Figure 2**).[8]

Looking at the data, the number of people who received meals increased considerably from February until the end of August compared to the previous year.

Notably, specific impacts of COVID-19 on people living on the streets occurred prior to the spread of infectious diseases and the loss of income due to the stagnation of economic activity and that especially the 'social distancing' policy deprived people of the opportunity to get together. Self-help activities in which people participate, such as soup kitchen or communal cooking (*kyōdō suiji*), are usually only possible when people gather together, from preparation to food distribution. This 'voluntary' lockdown and restraint before the official emergency call invited more people from a broader area to participate in the activities. The Japanese government has been repeatedly 'requiring' 'voluntary'

---

7 Based upon the data collected by the Homeless Information Centre with *Nojiren* as of 25 April 2020. See also my comment that appeared in NHK Politics Magazine 2020.

8 As of 13 June 2020, *Nojiren* confirmed that seven groups have continued to suspend their soup kitchen activities.

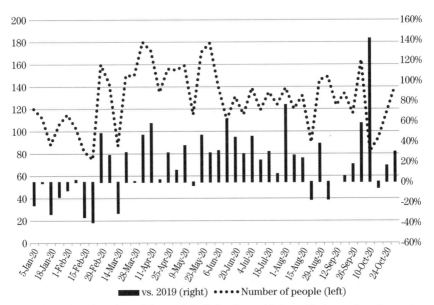

■■■ vs. 2019 (right) •••• Number of people (left)

Figure 2: Number of people receiving meals in *Nojiren*'s soup kitchen with changes from the previous year (January to October 2020)[9]

restraint (*jishuku yousei*) to the nations also later, as it is a contradictory use of language in a sense that many people felt it was practically mandatory.

Nojiren also changed its food distribution methods. The gathering of more than a hundred people in a small park[10] would generally have encouraged conversation, but to avoid proximity, we decided to switch to distributing packed rice *bentō* boxes as soon as they were ready so that participants could bring them back and eat at their places safer.[11] This makes it more challenging to understand the living conditions of the homeless.

When the decision was made to maintain our activities in the face of the COVID-19 pandemic, the greatest fear was that the supporters would become a

9   Although the number on 20 October 2020 was only 82, it was 141.2% higher than the previous year. This was because a large typhoon hit Tokyo on 12 October 2019, resulting in fewer participants, as many as 34.

10 Two-thirds of *Mitake Park*, which has a size of 2,888 m², was fenced off to prevent the homeless campers from entering.

11 This measure was introduced on 29 February 2020 and continued for three years until 25 February 2023.

source of infection because they had more contact with an unspecified number of people in their social life, such as commuting to work or school on crowded trains, while most homeless people lived in isolation. The average age of people living on the street is 63.6 (as of November 2021; see MHLW 2022), and the risk of severe illness or disability is known to be high. Therefore, various hygienic measures were taken in our soup–kitchen activities, such as washing hands, disinfecting cooking tables, wearing masks, gloves, and face guards during consultations, communicating online with medical doctors, and asking participants to avoid chatting and eating on the spot. We stopped tea services and prioritised the distribution of a minimum amount of food, and these changes caused consternation among the participants.

Living on the street, access to media was limited, and information gaps were often observed. With the help of medical practitioners, basic information on infectious diseases and their prevention was compiled into leaflets and distributed in March 2020. However, even in June, some people said that they did not know about the possibility of an asymptomatic infection or the effectiveness of wearing masks. Even when masks were distributed to participants and asked to wear, some people refused out of desperation, saying 'I'm just fine' or 'I don't care even if I get infected'. This reaction served as a reminder that self–esteem and the basic will to live are essential prerequisites for encouraging people to take minimum sanitary self–defence measures.

3.2 'Stay homeless' policy and emergency hotel for net café refugees

Although Japan has an exceptional number of hospital beds per population worldwide, the number of beds available for COVID-19 patients is very limited.[12] Hence, the TMG had adopted the above-referred 'stay home' policy by April 2020, stating that asymptomatic or mildly infected patients should be refused hospital treatment.

If they are told to 'stay home' but have nowhere to return to, they have no

---

12 In comparing the number of hospital beds in Organization for Economic Cooperation and Development member countries, Japan leads all member countries with 13.1 beds per 1,000 people. Still, as of December 2020, only 1.8% were beds for COVID-19 patients. This fact was revealed by Prof. Shigeto Yonemura, a medical doctor and jurist at the University of Tokyo, in an interview with Video News on 19 December 2020 (Yonemura 2020). It became widely known when the Video News journalist Tetsuo Jimbo pointed this out at the then Prime Minister Yoshihide Suga's press conference on 23 April 2021.

choice but to remain on the streets. Suppose an infected person has to 'stay on the street', not hospitalised, even with mild symptoms. In such cases, it becomes difficult to identify their whereabouts, and the spread of infections and prejudice cannot be prevented. In the U.S., where lockdown restrictions were already partly in place as of March 2020, there have been reports of the possibility of mass infection in tens of thousands of people among the vast number of unsheltered people.[13]

On 6 April *Nojiren* submitted a written request to the TMG to secure 1) evacuation centres under the Disaster Relief Act and the implementation of food service support; 2) places for quarantine and recovery for those who do not have homes; and 3) private rooms as well as support for the transition from shared accommodation (Nojiren 2000).

When a state of emergency was declared the following day, the MHLW issued an administrative communication instructing local authorities to secure 'temporary accommodation' for those who had moved out of Internet cafés and other facilities. On the weekend, when Internet cafés began to close, we came across approximately 15 people who were wandering in the park because they had nowhere to go and asked for help. We were informed that the TMG was offering to rent 100 hotel rooms, but that there was no information on their website. When I called the department in charge, I was told that they would not accept them unless they could prove that they had been in the city for more than six months and had continuously used Internet cafés and other facilities. Puzzled by the inflexible response, we advised the unhoused people to use accommodation support from other private organisations, but some of them were asleep out for the weekend to visit the city hall together with us to apply for public assistance the following Monday.

---

13 Especially in California, where the homeless population has skyrocketed in recent years due to the rise in land prices as a result of the expansion of IT companies, the governor held a press conference to announce that 56% of the state's 108,000 unsheltered population, namely about 60,000 people, could be afflicted with the COVID-19 for the next eight weeks, and the medical system was at risk of being overwhelmed (Reuter, 19 March 2020: 'California governor says 60,000 homeless in state could get coronavirus in next eight weeks'). It was further announced that he was planning to take budgetary measures to mitigate this risk, including renting trailers and motels for the homeless people (LA Times, 18 March 2020 'Coronavirus hitting California's homeless population could be what finally breaks hospitals').

3.3 Economic impacts on homeless labourers

Although not generally known, about half of the Japanese homeless people (48.9%, see MHLW 2022: 11) earn some income through day labour, scavenging, and so on. For this reason, we go on night patrols every Saturday to visit homeless people who do not visit soup kitchens, but live independently. Some move between Internet cafés and streets.

In March, people who had earned income from construction, cleaning, and event management also began to ask for assistance, saying they had no work, and those living on the streets collecting aluminium cans reported a sharp fall in their income due to a decrease in waste based on a plummeting unit price.[14] Some earned less than 8,000 yen per day several times a month by engaging in light work, such as park cleaning, through the TMG's measures against unemployment; however, as new recruitment was suspended from April to June, these people also lost their income.

The stagnation of economic and social activities led to an increase in unemployment and reduced income, which seriously impacted the lives of those living on the streets. In line with the closure of schools, libraries and other public facilities were temporarily closed, and restaurants and other retail stores refrained from operating. In addition, unstable weather conditions continued from January to March 2020, with snowfall observed in Tokyo every month. It became increasingly difficult to provide shelter from wind and rain in these places.

4. Questionnaire survey and analysis

Under these circumstances, in January and February 2022, I conducted a questionnaire survey of participants who used soup kitchen services in cooperation with our group, *Nojiren*, to better understand the impact of the COVID-19 pandemic on soup kitchen users and clarify the extent to which public support measures by local and national governments reached them.[15]

---

14 The average price of aluminium in April 2020 was 207.6 yen (per kg), 0.79 times the price for the same month a year earlier (263.33 yen) (Nissin 2019–2020). However, the end price traded by homeless workers is much lower, at 65 yen per kg as of May 2020, with a sharp decrease from 80 yen as compared with a month before. A homeless can collector complained that he could barely collect enough cans overnight to make 300 yen (Interviews on 2 and 23 May 2020).

Table 1: Age group of the soup kitchen users

	Age group	Frequency %	Valid %	
Valid	20s	1	1.2%	1.3%
	30s	5	6.0%	6.3%
	40s	20	24.1%	25.3%
	50s	21	25.3%	26.6%
	60s	20	24.1%	25.3%
	70s	11	13.3%	13.9%
	80s	1	1.2%	1.3%
	Total	79	95.2%	100.0%
Missing	NA	4	4.8%	
Total		83	100.0%	

Over three weeks, from the end of January to the beginning of February 2022, a gross headcount of 386 impoverished people visited soup kitchens and 83 answers were collected.[16] The basic attributes of the 83 respondents included 78 men (95.1%) and four women (4.9%), with an average age of 52.7 years (see **Table 1** for the age composition of the sample). This is considerably lower than the national survey showed (63.6 as of September 2011, according to HMLW 2022).

To understand the living situation of the respondents, the questionnaire covered four topical areas: 1) respondents' housing, jobs, and current state of health, 2) the impact of COVID-19, 3) their use of government support measures, and 4) their current and past use of public assistance programs.

4.1 Helpless homeless under the pandemic

In terms of housing, 55 respondents (66.3%) were currently 'homeless' (including those staying in cars, using Internet cafés, and similar facilities.), whereas 28 (33.7%) had an apartment, shelter, or other type of housing to which they could return. Of the 55 homeless respondents, 20 (38.5%) had been living

---

15 The primary results and part of the following analysis are also published on *Nojiren*'s website (2022). The survey was also reported in newspapers such as *Mainichi Shinbun* (Kurokawa 2022) and *Tokyo Shinbun* (Yamashita 2022).

16 The participants were 97 on 22 January, 155 on 29 January and 134 on 5 February. Due to the overlap of visitors, the exact response rate is unknown, but if limited to the first day of the survey, the response rate was 55.6% (54 out of 97 persons). The overall response rate can be estimated at 53.5, given that the largest number on 29 January is considered as the population.

on the street for 'less than one year' at the time of the survey, which meant that they became homeless after the COVID-19 outbreak.

With regard to employment, due to the pandemic, 21 (25.3%) of the total respondents have 'lost their jobs', and also the same percentage have 'lost their income', 9 (10.8%) have 'lost their housing', and 19 (22.9%) have had to 'reduce the number of their meals'. All these findings indicate that COVID-19 and the stay–at–home policy have had a severe impact directly related to impoverishment.

Then, I examined whether the government's various COVID-19-related support measures reached people in need on the street, such as the Special Cash Payment in 2020, *Abenomask*, vaccination, and public assistance, using multiple-choice questions combined with an open-ended text box. In April 2020, the Japanese government launched the Special Cash Payment Program to provide 100,000 yen per person to 'all residents' living in Japan for emergency economic measures related to the COVID-19 pandemic, especially to support household financing. Also, on April 1, then Prime Minister Shinzo Abe announced that all households would receive two cloth face masks each against a shortage of masks, later dubbed '*Abenomasks*' in reference to his economic policy *Abenomics*. As of April 30, the Housing Security Benefit (rent subsidy), which had previously been intended for the newly unemployed, was expanded to include those whose incomes had reduced owing to the economic contraction caused by the pandemic, and the duration of the benefit was also extended.

These policies were necessary for the economic assistance that should have been provided to those who lost their jobs or places of residence due to the pandemic. However, of the 83 respondents to the survey, only 48 (57.8%) received Special Cash Payment, 31 (37.3%) received *Abenomask*, and only one person (1.2%) used the Housing Security Benefit.[17] Among the 55 respondents who were homeless at the time of the survey, the utilisation rate of these programs was even lower: 25 (45.5%) for the Special Cash Payment and 13 (23.6%) for the mask, indicating that public support measures did not reach many homeless people.

---

17 The programme started in 2015 and provides a three-month benefit equal to public assistance if a person cannot pay rent due to unemployment. After the COVID-19 pandemic, the application and extension restrictions conditions were relaxed.

What about the free vaccination program for COVID-19, which started in February 2021 and was also for 'all residents'? Vaccination was a policy that directly linked the risk of life to impoverished people on the street, especially when many of them were elderly and lacked a convalescent environment after infection. At the time of the survey, one year after the start of the program, however, the vaccination rate among the respondents (the percentage of those who had completed two doses) was only 38.6% (32 persons), which was significantly lower than the vaccination rate among the total Japanese population (79.0% as of February 16, 2022 according to the MHLW).

The low uptake of these public support measures can be attributed to the system needing to be in sync with the actual situation of the most vulnerable, as Special Cash Payments, distribution of masks, and vaccination coupons were all based on the premise of resident registration. The Special Cash Payment was also intended to be applied for and paid to 'those homeless etc.' (Ministry of Internal Affairs and Communications (MIC) 2020a). However, the requirement was that 'the applicant be recorded in the basic resident register of the municipality of residence' to receive the money (ibid.) This has resulted in the exclusion of many people in need who have lost their registered addresses from the benefit list. This issue is discussed in section 5–2.

Last, but not the least, we will discuss the public assistance (*seikatsu hogo*) program, which is expected to play a role as a safety net to guarantee the country's 'national minimum'. Regardless of whether a person is registered as a resident, or she can receive public assistance from the local government in the current location where or she is in need. In Tokyo (a first-class area such as Shibuya), a single adult can receive 76,310 yen per month for living expenses and up to 53,700 yen[18] for housing expenses (rent). As long as the welfare system is functioning, there should be no need for people living on the streets. Why should homeless people not receive public assistance?

Of the 83 respondents who visited *Nojiren*'s soup kitchen, 18 (22.2%) were welfare recipients of public assistance and 55 (66.2%) were homeless at the time of the survey. Among 65 persons who did not receive public assistance, 39 (60.0%) had 'never used it before' and 24 (36.9%) had 'used it in the past'. Regarding their reasons for not applying, the highest percentage (36.9%) of

---

18   They amount to approximately $545 and $383, respectively, at an exchange rate of 140 JPY to USD).

respondents (24 people) answered that they did not want to use the welfare system while they could work, although the majority (19 people) were homeless. This indicates that many people did not use public assistance by their own will, at least in their recognition, because they wanted to be 'independent' despite living in poverty due to a lack of stable employment. This work ethic or the avoidance of 'dependence' among the Japanese homeless people was astonishingly evident even during the pandemic of COVID-19. Regarding work ethics, 35 (42.2%) of all respondents and 22 (40.0%) of those currently homeless worked as day labourers or in other income-earning jobs, including TMG's paid programs for the unemployed.[19] While various public support measures did not reach homeless people, it became clear that they tried very hard to do so, even during the pandemic, with the limited employment opportunities available and found support from private aid group activities such as soup kitchens.

To explain the legal application rate of public assistance, however, the following circumstances and normative attitudes toward independence must be considered among homeless Japanese people: In the case of those who apply for public assistance without a registered address, most of the 23 Special Wards in Tokyo send users to temporary shelters (*muryō teigaku shukuhakujo*, literally meaning free or low–cost lodging). There were concerns among homeless people that the risk of infection would increase by moving into a shared room because the number of shelters with private rooms was limited (Kimura 2020a: 33). This issue is discussed in more detail in section 5–1.

4.2 Non-homeless users of the soup kitchen

To identify long-term trends in soup kitchen users, we compared our findings with similar surveys conducted in cooperation with *Nojiren* in 2014 before the COVID-19 disaster.[20] Remarkably, the number of non-homeless soup

---

19 TMG has been running the Special Employment Measures Programme since 1969 as a measure against unemployment among day labourers. Those who register for the programme are offered jobs that pay around 8,000 yen daily, several times a month, cleaning streets and parks. Of the 55 people who were homeless, 17 (30.9%) said they were engaged in this work. However, this programme was also closed during the period of self-restraint from leaving the house and the declaration of a state of emergency.

20 *Nojiren* and I surveyed 8 and 15 March 2014. The participants were 109 and 163, and we collected 61 samples. The questionnaire are similar and comparable with the survey in 2022 except for the questions concerning COVID-19.

kitchen users will increase from 8.2% (5 of 61 respondents) in 2014 to 33.7% in 2022.[21] Let us now review the characteristics of non-homeless soup kitchen users.

Of the 28 non-homeless respondents, 15 had lived homeless outside the past and most of them (14) had experienced homelessness for a total of three years or more. The remaining 13 had never experienced homelessness and needed to visit a soup kitchen. While 16 (57.1% of the 28 respondents) were then using public assistance, 11 (39.3%) had never used it.

Thus, half of the current non-homeless respondents had been camping out for quite a long time and had subsequently found a place to return to mainly through public assistance.

Thirteen people who had never experienced homelessness and those who had never used welfare almost overlapped. All the above 11 had never stayed in a public shelter and had never been to a soup kitchen before the pandemic. Hence, they can be considered newcomers who fell into destitution for the first time, possibly because of the pandemic. To confirm this point in more detail, I examined their responses regarding how they were affected by the COVID-19 pandemic (**Figure 3**).

The questionnaire asked respondents to tick all that applied, asking them to 'Has the outbreak of the new coronavirus changed your work or life situation?'. Six of the 28 non-homeless persons (21.4%) lost their jobs, and nine persons (32.1%) had reduced incomes (excluding those who lost their jobs). Regarding their life situation, one (3.6%) lost his residence (now staying with an acquaintance), one (3.6%) went into debt, and seven (25.0%) had fewer meals than usual. The changes also affected their physical and psychological health and human relationships, with three respondents (10.7%) stating to have more health problems, four (14.3%) worried more than before, and three (10.7%) experiencing a worsening of their close relationships. In addition, four participants (14.3%) had other concerns about their lives, and three (10.7%) answered that their close relationships had deteriorated due to the pandemic. Therefore, even for non-homeless people, the pandemic's effects on their social and economic lives are considerably serious.

---

21 Those who were staying at an acquaintance's house or an Internet café but at the same time had a place to sleep on the street were here counted as 'homeless'.

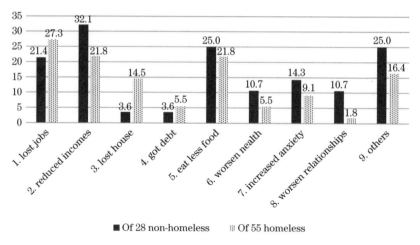

Figure 3: COVID-19 pandemic impacts on soup-kitchen users (MA, %)

4.3 Government's 'punishment' for being homeless

We confirmed that the economic impact of the COVID-19 pandemic was broad enough to spread to the non-homeless population who could not find enough food and had to rely on soup kitchens to get by. Low-income and insecurely housed people who are not counted as 'homeless' by the laws of Japan were at risk of becoming eventually 'homeless' with scarce public support.

Another vital fact comes to light when comparing soup-kitchen users with and without addresses. The percentage of those who utilised various public services was significantly higher among non-homeless people with registered residences than among those who did not. Of the 28 non-homeless respondents, 18 (64.3%) received *Abenomask*, 23 (82.1%) received benefits, and 21 (75.0%) received vaccinations twice (while only 20.0% of the unhoused respondents did) **(Figure 4)**.

Since the *Abenomasks* were distributed via postal mail to all residents but not to homeless people, it is assumed that their use in the case of unhoused people would be donations by their supporters, such as *Nojiren*. As noted above, special cash payments are conditional on resident registration. However, since our group offered temporary addresses for homeless applicants and assistance in contacting local authorities that have registered past residences, this rate (45.5) for utilisation as homeless people without fixed addresses is

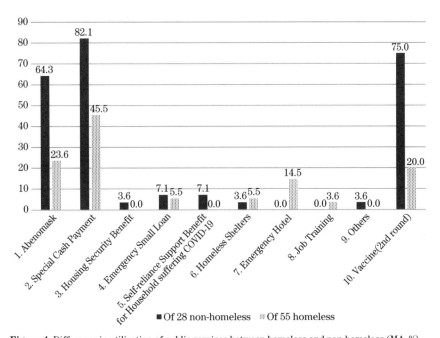

Figure 4: Difference in utilization of public services between homeless and non-homeless (MA, %)

considered exceptionally high compared to people without housing in other areas.

A significant difference was the rate of non-vaccination, which can be life-threatening; 75.0% of non-homeless people answered that they had completed the second round of vaccinations, whereas 76.4% of unhoused respondents had never received vaccinations at the time. The utilisation rate of other services for low-income people is also meagre, suggesting a mismatch between the living conditions and the needs of the impoverished and the conditions for using the system.

People lose their resident registration because they cannot afford rent due to unemployment or financial hardships. The state's responsibility is to guarantee the right to survive and deliver official assistance. However, the evidence presented in this chapter indicates that the Japanese government treats homelessness as if it were a crime and punishes those involved by excluding those who are unaddressed from many essential public services.

As mentioned earlier, the guiding principles of the SDGs are 'human rights-based approach' and 'leave no one behind'. The Japanese government left the poor behind on the streets, leaving them homeless, helpless, and infringing on their rights.

5. Further challenges and prospects

Based on the analysis above, clear recommendations can be made for what needs to be done to improve the situation of people living on the streets in Japan. After presenting a legal interpretation of public assistance and welfare facilities for homeless people (5.1), I introduce a social movement led by concerned people who aimed to improve the Special Cash Payment program (5.2).

5.1 Welfare facilities with 'three Cs': Legal interpretation of Public Assistance dysfunctions

As expected, the economic fallout from the COVID-19 pandemic increased hardship on the streets and increased the number of consultations for welfare benefits. To help with this, our organisation set up a counselling service during meal distribution. Surprisingly, the number of people who consulted soup-kitchen locations did not increase significantly. When we spoke to people who had been forced to live on the streets before the pandemic, we found that most were well informed about the welfare system and hesitant to apply for it. The biggest reason was their 'will to be independent' (36.9%), as seen above. However, many participants (25.8%) complained that 'receiving welfare would cause various inconveniences'.

Additional individual interviews revealed that respondents' concerns about the public assistance system were primarily directed at the 'various inconveniences' of the facilities where they could be institutionalised upon application.[22] Most of the 23 Special Ward authorities of Central Tokyo maintain that the only option for those seeking protection from living on the streets is to be admitted to an institution. At the same time, the number of institutions with private rooms is limited. Hence, there were concerns among respondents that sharing a room would increase the risk of COVID-19.

---

22 Responses included 'previous facility had faulty waterworks', 'forced to share a room in the facility', 'do not like caseworkers' requirement for job hunting', 'elderly roommates are noisy', and 'not allowed to move to an apartment'.

To control the number of infections, the government called on citizens to avoid the three Cs (*san mitsu*): (1) closed spaces with poor ventilation, (2) crowded places with many people nearby, and (3) close-contact settings, such as close-range conversation. However, many welfare facilities available for the homeless are shared accommodation facilities that do not meet these requirements. The poor condition of facilities at least partly explains why Japanese homeless people were hesitant to apply for welfare, even during the pandemic.

It has already been mentioned that when the state of emergency was declared in April 2020, Internet cafés ceased to operate, and people living there, so-called 'net café refugees', were forced to leave. TMG prepared hotels for them, but the conditions of use were strict. To qualify, they had to have a living history of at least six months in Tokyo and submit a written record of Internet café use. However, even those in need who had made it through strict conditions to move into hotels for a limited period were sent to shared–room facilities when they subsequently applied for and received public assistance. In response to protests from support groups, on 17 April 2020 the MHLW ordered local authorities to encourage the use of private rooms with good hygiene management when providing or introducing accommodation to needy people (MHLW 2020b). Following this, the TMG's Bureau of Social Welfare and Public Health instructed the local welfare departments 'to continue to consider using hotels if private rooms with good hygiene management in other emergency facilities cannot be secured' (TMG 2020b).

Although Internet cafés being used as housing for homeless people is a significant problem, the policy change was undoubtedly a step forward. However, the above-mentioned TMG guidance to the welfare office contained the following sentence in the Q&A section: 'In principle, the use of emergency temporary accommodation is limited to users of Internet cafés and other facilities in Tokyo who have lost their place of residence due to the closure of the facilities they use, and therefore, other people living on the streets cannot use the accommodation' (MHLW 2020b).

In short, the TMG authorities did not permit homeless people to use these private room emergency accommodations if they applied for public assistance directly from the street and not through the TMG temporary hotel. This measurement is clearly against the Public Assistance Law, which enshrines the principle of non-discrimination and equality in Article 2, and the restrictions placed on the facilities used by the applicant based on his or her place of residence immediately before the application for protection deviated from the principles of the law.

Most welfare offices in Tokyo have customary rules not to move homeless applicants directly from the street into private flats and often withhold a decision for three to six months on the provision of the security deposit required in most cases of new tenants moving into a flat (Kimura 2020a: 34; Inaba 2016: 89). After checking whether the person can live without difficulty in the facility, they allow the person to move into a flat if he or she requests it with information on available properties.

Indeed, there are cases where it is difficult for the person concerned to manage their finances because of factors such as dependence on alcohol and gambling, and it may seem unavoidable to direct them to a facility where meals are secured. However, in reality, even people with past experiences who live by themselves are uniformly sent to shared accommodation facilities. Furthermore, even after a three-month waiting period, it is often difficult for homeless people to move to a private room flat because the lack of public housing has made welfare offices dependent on the private rental housing market, and landlords often refuse to sign tenancy agreements for older people who have experienced homelessness. After applying for welfare assistance, homeless people in Tokyo are usually sent to 'free and low-cost accommodations', which are the facilities defined in Article 2 of the Social Welfare Law as 'a business that lets simple housing or provides accommodation and other facilities for people with livelihood difficulties free of charge or for a low fee'. These facilities, originally intended to be temporary places to live until they can live at home, have, in reality, become a place of last resort for people who have experienced homelessness and are refused in the rental housing market because of it. The root of the problem is the overwhelming shortage of public housing in Tokyo, which is necessary to provide all the needy with a national minimum standard of living. The country's guarantee of the right to a decent life is dysfunctional because of its dependence on public assistance in the private-rental-housing market, which is not required to comply with the system.

5.2 Exclusion from 'universal' benefits

While calling for citizens to stay at home, the TMG failed to establish sufficient emergency shelters for the homeless. 40.0% of homeless people work from the street, but day labourers have no unemployment benefits, even when they lose their jobs. Furthermore, facilities available for those applying for welfare from the streets are in poor condition, which increases the risk of infection. These circumstances were further worsened by the exclusion of homeless people from the Special Cash Payment Program approved by the cabinet on 20 April 2020.

The MIC (2020a) quickly announced that homeless people would not be excluded from benefits. However, this was only the case when they were newly registered residents and benefits were not granted while still living on the street.

Many support groups and concerned people petitioned for the benefits to be extended to those living on the street. However, the MIC (2020b) responded to these petitions on 17 June 2020, adding more confusion. The documents listed 1) homeless self-support centres, 2) Internet cafés, 3) day labourers' dormitories (*doya*), 4) free and low–cost accommodation, and 5) facilities of private support groups as examples of facilities where people could register as residents. However, this was misleading because the MIC did not relax the criteria for address recognition but reaffirmed its previous interpretation of the law, stating that resident registration at these facilities is only possible with the facility manager's consent and actual residence status.[23]

Having an address where one can register is synonymous with exiting homelessness under Japanese law, which exclusively defines homeless people as rough sleepers. Why do so many people live on the streets despite the various facilities mentioned?

First, self-support centres run by local authorities aim to help people become self-sufficient in employment. They cannot be used by the elderly, the physically challenged, or by others who have difficulty finding work. Furthermore, there are limits to the length and number of times they can stay in these centres.[24] Second, the existence of Internet cafés that allow resident

---

23 The following argument of this section was based upon my policy request to MIC (Kimura 2020b).

24 I have discussed this system in detail on another occasion (Kimura 2013: 89). It is a typical job-first approach that effectively prevents the homeless but potential workforce from applying for public assistance.

registration has not been confirmed,[25] and as of June 2020, the government requested 'voluntary restraints' on their businesses, meaning that they could not be used. Third and fourth, landlords of the day labourer's dormitory (*doya*) and free and low-cost accommodations often refuse to register their tenant's address with the city hall, even if they have moved in on welfare benefits.[26] As a result, homeless people can only register their addresses with a limited number of shelters run by support groups or find a flat after staying for several months in 3C facilities of free and low-cost accommodation during the pandemic without address registration. This requirement for address registration is an obstacle that cannot be easily overcome by people living on the street.

The MIC requires resident registration to prevent double payment. However, even if the resident registration has been cancelled, the history of residential transfers is recorded in the supplementary table of the family register (Japanese *koseki* system). Thus, a simple check at the municipality where the resident registration was last held or at the place of family registration can enable the application and benefits of the Special Cash Payment in the current location, with no risk of duplicated payments.[27] The government has identified 3,688 homeless people nationwide (as of January 2020, according to MHLW 2020c). Even if we consider the implicit number mentioned before (section 2), the additional procedures required were not unfeasible to fulfil the project's aim: to provide benefits to 'all residents' of the country.

After repeated negotiations with the MIC, *Nojiren*, together with other groups, held a rally in the office of the House of Representatives on 30 July 2020 to appeal to the MIC, MHLW, and the Ministry of Justice that homeless people should be eligible for benefits.[28] The MIC Minister Sanae Takaichi, however,

---

25 The only known exception was a case in 2008 in Soka city, Saitama Prefecture, where an Internet café owner allowed homeless persons to register as residents, which was widely reported as 'Internet café residents'. Today, the city does not permit new residents to register (An interview with the café conducted on 24 December 2023).

26 This finding is based on *Nojiren*'s casework activities since 1998. *Doya* falls under the 'simple lodging house business' category under the *Ryokan* (Japanese Inn) Law, not a residence. Hence, the authorities also require that proof of accommodation is provided when registering an address in these places. When accepting welfare applications, municipalities allow inconsistencies between the current address and the registered address (or even its absence) under the Basic Resident Registration Act, and they do not necessarily grasp these circumstances.

27 According to press reports, Shibuya Ward also made a similar suggestion to the MIC (*Mainichi Shinbun*, 19 August 2020).

remained adamant about the requirements for residence registration. As a result, many people living on the streets were left behind and unable to receive benefits until the application deadline passed.

6. Conclusion

While medical triage for COVID-19 patients has been discussed under limited healthcare resources worldwide, a severe disparity in life between those with and without an address is systematically tolerated and structured in Japan. It is the voluntary private support of NGOs and the self-help efforts of the people themselves, who are still working hard to patch the holes in public assistance systems, that should guarantee a minimum standard of living. These activities were supported by the goodwill of many citizens who volunteered to help people in need. However, this is by no means a beautiful story. By contrast, it shows how one of the world's wealthiest nations fails to grant the right to a decent life to all its citizens, leaving the survival and welfare of impoverished people in the hands of the uncertain charity of a few.

How social welfare should be approached is a central question in all societies and much time has been spent contemplating its primary function. When Robert Menzie, former prime minister of Australia, referred to 'forgotten people' in his well-known speech (Menzie 1942), he had in mind the middle class of salary-earners, shopkeepers, skilled artisans and the like, who were different from the capitalists, who could fend for themselves and also from the organised and politically represented proletariat.

He recognised the value of these forgotten people, amongst all, in their 'homes' because 'the real life of the nation is to be found ... in the homes of people who are nameless and unadvertised ...' He continued, '[t]he home is the foundation of sanity and sobriety; it is the indispensable condition of continuity; its health determines the health of society as a whole'.

Shortly after the start of the Pacific War, Menzie did not appeal to his people for the courage to sacrifice their lives to protect their home and country,

---

28 See my policy request addressed to the MIC at the negotiation meeting in Kimura 2020b. News media such as NHK (7 June 2020), *Tokyo Shinbun* (16 May, 18 June, and 25 August 2020), and *Nishinihon Shinbun* (16 September 2020) also reported on the issue with my comment.

let alone compare the nation to a single house and inspire totalitarian loyalty to the deified ruler. At this point, he envisioned a peaceful postwar nation, emphasising social solidarity and sustainability for the next generation. For him, the value of a home is not only the physical possession of a house and its economic benefits ('home material' in his expression) but also the human connection with the family and society through family members ('home human'). Moreover, as a 'home spiritual', it meant the possibility of social solidarity rather than individual or family isolation.

He maintained:

[W]e have homes spiritual ... Human nature is at its greatest when it combines dependence upon God with independence of man. We offer no affront – on the contrary we have nothing but the warmest human compassion – toward those whom fate has compelled to live upon the bounty of the State, when we say that the greatest element in a strong people is a fierce independence of spirit. (Menzies 1942)

Similarly, we can ask how forgotten people are in Japan and other countries during the COVID-19 pandemic. Social distancing of 1.5 meters to avoid infection has significantly narrowed the scope of our solidarity and society. The Japanese government found a base for social defence against the novel coronavirus in private homes and saw political value in it. However, adequate measures were not taken to help people who had already lost their homes because of unemployment or poverty. The guarantee of fundamental human rights is essential for ensuring the sustainability of societies. In this respect, Japan is failing those who are living on the streets, who have lost their homes, and who were kept homeless due to insufficient policies in times of crisis.

References

ARCH (Advocacy and Research Centre for Homelessness) (2020): Announcement of Tokyo Street Count 2020 Winter Survey Results, [in Japanese], www.archomelessness.org/, [Accessed 11 March 2023].

City of Berlin (2020): Erste Ergebnisse der Obdachlosenzählung: Senatorin Breitenbach will Hilfsangebote vor Ort für obdachlose Menschen verbessern, www.berlin.de/sen/ias/presse/pressemitteilungen/2020/pressemitteilung.892510.php, [Accessed 30 March 2023].

Inaba, Tsuyoshi (2016): *Encourage Social Change from the Scene of the Poverty Problem*, [in Japanese], Horinouchi Press.

Kimura, Masato (2013): Roofs or Jobs First?: On the Poor and Homeless People in Tokyo. In: German–Japanese Society for Social Sciences (ed.): *Life Course and Life Style in Comparison: Proceedings of the 11th Meeting of the German–Japanese Society for Social Sciences*, Asakusa Printing, 83–98.

Kimura, Masato (2019): Privatization and Protest of Commons: On the Gentrification and Homeless Movement in Shibuya, [in Japanese]. In: *Space, Society and Geographical Thought [Kūkan, Shakai, Chirishisou]* 22: 139–156.

Kimura, Masato (2020a): Stay homeless? Homelessness under COVID-19 disaster and the survival gap, [in Japanese]. In: *Gospel and world* 75 (12): 30–35.

Kimura, Masato (2020b): Policy proposals on procedures for the COVID-19 Special Cash Payment to the homeless people, [in Japanese], A document submitted to the MIC and MHLW on 30 June 2020, kimuramasato.wordpress.com, [Accessed 25 March 2023].

Kimura, Masato (2021): Who killed her? A Homicide of a Homeless Person in Hatagaya, [in Japanese]. In: Group of Citizens Opinion 30 (ed.), *Citizens Opinion* 184: 12–13.

Kimura, Masato (2023): Eviction and Robbery: What happened in a park. In: Group of Citizens Opinion 30 (ed.), *Citizens Opinion* 195: 12–13.

Mainichi Shinbun (2020): COVID-19: Homeless people kept away from 100,000 yen, which is supposed to be 'for all citizens of the country', but resident registration is a barrier, soon to expire, 19 August.

Menzies, Robert (1942): The Forgotten People: A Speech delivered on the radio on 22 May 1942, available on the website of Menzies research centre, www.menziesrc.org/the-forgotten-people, [Accessed 1 May 2023].

MHLW (Ministry of Health, Labor, and Welfare) (2003): The result of the national survey on the actual situation of the homeless (survey on actual living conditions), [in Japanese], www.mhlw.go.jp/houdou/2003/03/h0326-5.html, [Accessed 11 March 2023].

MHLW (2020a): Diamond Princess Local Task Force Report, [in Japanese], www.mhlw.go.jp/content/10900000/000627363.pdf, [Accessed 25 March 2023].

MHLW (2020b): Considerations in responding to the declaration of a state of emergency concerning New Coronavirus Infections, [in Japanese], www.mhlw.go.jp/content/000622762.pdf, [Accessed 11 May 2020].

MHLW (2020c): The result of the national survey on the actual situation of the homeless (survey of approximate numbers), [in Japanese], www.mhlw.go.jp/stf/newpage_12485.html [Accessed 25 March 2023].

MHLW (2022): The result of the national survey on the actual situation of the homeless (survey on actual living conditions), [in Japanese], www.mhlw.go.jp/stf/newpage_25330.html, [Accessed 11 March 2023].

MHLW (2023): Visualizing the data: information on COVID-19 infections, covid19.mhlw.go.jp/en/, [Accessed 25 March 2023].

MIC (Ministry of Internal Affairs and Communications) (2020a): Request for cooperation in publicizing the Special Cash Payment to the homeless, etc., [in Japanese], www.soumu.go.jp/main_content/000715542.pdf, [Accessed 23 May 2020].

MIC (2020b): Handling of address recognition for homeless persons, etc. (Notice), [in Japanese], www.soumu.go.jp/main_content/000693286.pdf, [Accessed 18 June 2020].

New York City (2022): Homeless outreach population estimate 2022 results, www.nyc.gov/site/dhs/outreach/hope.page, [Accessed 30 March 2023].

NHK Web (2020): (Read from data) Number of deaths from new coronas: Level on par with the peak of the first wave, [in Japanese], www3.nhk.or.jp/news/html/20201127/k10012734011000.html, [Accessed 30 March 2023].

NHK Politics Magazine (2020): A series of suspensions of soup kitchen activities, [in Japanese], www.nhk.or.jp/politics/articles/lastweek/34694.html, [Accessed 27 April 2020].

Nissin (Nihon Shinkan) 2019–2020: Aluminum bullion market price, www.nihonshinkan.co.jp, [Accessed 2 August 2023].

Nojiren (2020): A request for emergency assistance for people living on the streets amid the COVID-19 pandemic.

Nojiren (2022): Summary of the results of the survey on the living conditions of people in need concerning the impact of the new corona (preliminary report), [in Japanese], nojiren.wixsite.com/index, [Accessed 1 March 2023].

TMG (Tokyo Metropolitan Government) (2020a): List of approximate number of people living on the street by region (January 2020), [in Japanese], www.fukushi.metro.tokyo.lg.jp/seikatsu/rojo/gaisuchosa.html, [Accessed 10 March 2023].

TMG (2020b): Issueance of Q&As on the use of emergency temporary accommodation (Part 3), [in Japanese], unpublished.

Kurokawa, Shinji (2022): Over 70% of people living on the street are unvaccinated, [in Japanese], *Mainichi Shinbun* (Tokyo regional edition, 25 February 2022).

Yamashita, Hazuki (2022): People lined up to get food from the soup kitchen, [in Japanese], *Tokyo Shinbun* (10 February 2022).

Yonemura, Shigeto (2021): An interview broadcasted on the Video News with the title of 'What is fundamentally lacking in the discussion in Japan on countermeasures against Corona infections', [in Japanese], www.videonews.com/marugeki–talk/1028, [Accessed 20 February 2021].

Chapter 7

Cyber- and Traditional Bullying as Global Challenges? Findings from Germany, Hong Kong, and Japan

Fabian Schunk
Gisela Trommsdorff
Natalie Wong
Gen Nakao

Bullying, including cyberbullying, constitutes a worldwide phenomenon with grave consequences for well-being, mental health, and educational outcomes (Kowalski et al. 2014; Kowalski & Limber 2013; Schunk et al. 2022). In 2014, the General Assembly of the United Nations adopted a resolution that recognized bullying as a global concern and encouraged member states to take measures for preventing and responding to bullying (UN General Assembly 2014). Marta Santos Pais, UN Special Representative of the Secretary-General on Violence against Children, emphasized the importance of reducing bullying for attaining the Sustainable Development Goals, saying that 'preventing and addressing bullying will no doubt contribute to the promotion of the safe and non-violent learning environments and to the elimination of physical, sexual and emotional violence that the [Sustainable Development Goals] seek to guarantee' (UN News 2015). Research on cultural differences in cyberbullying has grown in recent years, given that cyberbullying is a global phenomenon (Sittichai & Smith 2015). Yet, research on cyberbullying is still typically conducted within a culture as opposed to across cultures. This chapter explores the role of culture in shaping bullying and presents empirical findings based on direct comparisons among university students from Germany, Hong Kong, and Japan.

1. Two types of bullying: Cyber- and traditional bullying

Research often distinguishes two types of bullying, traditional bullying and cyberbullying. Based on the conceptualization by Olweus (1993), traditional bullying can be defined as 'an aggressive, intentional act or behaviour that is carried out by a group or an individual repeatedly and over time against a victim who cannot easily defend him or herself' (Smith et al. 2008: 376). Cyberbullying refers to 'an aggressive, intentional act carried out by a group or individual, *using electronic forms of contact*, repeatedly and over time against a victim who cannot easily defend him or herself' (Smith et al. 2008: 376). The importance of cyberbullying has increased due to the enhanced use of information and communication technologies (ICT; Smith & Slonje 2009). In contrast to traditional bullying, cyberbullying is more often enacted anonymously and publicly (Sticca & Perren 2013). These typical characteristics of cyberbullying may seem appealing to aggressors who want to hurt or embarrass a person in front of a large audience with less risk of retaliation. Notably, a cyberbullying act can have a repetitive effect as offending posts or embarrassing pictures might stay online for a prolonged time which may then further torment a victim (Smith & Slonje 2009).

2. Bullying across cultures

The concept of bullying is known across cultures, for instance, as *Mobbing* in Germany, *qiling* in China, and *ijime* in Japan. A meta-analysis across 80 studies from various cultures found an average prevalence rate of 35% for traditional bullying involvement and 15% for cyberbullying involvement among adolescents (Modecki et al. 2014). The EU Kids Online survey collected data in 25 European countries and found that 12% of 9–16-year-old children in Europe reported having bullied someone either online or offline in the last year (Livingstone et al. 2011). In the same survey, 19% reported having experienced some form of bullying themselves. Importantly, the prevalence of bullying varied considerably across countries, with a victimization rate of 9% in Portugal, 16% in Germany, and 43% in Estonia. Further, a review of 49 studies on cyberbullying among adolescents found striking differences in cyberbullying prevalence across studies, with rates between 1.9% and 79.3% of cyberbullying perpetration in the last 6 months (Brochado et al. 2017).

More recently, a survey among 4,418 German children and adolescents found a lifetime cyberbullying perpetration rate of 12.7% (Bündnis gegen Cybermobbing 2020). For Hong Kong, one study found that 17.5% of adolescents perpetrated cyberbullying in the last month (Chan & Wong 2020), while another study found that 20.4% engaged in at least one cyberbullying act during the last semester (Chen & Chen 2020). According to Wong et al. (2011), the traditional bullying perpetration rate was considerably higher with 36% of high school students reporting traditional bullying behaviour within a month. As for Japanese adolescents, cyberbullying rates of 7.9% (Udris 2014) and 18% (Aoyama et al. 2012) were reported, whereas 11.8% replied having engaged in traditional bullying perpetration in the last 3 months (Osuka et al. 2019). Unfortunately, meaningful cultural comparisons based on these studies are not possible due to variations in the conceptualization and measurement of bullying across surveys (Görzig et al. 2021). While there have been some cross-cultural studies directly comparing bullying across cultures (e.g., Barlett et al. 2021), few studies have examined both traditional (offline) and cyberbullying simultaneously. To achieve a more comprehensive understanding of how bullying varies across cultures, we attempt a systematic comparison of factors contributing to cyber- and traditional bullying among students from different cultures.

3. Predictors of cyber- and traditional bullying perpetration across cultures

Previous research suggests that some risk factors for bullying perpetration are culturally universal. For instance, cyber- and traditional bullying as well as bullying roles (victim or bully) were shown to highly overlap across cultural samples (Kowalski et al. 2014; Smith et al. 2008; Waasdorp & Bradshaw 2015). That is, victims of cyberbullying were more likely to be also victims of traditional bullying, and perpetrators of cyberbullying were more likely to be perpetrators of traditional bullying.

These similarities notwithstanding, the cultural context may shape the frequency of specific bullying types and how supposed predictors relate to bullying perpetration. Bronfenbrenner's socio-ecological theory describes human development within a broader social context of four types of environmental systems that interact with each other: the micro-, meso-, exo-, and macrosystem (Bronfenbrenner 1977). In line with Bronfenbrenner's model, we understand culture as overarching institutional patterns that influence human development on the broadest and most distal level, the macrosystem. The cultural level includes both explicit and implicit information that is manifested in the minds of the society's members (e.g., values, norms, customs) and shapes individuals' behaviour, including aggression (e.g., Kornadt 2011).

In the next section, we outline several factors that have been linked to cyber- and traditional bullying by past research and elucidate how culture may shape the relations of these factors to bullying perpetration. In particular, we focus on normative beliefs about (cyber-)aggression, moral disengagement, and fun-seeking tendencies.

3.1. Normative beliefs about (cyber-)aggression

Normative beliefs refer to 'individualistic cognitive standards about the acceptability of a behaviour' (Huesmann & Guerra 1997: 409). Normative beliefs about aggression, in particular, were shown to be one of the strongest predictors of both cyber- and traditional bullying (Kowalski et al. 2014; Burton et al. 2013). In other words, when believing that aggression and specifically bullying, is acceptable and normative, the probability of individuals engaging in bullying may be increased (or less inhibited). Members of East Asian cultures are more likely to prioritize group goals over personal beliefs when compared to members of Western cultures (Markus & Kitayama 1991). Thus, individual normative beliefs about aggression might be comparatively more powerful in predicting bullying in Western than East Asian cultures.

3.2. Moral disengagement

Moral disengagement describes processes through which individuals cognitively restructure unethical behaviour to convince themselves that actions are less harmful or justified in a given situation (Moore et al. 2012; Bandura 2002). Cyber- and traditional bullying perpetration were shown to be highly related to increased moral disengagement (Kowalski et al. 2014; Robson & Witenberg 2013). Interestingly, Pornari & Wood 2010 found moral disengagement to be more strongly related to traditional bullying than cyberbullying.

Their results also suggested that cyberbullying may require comparatively lower levels of moral disengagement because the anonymity and distance from the victim in cyberspace might render the perceived consequences of bullying less harmful. As a result, cyberbullies might feel less empathy toward their victims and need less justification for committing aggressive actions.

One major mechanism of moral disengagement is the displacement or diffusion of one's responsibility in intending to harm others (Bandura 2002). Self-condemning feelings can be reduced by viewing actions as originating from authorities or as part of collective behaviour that is undertaken by a group. Thus, it might be conceivable that moral disengagement is more powerful in predicting bullying perpetration among individuals from collectivistic societies where bullying tends to emerge within group processes. For instance, Strohmeier et al. (2016) found that Japanese victims of bullying are more likely to suspect at least two people or a group as joined perpetrators, whereas most Austrians identified a single bully. Therefore, it seems that bullies in individualistic societies are more likely to act alone, whereas bullies in collectivistic societies act in groups.

3.3. Fun-seeking tendencies in (cyber-)aggression

Kornadt's motivation theory on aggression links the aggression motive to negative emotions such as anger which emerge in reaction to a frustration (Kornadt 2011). Expanding his theory, bullying research recently focused on the function of positive emotions (e.g., fun and thrill) for the aggression motive (Runions et al. 2018; Fluck 2017; Graf et al. 2022). In particular, fun-seeking tendencies in (cyber-)aggression were shown to constitute a critical predictor of bullying across samples from various cultural contexts (Chou et al. 2018; Wong & McBride 2018; Wang & Ngai 2021). Fun-seeking tendencies in (cyber-) aggression describe the tendency to perceive (cyber-)aggressive behaviour as fun and are considered a type of motivation that belong to the behavioral activation system (BAS; Wong & McBride 2018). Fun has been proposed to be particularly powerful in shaping the motivation for cyberbullying (Graf et al. 2022; Wong & McBride 2018) as individuals tend to be less restrained in cyberspace which is known as the online disinhibition effect (Suler 2004). Notably, Wong and McBride (2018) emphasized the role of fun-seeking in shaping cyberbullying by showing that the positive link between fun-seeking tendencies and cyberbullying perpetration was stronger than that between normative beliefs and cyberbullying perpetration. We aim to compare whether fun-seeking tendencies are differently related to bullying perpetration across cultural groups since previous research suggests cultural differences in how individuals from different cultures want to regulate or express their emotions (Schunk et al. 2021; Schunk et al. 2023).

4. The present research

Based on past research, the objective of this chapter is to explore how cyber- and traditional bullying differ across cultural contexts. We examined differences among university students from three cultures, namely Germany, Hong Kong, and Japan. Germany can be described as a Western and individualistic culture that emphasizes autonomy and self-expression. In turn, Hong Kong and Japan represent Confucian East Asian and collectivistic cultural contexts, with Hong Kong placing comparatively more value on hierarchy and Japan placing more value on harmonious social relations (Schwartz 2006). With regard to the educational context, Hong Kong is a highly competitive and achievement-oriented culture that emphasizes accomplishments and outperforming others to gain social benefits (Brown & Wang 2016; Lau & Lee 2008). The judgment of social others is also important in the Japanese culture, but instead of competitiveness, individuals are more strongly motivated by face-saving concerns to meet social standards. That is, individuals focus on avoiding losing their social status by cooperating with others to maintain their face (Boiger et al. 2014; Trommsdorff 2022). In contrast to these two East Asian contexts, individuals in the German culture are less viewed as embedded in a social collectivity and are instead motivated to act autonomously by pursuing their own goals and expressing their unique preferences and opinions (Schwartz 2006). The inclusion of samples from two East Asian regions allows us to expand the often-assumed East-West dichotomy (see Vignoles et al. 2016) by examining culture-psychological similarities and differences between two East Asian contexts. Furthermore, the focus on university students might provide additional insights due to past research's focus on bullying among high school students. Notably, Kowalski et al. (2019) pointed out that cyberbullying is similarly prevalent among university students as compared to high school students. The aims of this exploratory study were:

(1) to identify cultural differences in the prevalence of cyber- and traditional bullying.

(2) to identify cultural differences in the underlying motives of cyber- and traditional bullies (i.e., anger, fun, and affiliation).

(3) to identify cultural mean differences in the determinants of bullying perpetration (i.e., fun-seeking tendencies, normative beliefs, and moral disengagement).

(4) to analyse and compare how these presumed determinants (see point 3) are related to cyber- and traditional bullying perpetration across cultural groups.

5. Method

5.1. Participants and procedure

We conducted an online survey among university students from Germany, Hong Kong, and Japan. Data were collected at the University of Konstanz, the Chinese University of Hong Kong, and Otemon Gakuin University, respectively. Participants gave informed consent and were compensated for their participation with course credits (Germany and Japan) or the chance to win a voucher for an online marketplace (Hong Kong). To enhance comparability between cultural samples, we excluded data from participants who were younger than 18 years or older than 29 years. The final sample included 129 Germans (M_{age} = 21.26 years, SD_{age} = 2.74; 70.5% female), 136 Hong Kong Chinese (M_{age} = 19.94 years, SD_{age} = 1.44; 69.9% female), and 123 Japanese (M_{age} = 18.91 years, SD_{age} = 0.61; 32.5% female). The study was approved by the Ethics Committee of the University of Konstanz.

5.2. Measures

All measures were translated into German, Chinese, and Japanese, respectively, by the authors. Descriptive statistics and Cronbach's alphas per cultural group are given in **Table 1**.

Cyberbullying perpetration and victimization. We used the scales by Wong and McBride (2018) to assess participants' involvement in cyberbullying perpetration and experience of cyberbullying victimization during the last three months with 15 items each (1 = *never*, 2 = *once or twice*, 3 = *two to three times in a month*, 4 = *once a week*, 5 = *few times in a week in the past 3 months*). Items cover four distinguishable types of cyberbullying: pictorial (e.g., 'I make fun of others by uploading unflattering photos of them'), verbal (e.g., 'I write insulting posts to offend others'), relational (e.g., 'I isolate or boycott people I do not like'), and extortion (e.g., 'I steal or hack into other people's accounts').

Traditional bullying perpetration and victimization. Frequencies of traditional bullying perpetration and victimization during the last three months were measured with nine items, respectively (1 = *never*, 2 = *once or twice*, 3 = *two to three times in a month*, 4 = *about once a week*, 5 = *few times a week*; adapted from Wong et al. 2011). Analogous to cyberbullying, items include statements about three distinct types of traditional bullying: physical (e.g., 'I intentionally push or shove somebody'), verbal (e.g., 'I verbally threaten others'), and relational (e.g., 'I gossip about someone I don't like behind their back').

Motives for cyber- and traditional bullying. Participants who replied positively to at least one cyber- or traditional bullying perpetration item were presented with an additional question asking them about their motives for committing bullying ('Why did you act like you did?' for cyber- and traditional bullying, respectively). The assessed motives were based on previous research on underlying motives of bullying behaviour (Gradinger et al. 2012): anger ('I did it because I was angry'), fun ('I did it because it was fun'), and affiliation ('I did it to be accepted by my friends'). Participants rated each item on a scale from 1 (*strongly disagree*) to 4 (*strongly agree*), thus making it possible for individuals to agree with multiple motives. We also measured power and revenge as motives but decided to exclude them from analyses due to low prevalence rates and conceptual overlap with the anger motive.

Fun-seeking tendencies. We applied the fun-seeking tendencies in cyberaggression scale (11 items; Wong & McBride 2018) and the fun-seeking tendencies in aggression scale (11 items; based on Wong & McBride 2018) to assess the level to which participants perceive bullying behaviours as being funny (1 = *strongly disagree*; 5 = *strongly agree*). The scales refer to cyberbullying (e.g., 'I think it is fun to make unflattering edits of other people's pictures') and traditional bullying (e.g., 'I think it is fun to laugh at people'), respectively.

Table 1: Descriptive statistics and cultural mean differences controlled for gender and age

	Germany			Hong Kong			Japan			ANCOVAs	
Variable	α	M	SD	α	M	SD	α	M	SD	F	p
Cyberbullying perpetration	.63	1.04a	0.09	.91	1.26b	0.46	.95	1.13a	0.36	14.13	< .001
Cyberbullying victimization	.92	1.06	0.21	.92	1.10	0.29	.96	1.13	0.37	1.26	.284
Traditional bullying perpetration	.50	1.20a	0.19	.80	1.29b	0.39	.88	1.15a	0.33	8.39	< .001
Traditional bullying victimization	.76	1.17	0.29	.83	1.15	0.31	.93	1.13	0.33	0.40	.670
Fun-seeking tendencies in CA	.84	1.13a	0.27	.92	1.60b	0.71	.98	1.16a	0.46	35.39	< .001
Fun-seeking tendencies in A	.78	1.46	0.39	.91	1.47	0.56	.94	1.51	0.70	0.52	.593
Normative beliefs about CA	.71	1.63a	0.57	.86	2.66b	0.97	.86	2.06c	1.00	56.40	< .001
Normative beliefs about A	.80	1.67a	0.67	.79	2.67b	0.85	.86	2.10c	1.06	49.38	< .001
Moral disengagement	.74	1.87a	0.69	.81	1.98a	0.86	.85	2.46b	1.08	4.59	.011

Note: α = Cronbach's alpha; CA = Cyberaggression; A = Aggression.
Different subscripts indicate significant cultural differences. Mean values sharing the same subscript are not significantly different; degrees of freedom of ANCOVAs: $df1 = 2$, $df2 = 383$.

Normative beliefs. The normative beliefs about aggression scale (12 items; Huesmann & Guerra 1997) was applied to assess participants' perception of how acceptable traditional bullying is on a scale from 1 (*strongly disagree*) to 7 (*strongly agree*; e.g., 'If you're angry, it's OK to say mean things to other people'). An adapted version of the scale was used to assess normative beliefs about cyberaggression (15 items; Wong & McBride 2018), referring to the perceived normativity of cyberbullying behaviour (e.g., 'If you're angry, it is OK to say mean things to other people online').

Moral disengagement. We used the scale by Moore et al. (2012) to measure moral disengagement with eight items (1 = *strongly disagree*; 7 = *strongly agree*; e.g., 'It is okay to spread rumours to defend those you care about').

5.3. Data processing and analytic strategies

We analysed bullying variables both as metric variables by calculating mean scores and as dichotomous variables to identify percentages of bullies and victims per culture. Participants who reported that they committed or experienced a bullying act more than once (i.e., answering an item with 'two to three times in a month' or higher on the respective scale) were categorized as bullies or victims, respectively. We chose this categorization to meet the criteria of repetition which is a core aspect of bullying (Olweus 1993). Additionally, the dichotomized scores provide an alternative to the mean scores which were partly based on scales showing low internal reliability. Further, motives were dichotomized to indicate agreement versus disagreement with a certain motive and to simplify the interpretation of findings by collapsing the first and last two answer categories (0 = *disagreement with motive*, 1 = *agreement with motive*). We used chi-square tests and ANCOVAs to explore cultural differences in bullying roles, motives of bullies, and mean scores of variables. Finally, we calculated Pearson correlations between cyber- and traditional bullying scales and the assumed predictors per cultural group. Correlation coefficients were compared using Fisher's z-transformation to identify cultural differences in relationships.

6. Results

6.1. Identification of bullies and victims across cultures

Table 2 shows the percentages of bullies and victims of cyber- and traditional bullying across cultures. Chi-square tests were applied to examine cultural differences. Cyberbullies were more prevalent among Hong Kong Chinese (33.8%) as compared to Germans (3.9%) and Japanese (10.6%). Similar percentages were found for traditional bullies, except for Germans. Both Germans (32.6%) and Hong Kong Chinese (33.1%) were more likely to be classified as traditional bullies than Japanese (11.4%). Correspondingly, traditional victims were significantly more prevalent among Germans (17.1%)

and Hong Kong Chinese (16.2%) as compared to Japanese (4.1%). We found no cultural difference in the percentage of cybervictims with 4.7% among Germans, 9.6% among Hong Kong Chinese, and 9.8% among Japanese. Notably, chi-square tests revealed no gender differences for being categorized as (cyber)bully or (cyber)victim.

6.2. Motives for cyber- and traditional bullying across cultures

As stated above, each motive (anger, fun, and affiliation) was dichotomized to indicate agreement or disagreement. As can be seen in **Table 2**, affiliation was the least prevalent motive for cyber- and traditional bullying across cultures, with 4.3% to 15.6% of bullies agreeing to this motive. In contrast, anger was the most frequent motive across cultures and bullying forms, with the exception of cyberbullying among Japanese. Specifically, Japanese cyberbullies reported higher agreement for having perpetrated cyberbullying out of fun (28.9%) than of anger (13.3%). We used chi-square tests to explore cultural differences for each motive and bullying form (cyber- and traditional bullying).

Table 2: Frequency of bullies, victims, and motives of bullies across cultures

Variable	Germany	Hong Kong	Japan	$\chi^2(df)$	p
Bullies					
Cyberbullies	3.9% a	33.8% b	10.6% a	47.70(2)	< .001
Traditional bullies	32.6% a	33.1% a	11.4% b	20.08(2)	< .001
Victims					
Cybervictims	4.7%	9.6%	9.8%	2.93(2)	.231
Traditional bully victims	17.1% a	16.2% a	4.1% b	12.02(2)	.002
Motives of cyberbullies					
Anger	51.6% a	41.9% a	13.3% b	14.63(2)	< .001
Fun	35.5%	33.7%	28.9%	0.45(2)	.800
Affiliation	9.7%	7.0%	15.6%	2.44(2)	.295
Motives of traditional bullies					
Anger	44.0%	44.6%	34.7%	1.47(2)	.479
Fun	27.0%	17.4%	18.4%	2.99(2)	.224
Affiliation	15.0% a	4.3% b	6.1% a,b	7.22(2)	.027

Note: Different subscripts indicate significant cultural differences. Mean values sharing the same subscript are not significantly different.

Compared to Germans (51.6%) and Hong Kong Chinese (41.9%), Japanese cyberbullies were significantly less likely to report anger as a motive (13.3%). Interestingly, German traditional bullies (15.0%) agreed significantly more often with the affiliation motive as compared to Hong Kong Chinese (4.3%). We found no other significant differences in motives between cultural samples. Moreover, we found no significant gender differences when conducting chi-square tests for motives within each cultural group.

6.3. Cultural mean differences in the level of variables

We examined cultural differences in the means of variables using a series of ANCOVAs to control for age and gender (see **Table 1**). We also tested for differences in the non-dichotomized, metric bullying variables that indicate the degree (i.e., more or less frequent) to which individuals committed or experienced bullying acts. Compared to Germans and Japanese, Hong Kong Chinese were higher in cyber- and traditional bullying perpetration, while no cultural differences were found for victimization. Hong Kong Chinese reported also higher fun-seeking tendencies in cyberaggression than Germans and Japanese, whereas the endorsement of fun-seeking tendencies in aggression did not differ across samples. Further, Hong Kong Chinese were significantly higher in normative beliefs (i.e., the perceived social acceptability of bullying) about both cyber- and traditional aggression than Germans and Japanese. Japanese, in turn, reported higher normative beliefs about both types of aggression than Germans. Finally, moral disengagement was higher among Japanese as compared to Hong Kong Chinese and Germans.

6.3.1. Distinguishing bullying types

To gain further insight into cultural differences in bullying, we analysed each type of cyberbullying (pictorial, verbal, relational, extortion) and traditional bullying (physical, verbal, relational), separately. **Figure 1** shows the distribution of mean scores per bullying type and culture. Across cultures, relational bullying was the most frequent type of perpetrating traditional bullying, whereas verbal bullying tended to be the most frequent type of perpetrating cyberbullying. Interestingly, the different bullying types were more evenly distributed for victimization than for perpetration. We used ANCOVAs to examine significant cultural differences in the frequency of bullying types.

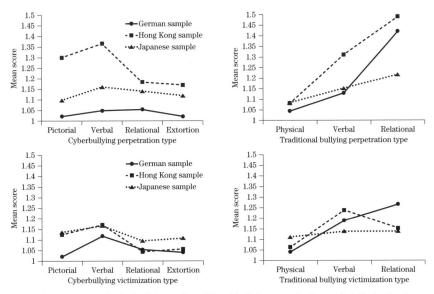

Figure 1: Frequency of cyberbullying and traditional bullying perpetration and victimization types per sample

Compared to Germans and Japanese, Hong Kong Chinese reported higher pictorial, F (1, 383) = 17.23, p < .001, and verbal, F (1, 383) = 15.90, p < .001, cyberbullying perpetration and higher verbal traditional bullying perpetration F (1, 383) = 11.85, p < .001. Further, Hong Kong Chinese reported higher relational, F (1, 383) = 4.35, p = .014, and extortion, F (1, 383) = 5.26, p = .006, cyberbullying perpetration than Germans. Japanese reported lower relational traditional bullying perpetration than Germans and Hong Kong Chinese, F (1, 383) = 9.09, p < .001. Neither cyberbullying victimization nor traditional bullying victimization types differed significantly across cultures.

6.4. Associations of cyber- and traditional bullying with potential predictors across cultures

Figure 2 shows the Pearson correlations between the mean scores of cyber- and traditional bullying perpetration with the other variables across cultural groups. All correlations were significant except for the correlation between moral disengagement and cyberbullying perpetration among Japanese (p = .093). Notably, involvement in any form of bullying predicted higher cyber-

and traditional bullying. Additionally, perceiving (cyber-)aggression as fun, believing (cyber-)aggression to be normative, and higher moral disengagement (except for cyberbullying among Japanese) were positively correlated with cyber- and traditional bullying perpetration, respectively.

Cyberbullying victimization correlated more strongly with cyberbullying perpetration for Hong Kong Chinese ($r = .81$) as compared to Germans ($r = .51$, $z = -4.63$, $p < .001$) and Japanese ($r = .48$, $z = 4.87$, $p < .001$). The correlation of traditional bullying perpetration with cyberbullying perpetration was weaker among Germans ($r = .22$) as compared to Hong Kong Chinese ($r = .63$, $z = -4.26$, $p < .001$) and Japanese ($r = .70$, $z = -5.13$, $p < .001$). Further, traditional bullying victimization correlated more weakly with cyberbullying perpetration among Germans ($r = .38$) than among Japanese ($r = .58$, $z = -2.09$, $p < .04$). Fun-seeking tendencies were more predictive of cyberbullying perpetration among Hong Kong Chinese ($r = .60$) as compared to Germans ($r = .35$, $z = -2.58$, $p < .010$). The correlations of normative beliefs about cyberaggression and moral disengagement with cyberbullying perpetration did not differ significantly across cultures ($ps > .07$).

Traditional bullying victimization was more strongly related to traditional bullying perpetration among Japanese ($r = .57$) than among Germans ($r = .34$, $z = -2.36$, $p < .019$). The correlations of cyberbullying perpetration and victimization with traditional bullying perpetration were weaker among Germans ($r = .22$ and $r = .18$, respectively) as compared to Hong Kong Chinese ($r = .63$, $z = -4.26$, $p < .001$; $r = .65$, $z = -4.71$, $p < .001$) and Japanese ($r = .70$, $z = -5.13$, $p < .001$; $r = .45$, $z = -2.36$, $p < .018$). Further, cyberbullying victimization was more strongly related to traditional bullying perpetration for Hong Kong Chinese than for Japanese ($z = 2.27$, $p < .023$). Neither the correlation of traditional bullying perpetration with fun-seeking tendencies in aggression nor with normative beliefs about aggression nor with moral disengagement did differ across cultural groups ($ps > .26$).

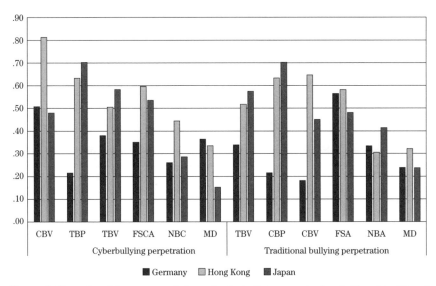

Figure 2: Strengths of Pearson correlations of cyberbullying perpetration (left) and traditional bullying perpetration (right) with assumed predictors

Note: CBV = cyberbullying victimization; CBP = cyberbullying perpetration; TBV = traditional bullying victimization; TBP = traditional bullying perpetration; FSCA = fun-seeking tendencies in cyberaggression; FSA = Fun-seeking tendencies in aggression; NBC = normative beliefs in cyberaggression; NBA = normative beliefs in aggression; MD = moral disengagement. All correlations are statistically significant ($p < .05$), except for the correlation between moral disengagement and cyberbullying perpetration among Japanese ($p = .093$).

7. Discussion

The present study explored cultural similarities and differences in the prevalence and predictors of cyber- and traditional bullying among university students from Germany, Hong Kong, and Japan. Participants from Hong Kong were significantly more likely to be categorized as cyberbullies (33.8%) than participants from Germany (3.9%) and Japan (10.6%), while participants from both Hong Kong (33.1%) and Germany (32.6%) were more likely to be traditional bullies than participants from Japan (11.4%). As for the underlying motives of bullies, anger was the most frequent motive across cultures and bullying forms (i.e., cyber- and traditional bullying), except for cyberbullying in the Japanese sample. Specifically, Japanese cyberbullies reported higher agreement for having perpetrated cyberbullying out of fun (28.9%) than of anger (13.3%).

Compared to German and Hong Kong Chinese cyberbullies, Japanese cyberbullies were also significantly less likely to report anger as a motive. Further, compared to the other cultural groups, Japanese participants reported higher moral disengagement, while Hong Kong Chinese participants reported higher fun-seeking tendencies in cyberaggression and more normative beliefs about both cyberaggression and aggression. Importantly, fun-seeking tendencies in (cyber-)aggression, normative beliefs about (cyber-)aggression, and moral disengagement (except for cyberbullying among Japanese) were related to higher cyber- and traditional bullying perpetration, respectively.

7.1. Cultural differences in bullying prevalence

Both cyber- and traditional bullying perpetration were comparatively high among Hong Kong Chinese participants and low among Japanese participants. German participants were particularly low in cyberbullying but higher in traditional bullying. Notably, results differed slightly depending on whether the dichotomized variables (bully vs. no bully) or mean score of bullying perpetration were compared. Specifically, both Germans and Hong Kong Chinese were more often categorized as traditional bullies than Japanese in our sample; yet Hong Kong Chinese were higher in the mean level of traditional bullying perpetration compared to both Japanese and Germans. This finding suggests that the number of traditional bullies was similar for the samples from Germany and Hong Kong, but traditional bullies from Hong Kong engaged in comparatively more bullying behaviour and thus had higher mean scores.

The high prevalence of bullying among Hong Kong Chinese in our study seemingly contradicts recent research that reported higher school bullying among German as compared to Chinese participants (Lin et al. 2020). Lin et al. (2020) presumed that bullying would receive more disapproval in collectivistic cultures which would be consistent with findings linking higher endorsement of individualism to more aggression and higher endorsement of collectivism to less aggression among Chinese adolescents (Li et al. 2010). We argue that this reasoning may not apply to bullying among Hong Kong Chinese university students because bullying may be regarded as a distinct form of aggression that is characterized by repetition and often develops within a group-interaction process (Strohmeier et al. 2016; Toda 2016). Depending on the respective social norms, bullying might be promoted in collectivistic societies if this kind of behaviour is perceived as acceptable, thus leading to several perpetrators harassing a single victim who deviates from social standards (Strohmeier et al. 2016; Akiba 2004). The strong focus on competitiveness and outperforming others in Hong Kong's education system may further encourage aggressive behaviour such as bullying (Brown & Wang 2016; Lau & Lee 2008; Tam & Taki 2007). Notably, we found low bullying perpetration rates among Japanese which might be explained by lower normative beliefs about (cyber-)aggression, indicating that bullying is perceived as less acceptable in this society as compared to Hong Kong. Face-saving tendencies may then inhibit aggressive behaviour to comply with social rules and to maintain harmonious relationships (Trommsdorff 2022). The comparatively lower normativity of (cyber-)bullying in Japan (versus Hong Kong) might be possibly explained by increased prevention and intervention efforts in the Japanese society (e.g., Toda & Oh 2019).

As mentioned before, empirical evidence suggests that competitive education systems in many Asian societies may promote bullying through increased stress (Tam & Taki 2007). Although the Japanese education system is relatively competitive as well, academic stress might accumulate during high school and decrease after entering university. For instance, the intense period of studying at the end of Japanese high school is referred to as *juken jigoku*, meaning 'examination hell', yet postsecondary education is rather relaxed for university students (Hill 1996). Systematic differences between school and postsecondary education in Japan (e.g., lower academic competition, more flexible social groups) might be one possible explanation for why we obtained relatively low levels of cyber- and traditional bullying perpetration for Japanese university students. These findings are intriguing considering the social concerns about bullying incidents among Japanese high school students that gained particular awareness after several bullying-related cases of suicide in the last decades (Toda 2016; Trommsdorff 1998). One may presume that the prevalence of bullying rapidly decreases in Japan after graduating from high school which would be consistent with survey results reported by the Japanese company Kanko (2018). Yet, more research across different age groups is needed to answer how bullying changes from adolescence until adulthood.

The prevalence of traditional bullies among German participants was similar to Hong Kong Chinese participants (around one third), while the prevalence of cyberbullying was almost non-existent in our German sample. A possible explanation for the particularly low prevalence of cyberbullying among German participants and the high prevalence of cyberbullying among Hong Kong Chinese participants might reside in the availability and endorsement of different online communication services. For instance, public group chats and online forums are popular among Hong Kong Chinese youth (Chan 2020). One may presume that individuals from cultures with higher acceptance of using digital communication devices in everyday life are more likely to transfer social interactions, including aggressive behaviour, to the online world. For instance, Fung et al. (2021) suggested that the high prevalence of online forum usage among Hong Kong Chinese created a new internet phenomenon called *doxing* which refers to the disclosure of an individual's private information online. This example illustrates that the use of specific types of online communication (e.g., online forums) may promote certain cyberbullying behaviour (e.g., spreading personal information online). Future studies may examine whether specific cultural values facilitate cultural differences in social media affordances as these have been proposed to influence cyberbullying victimization (Nesi et al. 2018).

The characteristics of digital communication may further shape how exactly bullying is perpetrated in the online world. Specifically, in our study, traditional bullying was most likely reported as being relational (e.g., isolating or gossiping about others), whereas cyberbullying tended to be perpetrated verbally (e.g., insulting others through text messages across cultures). For cyberbullying (as opposed to traditional bullying), individuals might be more likely to directly insult others because of the online disinhibition effect (Suler 2004) and the reduced likelihood of immediate retribution by the victim. Interestingly, Hong Kong Chinese participants reported higher verbal and pictorial cyberbullying perpetration than German and Japanese participants. The comparatively high prevalence of verbal and pictorial cyberbullying among Hong Kong Chinese is consistent with previous findings on the relatively high endorsement of these strategies among older secondary school students in Hong Kong (Wong & McBride 2018). The high level of fun-seeking tendencies observed in the Hong Kong sample may explain the prevalence of verbal and pictorial cyberbullying strategies in the sample, since these strategies may be perceived as more fun, as indicated in previous research (e.g., Steer et al. 2020).

Notably, Japanese university students reported lower relational traditional bullying perpetration than German and Hong Kong Chinese students. One possible explanation for this finding might be that relational bullying strategies (e.g., public shaming, ostracism) are seen as more harmful and offensive among face-saving and harmony-oriented Japanese who reported relatively low levels of normative beliefs about aggression (i.e., perceived aggression as socially unacceptable). In addition to norms about the social acceptability of (cyber-) aggression, the cultural emphasis on face-saving may be particularly relevant for inhibiting aggression in Japanese culture (Trommsdorff 2022).

7.2. Determinants of bullying perpetration

In line with past research on predictors of bullying perpetration (Kowalski et al. 2014; Wong & McBride 2018; Robson & Witenberg 2013; Burton et al. 2013), fun-seeking tendencies in (cyber-)aggression, normative beliefs about (cyber-) aggression, and moral disengagement (except for cyberbullying among Japanese) predicted higher engagement in cyber- and traditional bullying, respectively. These findings extend past studies by suggesting that these factors may contribute to higher bullying perpetration across individuals from different cultures. Notably, the comparatively high bullying perpetration rate among Hong Kong Chinese might be largely accounted for by a high endorsement of such factors. Specifically, compared to German and Japanese university students, Hong Kong Chinese students perceived cyberbullying as more fun and viewed both cyber- and traditional bullying as more normative. Moreover, fun-seeking tendencies were significantly more strongly related to cyberbullying among Hong Kong Chinese participants as compared to German participants, underscoring that perceiving cyberbullying as fun is a critical predictor of cyberbullying in Hong Kong. This result is consistent with past findings suggesting that online schadenfreude is more common in regions with high political tension such as Hong Kong (Au & Ho 2022). Specifically, tension within societies may lead to a stronger legitimization of aggression in the form of schadenfreude which may relate to an increased tendency of individuals to act on their fun-seeking tendencies in cyberaggression by perpetrating cyberbullying. In turn, Japanese university students reported higher moral disengagement than Hong Kong Chinese and German students. Moral disengagement might be particularly endorsed among Japanese to justify prohibited or socially undesirable behaviour to avoid self-punishment (Toda

2016). Yet, moral disengagement related to higher traditional bullying perpetration but was unrelated to cyberbullying perpetration for Japanese, indicating that in Japan moral justification might be more relevant for perpetrating bullying in the offline as compared to the online world.

7.3. Underlying motives of bullies

Western research on bully motives among Austrian adolescents showed that anger was the most prevalent motive, followed by fun, and low levels of affiliation (Gradinger et al. 2012). We found some support for this finding among individuals from an East Asian cultural context. Yet, Japanese cyberbullies were an exception to this sequence, as they reported fun more often than anger as a motive for perpetrating cyberbullying. Japanese cyberbullies were also significantly less likely to report anger as a motive compared to cyberbullies from Germany and Hong Kong. This is in line with research suggesting that Japanese are less likely to act aggressively even if they feel anger (Kornadt 2011). Although anger seems to be an important driving force behind bullying perpetration in the other two cultures, fun constitutes an almost as important bullying motive. Notably, fun was comparatively more often stated by cyberbullies than traditional bullies which is in line with our findings on fun-seeking tendencies and past research emphasizing the disinhibiting effect of online communication (Suler 2004) and the role of sensation-seeking in cyberbullying (Graf et al. 2019).

7.4. Limitations and future directions

Importantly, the generalizability of our findings is limited due to the small sample sizes per culture and the exploratory focus of our design that focused on university students. Future studies may examine cultural differences in cyber- and traditional bullying using larger samples that include participants of different ages who have various cultural and socioeconomic backgrounds. It might be advisable to apply different methodological approaches to assess bullying perpetration since participants' responses might be heavily influenced by social desirability. Further, the cross-sectional research design prohibits us from making definite claims about the causation underlying the relationships between variables. Finally, future research may examine how psychological characteristics of individuals interact with structural factors (e.g., technological infrastructures, education systems, anti-bullying campaigns) in shaping cyber- and traditional bullying across cultures (see also Görzig et al. 2021 and Wong 2016).

7.5. Implications and conclusion

Our findings provide insights into the prevalence and predictors of cyber- and traditional bullying among university students from three different cultures. It is important to note that bullying occurred in all three cultural groups but with different frequency concerning the context (cyber- versus traditional bullying) and bullying strategies (e.g., verbal, pictorial). Hong Kong Chinese were more often categorized as cyberbullies than Germans and Japanese, whereas both Hong Kong Chinese and Germans were more likely to be traditional bullies than Japanese participants. Notably, bullying was predicted by similar attitudes and beliefs (e.g., fun-seeking tendencies, normative beliefs) across cultures, yet their relative endorsement and strength in predicting cyber- and traditional bullying perpetration varied among samples. In particular, Hong Kong Chinese participants (versus Germans and Japanese) reported higher fun- seeking tendencies in cyberaggression and more normative beliefs about both cyberaggression and traditional aggression, suggesting that bullying might be perceived as more acceptable in this sample. A better understanding of the mechanisms between how and why individuals perpetrate bullying across diverse cultures will hopefully benefit the development of culture-sensitive prevention and intervention programs for reducing bullying and thereby create a safe learning environment that the Sustainable Development Goals seek to acquire.

References

Akiba, Motoko (2004): Nature and Correlates of Ijime: Bullying in Japanese Middle School. In: *International Journal of Educational Research* 41 (3): 216–236.

Aoyama, Ikuko/Utsumi, Shoka/Hasegawa, Motohiro (2012): Cyberbullying in Japan: Cases, Government Reports, Adolescent Relational Aggression, and Parental Monitoring Roles. In: Li, Qing/Cross, Donna/Smith, Peter K. (eds.): *Cyberbullying in the Global Playground: Research from International Perspectives*, Hoboken: Wiley Blackwell, 183–201.

Au, Cheuk H./Ho, Kevin K. W. (2022): Online Schadenfreude as an Outcome of Ideological Polarization: A Case in Hong Kong. In: *Online Information Review* 46 (4): 678–697.

Bandura, Albert (2002): Selective Moral Disengagement in the Exercise of Moral Agency. In: *Journal of Moral Education* 31 (2): 101–119.

Barlett, Christopher P./Seyfert, Luke W./Simmers, Matthew M./Hsueh Hua Chen, Vivian/ Cavalcanti, Jaqueline Gomes/Krahé, Barbara/Suzuki, Kanae/Warburton, Wayne A./Wong, Randy Yee Man/Pimentel, Carlos Eduardo/Skowronski, Marika (2021): Cross-Cultural Similarities and Differences in the Theoretical Predictors of Cyberbullying Perpetration: Results from a Seven-Country Study. In: *Aggressive Behavior* 47 (1): 111–119.

Boiger, Michael/Güngör, Derya/Karasawa, Mayumi/Mesquita, Batja (2014): Defending Honour, Keeping Face: Interpersonal Affordances of Anger and Shame in Turkey and Japan. In: *Cognition and Emotion* 28 (7): 1255–1269.

Brochado, Sandra/Soares, Sara/Fraga, Sílvia (2017): A Scoping Review on Studies of Cyberbullying Prevalence among Adolescents. In: *Trauma, Violence, & Abuse* 18 (5): 523–531.

Bündnis Gegen Cybermobbing (2020): Cyberlife III Spannungsfeld zwischen Faszination und Gefahr: Cybermobbing bei Schülerinnen und Schülern. www.buendnis-gegen-cybermobbing.de/fileadmin/pdf/studien/Cyberlife_Studie_2020_END1__1_.pdf, [Accessed 23 June 2022].

Bronfenbrenner, Urie (1977): Toward an Experimental Ecology of Human Development. In: *American Psychologist* 32 (7): 513–531.

Brown, Gavin T. L./Wang, Zhenlin (2016): Understanding Chinese University Student Conceptions of Assessment: Cultural Similarities and Jurisdictional Differences between Hong Kong and China. In: *Social Psychology of Education* 19 (1): 151–173.

Burton, K. Alex/Florell, Dan/Wygant, Dustin B. (2013): The Role of Peer Attachment and Normative Beliefs About Aggression on Traditional Bullying and Cyberbullying. In: *Psychology in the Schools* 50 (2): 103–115.

Chan, Gloria Hongyee (2020): Intimacy, Friendship, and Forms of Online Communication among Hidden Youth in Hong Kong. In: *Computers in Human Behavior* 111. DOI: 10.1016/j.chb.2020.106407

Chan, Heng Choon/Wong, Dennis S. W. (2020): The Overlap between Cyberbullying Perpetration and Victimisation: Exploring the Psychosocial Characteristics of Hong Kong Adolescents. In: *Asia Pacific Journal of Social Work and Development* 30 (3): 164–180.

Chen, Ji-Kang/Chen, Li-Ming (2020): Cyberbullying among Adolescents in Taiwan, Hong Kong, and Mainland China: A Cross-National Study in Chinese Societies. In: *Asia Pacific Journal of Social Work and Development* 30 (3): 227–241.

Chou, Wen-Jiun/Liu, Tai-Ling/Yang, Pinchen/Yen, Cheng-Fang/Hu, Huei-Fan (2018): Bullying Victimization and Perpetration and Their Correlates in Adolescents Clinically Diagnosed with ADHD. In: *Journal of Attention Disorders* 22 (1): 25–34.

Fluck, Julia (2017): Why Do Students Bully? An Analysis of Motives Behind Violence in Schools. In: *Youth & Society* 49 (5): 567–587.

Fung, Annis Lai Chu/Zhou, Guangdong/Tsang, Eileen Yuk Ha/Low, Andrew Yiu Tsang/Lam, Bess Yin Hung (2021): The Age and Gender Effect on Four Forms of Peer Victimization among Chinese Children and Adolescents. In: *Applied Research in Quality of Life* 16 (6): 2439–2456.

Görzig, Anke/Wachs, Sebastian/Wright, Michelle (2021): Cultural Factors and Bullying. In: Smith, Peter K./Norman, James O'Higgins (eds.): *The Wiley Blackwell Handbook of Bullying*, UK: Wiley, 519–537.

Gradinger, Petra/Strohmeier, Dagmar/Spiel, Christiane (2012): Motives for Bullying Others in Cyberspace: A Study on Bullies and Bully-Victims in Austria. In: Li, Qing /Cross, Donna / Smith, Peter K. (eds.): *Cyberbullying in the Global Playground: Research from International Perspectives*, Malden, MA: Blackwell, 263–284.

Graf, Daniel/Yanagida, Takuya/Runions, Kevin/Spiel, Christiane (2022): Why Did You Do That? Differential Types of Aggression in Offline and in Cyberbullying. In: *Computers in Human Behavior* 128: 1-8.

Graf, Daniel/Yanagida, Takuya/Spiel, Christiane (2019): Sensation Seeking's Differential Role in Face-to-Face and Cyberbullying: Taking Perceived Contextual Properties into Account. In: *Frontiers in Psychology* 10: 1-12. DOI: 10.3389/fpsyg.2019.01572.

Hill, Benjamin (1996): Breaking the Rules in Japanese Schools: Kōsoku Ihan, Academic Competition, and Moral Education. In: *Anthropology & Education Quarterly* 27 (1): 90–110.

Huesmann, L Rowell/Guerra, Nancy G (1997): Children's Normative Beliefs About Aggression and Aggressive Behavior. In: *Journal of Personality and Scial Pychology* 72 (2): 408–419.

Kanko (2018): Reality of bullying in school days. kanko-gakuseifuku.co.jp/media/homeroom/ vol149, [Accessed 23 July 2023].

Kornadt, Hans-Joachim (2011): *Aggression: Die Rolle der Erziehung in Europa und Ostasien*, Wiesbaden: VS Verlag.

Kowalski, Robin M/Giumetti, Gary W/Schroeder, Amber N/Lattanner, Micah R (2014): Bullying in the Digital Age: A Critical Review and Meta-Analysis of Cyberbullying Research among Youth. In: *Psychological Bulletin* 140 (4): 1073–1137.

Kowalski, Robin M/Limber, Susan P/Mccord, Annie (2019): A Developmental Approach to Cyberbullying: Prevalence and Protective Factors. In: *Aggression and Violent Behavior* 45: 20–32.

Kowalski, Robin M./Limber, Susan P. (2013): Psychological, Physical, and Academic Correlates of Cyberbullying and Traditional Bullying. In: *Journal of Adolescent Health* 53: 13–20.

Lau, Kit-Ling/Lee, John C. K. (2008): Validation of a Chinese Achievement Goal Orientation Questionnaire. In: *British Journal of Educational Psychology* 78 (2): 331–353.

Li, Yan/Wang, Mo/Wang, Cixin/Shi, Junqi (2010): Individualism, Collectivism, and Chinese Adolescents' Aggression: Intracultural Variations. In: *Aggressive Behavior* 36 (3): 187–194.

Lin, Muyu/Wolke, Dieter/Schneider, Silvia/Margraf, Jürgen (2020): Bullies Get Away with It, but Not Everywhere: Mental Health Sequelae of Bullying in Chinese and German Students. In: *Journal of Cross-Cultural Psychology* 51 (9): 702–718.

Livingstone, Sonia/Haddon, Leslie/Görzig, Anke/Ólafsson, Kjartan (2011): Risks and Safety on the Internet: The Perspective of European Children - Full Findings and Policy Implications from the Eu Kids Online Survey of 9-16 Year Olds and Their Parents in 25 Countries. http:// eprints.lse.ac.uk/33731/, [Accessed 23 June 2022].

Markus, Hazel R./Kitayama, Shinobu (1991): Culture and the Self: Implications for Cognition, Emotion, and Motivation. In: *Psychological Review* 98 (2): 224–253.

Modecki, Kathryn L./Minchin, Jeannie/Harbaugh, Allen G./Guerra, Nancy G./Runions, Kevin C. (2014): Bullying Prevalence across Contexts: A Meta-Analysis Measuring Cyber and Traditional Bullying. In: *Journal of Adolescent Health* 55 (5): 602–611.

Moore, Celia/Detert, James R/Klebe Treviño, Linda/Baker, Vicki L/Mayer, David M (2012): Why Employees Do Bad Things: Moral Disengagement and Unethical Organizational Behavior. In: *Personnel Psychology* 65 (1): 1–48.

Nesi, Jacqueline/Choukas-Bradley, Sophia/Prinstein, Mitchell J. (2018): Transformation of Adolescent Peer Relations in the Social Media Context: Part 1 - A Theoretical Framework and Application to Dyadic Peer Relationships. In: *Clinical Child and Family Psychology Review* 21 (3): 267–294.

Olweus, Dan (1993): *Bullying at School: What We Know and What We Can Do*, Malden: Blackwell Publishing.

Osuka, Yuko/Nishimura, Tomoko/Wakuta, Manabu/Takei, Nori/Tsuchiya, Kenji J. (2019): Reliability and Validity of the Japan Ijime Scale and Estimated Prevalence of Bullying among Fourth through Ninth Graders: A Large-Scale School-Based Survey. In: *Psychiatry and Clinical Neurosciences* 73 (9): 551–559.

Pornari, Chrisa D./Wood, Jane (2010): Peer and Cyber Aggression in Secondary School Students: The Role of Moral Disengagement, Hostile Attribution Bias, and Outcome Expectancies. In: *Aggressive Behavior* 36 (2): 81–94.

Robson, Claire/Witenberg, Rivka T. (2013): The Influence of Moral Disengagement, Morally Based Self-Esteem, Age, and Gender on Traditional Bullying and Cyberbullying. In: *Journal of School Violence* 12 (2): 211–231.

Runions, Kevin C./Salmivalli, Christina/Shaw, Therese/Burns, Sharyn/Cross, Donna (2018): Beyond the Reactive-Proactive Dichotomy: Rage, Revenge, Reward, and Recreational Aggression Predict Early High School Bully and Bully/Victim Status. In: *Aggressive Behavior* 44 (5): 501–511.

Schunk, Fabian/Trommsdorff, Gisela/Wong, Natalie/Nakao, Gen (2021): Associations Between Emotion Regulation and Life Satisfaction Among University Students From Germany, Hong Kong, and Japan: The Mediating Role Of Social Support. In: *Frontiers in Psychology* 12: Article 745888.

Schunk, Fabian/Wong, Natalie/Nakao, Gen/Trommsdorff, Gisela (2023): Different Functions of Emotion Regulation in Linking Harmony Seeking And Rejection Avoidance to Life Satisfaction and Social Support in Germany, Hong Kong, and Japan. In: *Asian Journal of Social Psychology* 26 (2): 254–269.

Schunk, Fabian/Zeh, Franziska/Trommsdorff, Gisela (2022): Cybervictimization and Well-Being among Adolescents During the Covid-19 Pandemic: The Mediating Roles of Emotional Self-Efficacy and Emotion Regulation. In: *Computers in Human Behavior* 126. DOI: 10.1016/j.chb.2021.107035.

Schwartz, Shalom (2006): A Theory of Cultural Value Orientations: Explication and Applications. In: *Comparative Sociology* 5 (2–3): 137–182.

Sittichai, Ruthaychonnee/Smith, Peter K. (2015): Bullying in South-East Asian Countries: A Review. In: *Aggression and Violent Behavior* 23: 22–35.

Smith, Peter K/Slonje, Robert (2009): Cyberbullying: The Nature and Extent of a New Kind of

Bullying, in and out of School. In: Jimerson, Shane R./Swearer, Susan M./Espelage, Dorothy L. (eds.), *Handbook of Bullying in Schools: An International Perspective*. New York: Routledge, 249–261.

Smith, Peter K./Mahdavi, Jess/Carvalho, Manuel/Fisher, Sonja/Russell, Shanette/Tippett, Neil (2008): Cyberbullying: Its Nature and Impact in Secondary School Pupils. In: *Journal of Child Psychology and Psychiatry* 49 (4): 376–385.

Steer, Oonagh L./ Betts, Lucy R./Baguley, Thomas/Binder, Jens F. (2020): 'I Feel Like Everyone Does It'- Adolescents' Perceptions and Awareness of the Association between Humour, Banter, and Cyberbullying. In: *Computers in Human Behavior* 108. DOI: 10.1016/j.chb.2020.106297.

Sticca, Fabio/Perren, Sonja (2013): Is Cyberbullying Worse Than Traditional Bullying? Examining the Differential Roles of Medium, Publicity, and Anonymity for the Perceived Severity of Bullying. In: *Journal of Youth and Adolescence* 42 (5): 739–750.

Strohmeier, Dagmar/Yanagida, Takuya/Toda, Yuichi (2016): Individualism/Collectivism as Predictors of Relational and Physical Victimization in Japan and Austria. In: Kwak, Keumjoo/Smith, Peter K./Toda, Yuichi (eds.), *School Bullying in Different Cultures: Eastern and Western Perspectives*, Cambridge: Cambridge University Press, 259–279.

Suler, John (2004): The Online Disinhibition Effect. In: *Cyberpsychology & Behavior* 7 (3): 321–326.

Tam, Frank Wai-Ming/Taki, Mitsuru (2007): Bullying among Girls in Japan and Hong Kong: An Examination of the Frustration-Aggression Model. In: *Educational Research and Evaluation* 13 (4): 373–399.

Toda, Yuichi (2016): Bullying (Ijime) and Related Problems in Japan: History and Research. In: Kwak, Keumjoo/Smith, Peter K./Toda, Yuichi (eds.), *School Bullying in Different Cultures: Eastern and Western Perspectives*, Cambridge: Cambridge University Press, 73–92.

Toda, Yuichi/Oh, Insoo (2021): *Tackling Cyberbullying and Related Problems: Innovative Usage of Games, Apps and Manga*, London: Routledge.

Trommsdorff, Gisela (1998): Social and Psychological Aspects of Ongoing Changes in Japan: Introduction. In: G. Trommsdorff/W. Friedlmeier/Kornadt, H.-J. (eds.) *Japan in Transition: Social and Psychological Aspects*, Lengerich: Pabst Science, 11–21.

Trommsdorff, Gisela (2022): Zwischen Tradition Und Moderne: Aufwachsen in Japan in Zeiten Von Krisen Und Gefährdungen. In: Blechinger-Talcott, Verena and Chiavicci, David and Schwentker, Wolfgang (ed.) *Japan: Ein Land Im Umbruch*, Berlin: be.bra Verlag, 181–198.

Udris, Reinis (2014): Cyberbullying among High School Students in Japan: Development and Validation of the Online Disinhibition Scale. In: *Computers in Human Behavior* 41: 253–261.

UN General Assembly (2014): Resolution Adopted by the General Assembly on 18 December 2014. daccess-ods.un.org/tmp/3988203.70435715.html, [Accessed 23 June 2022].

UN News (2015): UN Envoy Calls for Concerted Efforts to Eliminate Bullying in All Regions. news.un.org/en/story/2015/10/512882-un-envoy-calls-concerted-efforts-eliminate-bullying-all-regions#.ViUNoH6rTcs, [Accessed 23 June 2022].

Vignoles, Vivian L./Owe, Ellinor/Becker, Maja/Smith, Peter B./Easterbrook, Matthew J./Brown, Rupert/González, Roberto/Didier, Nicolas/Carrasco, Diego/Cadena, Maria Paz/Lay, Siugmin/Schwartz, Seth J./Des Rosiers, Sabrina E./Villamar, Juan A./Gavreliuc, Alin/ Zinkeng, Martina/Kreuzbauer, Robert/Baguma, Peter/Martin, Mariana/.../Bond, Michael Harris (2016): Beyond the 'East–West' Dichotomy: Global Variation in Cultural Models of Selfhood. In: *Journal of Experimental Psychology: General* 145 (8): 966–1000.

Waasdorp, Tracy E./Bradshaw, Catherine P. (2015): The Overlap between Cyberbullying and Traditional Bullying. In: *Journal of Adolescent Health* 56 (5): 483–488.

Wang, Lin/Ngai, Steven Sek-Yum (2021): Cyberbullying Perpetration among Chinese Adolescents: The Role of Power Imbalance, Fun-Seeking Tendency, and Attitude toward Cyberbullying. In: *Journal of Interpersonal Violence*. DOI: 10.1177/08862605211062988.

Wong, Dennis Sw/Cheng, Christopher Hk/Ngan, Raymond Mh/Ma, Stephen K (2011): Program Effectiveness of a Restorative Whole-School Approach for Tackling School Bullying in Hong Kong. In: *International Journal of Offender Therapy and Comparative Criminology* 55 (6): 846–862.

Wong, Natalie (2016): Risks Factors in Cyberbullying: The Moderating Role of Culture. *In:* Wright, Michelle F. (ed.) *A Social-Ecological Approach to Cyberbullying*, New York: Nova Science Publishers, 269–294.

Wong, Natalie/McBride, Catherine (2018): Fun over Conscience: Fun-Seeking Tendencies in Cyberbullying Perpetration. In: *Computers in Human Behavior* 86: 319–329.

Chapter 8

Sustainable Democracy and Value Change: Europe, East Asia, and Southeast Asia in Comparison

Carmen Schmidt
Defny Holidin

1. Introduction

Cross-cultural research on value change and democracy has long focused on Europe and – recently also – East Asia. In this chapter, we extend this discussion by also including Southeast Asia. In particular, we want to investigate whether or how ethic-religious background influences the direction of value change. In addition, we seek to explain why nations with different cultural backgrounds similarly reinterpret authoritarian traits into democratic ones. For our analysis, we use data from wave 7 of the World Values Survey (2017-2022) because it is the most recent data that allows for cultural mapping of values in different countries. We examine value change in Germany representing Europe,[1] Japan, Korea, and China representing East Asia, and Indonesia and the Philippines representing Southeast Asia. During the course of modernization and technological development, European societies have changed from traditional-religious, to rational-secular societies, to post-material societies, placing non-material goals such as self-expression, autonomy, freedom of speech, gender equality, and environmentalism above the goal of economic growth (Inglehart and Welzel 2010: 552 f.). However, this is not the case in East and Southeast Asian societies. East Asian societies have maintained their Confucian traditions while their educational levels have increased, and

---

1   We only include Germany to represent Europe, because there already is extensive research on value change for the European context, based on which we can be confident to use Germany as a proxy for the European context.

technology-intensive industrialization has been successful. Nevertheless, Authoritarian Notions of Democracy (AND) have persisted over time. Southeast Asian societies come with different cultural backgrounds, and educational levels are lower than those of their East Asian counterparts. Here, socio-political legacies inherited from their colonial masters prevail. However, regardless of their socio-cultural background, societies in these two cultural spheres have pragmatically moved closer to democratic values, which in turn leads to AND, and even Democratic Notions of Authoritarianism (DNA).[2] Therefore, we refute the Western value change discourse that expects value change towards sustainable democracy in the second modernity. We point to the importance of the cultural-religious background driving value change in different ways during democratization in Eastern and Southeastern societies, which is grounded in educational traditions in the different countries. It is also worth noting that in all these Asian countries, the concept of democracy in the Western sense is not native. This results in a different understanding of democracy in Asia and Europe. In Asia, we find evidence for Democratic Notions of Authoritarianism (DNA), which leads to authoritarian government practices. In the following, we discuss the different trajectories of value change and democratization to be found in European as well as East and Southeast Asian contexts.

2. Modernization, value change, and sustainability: Western value change research

In 1981, the World Value Surveys started with the goal of studying value change and its impact on social and political life in cross-cultural comparisons. It was designed by scholars of value change such as Ronald Inglehart (e.g., 1971; 1990) to test the hypothesis that economic and technological changes are transforming the basic values and motivations of industrialized societies' publics, namely from materialistic to post-materialistic values, that place non-material goals such as self-expression, autonomy, freedom of speech, gender equality and environmentalism above the goal of economic growth.[3] The Green

---

2   For more detailed definitions of ANDs and Liberal Notions of Democracy (LND) see subchapter 2.

3   See www.worldvaluessurvey.org.

parties that emerged in Western societies in the early 1980s were the political expression of this value change. In this sense, a post-materialistic value orientation seemed like a precondition for sustainable politics in terms of peace, justice, and strong institutions.

In 2010, Inglehart and Welzel (2010: 552) introduced a revised modernization theory, in which they acknowledge that religious and ethnic traditions did not die out, but rather continue to have a long-lasting imprint on people's world views and values. They also acknowledged that modernization is not necessarily Westernization, as the example of East Asia shows, which by then had the highest economic growth rate and Japan the world's highest life expectancy.[4] They further differentiate between value change that was triggered by industrialization bringing bureaucratization, centralization of authority, secularization, and a shift from traditional to secular values, i.e. the value change that occurred in the 'first' or 'simple modernity' (Beck 2001: 13f.), and the value change that occurred in the post-industrial phase, or the 'second modernity'. This latter value change is predicted to facilitate individual autonomy and self-expression values, which will lead to an erosion of the legitimacy of authoritarian regimes and more support for liberal democratic ideas. This so-called 'enlightenment force' (Welzel & Kirsch 2017: 3), i.e., cognitive and moral liberation through education, enforces self-expression and free choice. Thus, the argument is made that even though modernization and industrialization did not automatically lead to democracy, the cultural change of the second modernity will make democracy increasingly probable since it produces a culture of trust and tolerance, in which people place a relatively high value on individual freedom, self-expression, and post-materialistic values. In other words, people will increasingly show support for Liberal Notions of Democracy (LNDs), supporting sustainable politics in terms of peace, justice, and strong institutions in contrast to Authoritarian Notions of Democracy (ANDs).[5]

---

4   Thus, they concede that there are different paths of modernity, as also pointed out by Eisenstadt (2000).

5   While LNDs are measured by support for gender equality, human rights, and fair elections, ANDs are measured by support for the positions that religious leaders should interpret the laws, that the army should take over when the government is incompetent, and that people should obey their rulers (Welzel and Kirsch 2017).

3. Confucianism, modernization, and value change in East Asian societies[6]

Based on these assumptions, Welzel and Kirsch (ibid.) present their empirical findings in the Inglehart-Welzel cultural map (ibid., p. XY). It shows the distribution of traditional vs. secular-rational and survival versus self-expression values by country arranged according to religious-cultural backgrounds such as Protestant, Catholic, or Confucian (see **Figure 1**). In a 2018 article, we investigated value change in East Asia to test the hypothesis whether the cultural-religious background of a society affects the direction of value change and whether this influence is stronger than the impact of the structural setting of a society. In other words, whether there is a link between value change, ethic-religious background, and democracy as had been shown to be the case in Japan (Schmidt 2018).

Regarding the traditional versus secular rational dimension, which mainly reflects the contrast between societies, in which religion is very important (traditional) and those in which it is not (secular rational), Japan is the most secular and rational country in the world (**Figure 1**). Overall, nearly all Confucian countries are more rational and more secular than most European countries. Regarding the second dimension (survival versus self-expression), however, East Asian countries (including affluent societies like Japan, Taiwan, or Hong Kong) show relatively low levels of self-expression values.

This suggests that while Confucianism seems to facilitate a shift towards rational values over the course of modernization, it is detrimental to a shift towards self-expression values as observed in Europe.[7] We argue that this is likely to be due to the strong link between Confucianism and the bureaucratic and rational principles of modernity. Since Confucianism promotes traditional family relationships and social hierarchies, the associated values can be seen as an obstacle to values of self-realisation. As a result, democracy finds relatively little support in these countries (Schmidt 2018: Figure 2). According to value-change theory, educational expansion enhances preferences for self-

---

6   This subchapter summarizes findings of Schmidt (2018) published in *Asian Journal of German and European Studies* (*AJGES*). We are grateful for the permission to reprint the findings.

7   For a discussion of value change over time, see Schmidt 2018.

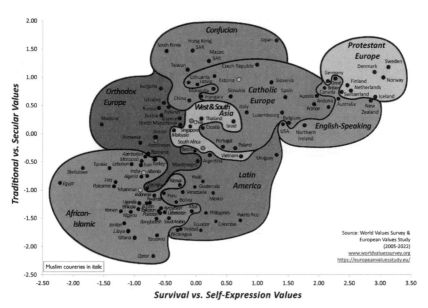

Figure 1: The Inglehart-Welzel World Cultural Map 2023
Source: modified from WVS (2023)

development values, support for liberal ideas of democracy, and rejection of authoritarian ideas of democracy. However, our previous research did not find support for this claim in the context of Confucian societies. Instead, we found that the people in authoritarian countries like China were more likely to support LNDs while this support was comparatively low in South Korea, but specifically in Japan. What is more, although Confucian societies place a high value on education, this did not lead to a higher demand for democracy. Especially in Japan, where the level of education is as high as in Germany, support for liberal ideas of democracy was comparatively low (Schmidt 2018: 10ff). The expectations of the Western discourse on changing values, which predicts a general turn towards more democracy in the 'second' modern age, thus do not hold within the East Asian context. Overall, our previous analysis showed that the ethic-religious background plays a key role in the change of values and seems to be as influential as the structural environment.

However, despite the similarities due to the common ethic-religious background, we also found country-specific features that deserve attention. In the case of China, we need to take into account that communism challenged the tenets of Confucianism, especially gender inequality and the traditional family system. So, it remains unclear whether other values are also changing in the course of the current structural change in China.

South Korea has seen a strengthening of civil society in recent years. In the so-called "candlelight protests", millions of people protested against the free trade agreement of the Transatlantic Trade and Investment Partnership (TTIP) or for the impeachment of then-President Park Geun-hye. This might indicate a shift from an elite-directed, top-down form of democracy to more elite-directing, bottom-up form of democracy through civil society.

In Japan, a consolidated democracy and a highly developed country in terms of industry and education, there is no significant correlation between education and preference for self-expression values and support for democracy. We can blame elite education and its associated educational ideals, such as the subjugation of individual desires in favour of learning for entrance exams or copying and memorising. This form of education stands in stark contrast to the Western ideal of reflexive questioning, which is considered as necessary foundation for democratic ideas.

Despite these country-based patterns, it seems that structural differences alone cannot explain the different trajectories of value change we are witnessing. Instead, values seem to be deeply rooted in the ethic-religious context and have a strong influence on the attitudes towards democracy. In the following, we test these findings by adding cases for Southeast Asia (Indonesia and the Philippines), which are highly contrasting in terms of both social structure and ethic-religious background (Muslim and Christian).

4. Value change and democracy in Southeast Asia

An awareness of the sociocultural foundations of the various kinds of polities seen in Southeast Asian countries is indispensable when trying to understand value change in these societies. Compared to their East Asian counterparts, not only are the Southeast Asian political realms so diverse that we cannot simplify them as a single polity and governance, they also share different socio-cultural imprints from one to another, greatly influenced by their own diverse colonial masters (see patterns and paths generating varieties of governance and development models as discussed in Cheung 2013: 258; Hill

2014: 22; Kim 2010: 15). The most striking similarity between Southeast Asian nations under the lens of government is their undermined sustainability within their policy agendas, although there is a growing trend among young individuals to exhibit heightened levels of care towards matters outside their subsistence needs, such as ecological protection, gender equality, and freedom of speech. The situation maintains state capture predominantly by oligarchs, who exploit natural resources and labour for their extractive industries hence preventing the nations from advancing into sustainable high-technology societies (Holidin 2022: 3).

Periodic sociocultural trend mapping based on the results of the World Values Survey (WVS) reaffirms this picture of diversity. When viewed through the perspective of the Inglehart-Welzel cultural map, the differences between Southeast Asian societies are rather sharp. With such a wide range of historically based nation-building and reform trajectories among prominent Southeast Asian nations (Malaysia, Singapore, Thailand, the Philippines, and Indonesia), it is no coincidence that they are dispersed over the cultural map (WVS 2023)[8]. The data of wave 7 of the WVS conducted in 2017-2022 divides the most prominent Southeast Asian nations into three cultural groups: culturally West-and-South Asian (Malaysia, Singapore, Thailand), culturally African-Islamic (Indonesia), and culturally Latin American (the Philippines[9]).

According to the cultural map (**Figure 1**), the three culturally West-and-South Asian nations (Malaysia, Singapore, and Thailand) appear to be at the crossroads of the transitions from traditional to rational-secular values, as well as from survival to self-expression values. They suffer from continually delayed democracy, which makes them susceptible to the growth of autocracies in the region. Regardless of their classification on the WVS cultural map, Indonesia's western and central areas have ethnic similarities with Malaysia and Singapore's predominant groups. The Philippines, in contrast, remains in the quadrant of traditional values but is beginning to transition toward self-expression

---

8   See the findings data refinement in Version 4.0 comprising all countries under investigation, edited by Haerpfer et al. (2022).

9   The Philippines is placed in this zone to reflect the fact that despite their geographical remoteness, the Philippines and Latin America share the imprint of Hispanic colonial rule and the Roman Catholic Church. See WVS 2022. https://www.worldvaluessurvey.org/WVSContents. jsp?CMSID=Findings.

determination. The Philippines and Indonesia have similar ethnic origins and core beliefs, notably in their central and eastern areas (Setyaningrum 2018: 112-113). In contrast to their culturally West/South Asian nation counterparts, both had been promising democracies in the region, despite the fact that their governments continue to struggle to reach the reform levels necessary for democracy consolidation.

Notable fact is that Indonesia continues to adhere to survivalist and traditional values that have been associated with weak democratic values. Even before the COVID-19 pandemic shocked the country, both the government and the general public prioritized economic growth over humane development and environmental protection (Ngarayana et al. 2021: 6). Indonesian government has cemented this preference by stipulating the Omnibus Law of Job Creation in 2020 amidst the early phase of the pandemic, seeking to speed up cross-sectoral regulatory framework harmonization. Aside from disregarding proper legislation processes, the law also bears substantial deficiencies, such as abolishing employees' rights to bargain with their employers and undermining obligatory environmental impact analysis before issuing business permits (Sembiring et al. 2020: 104-105; Marilang et al. 2021: 6-7). Meanwhile, in the Philippines, the privileged regions on Luzon Island remain benefitting from competitive development amidst the rampant political dynasties, while those outside Luzon hitherto miss any institutional mechanisms to create competitiveness in development. This allows political dynasties to remain in office implementing development agendas which undermine sustainable and humane development (Mendoza 2022: 8-9). That large parts of the population still focus on subsistence needs over environmental issues and humane development is also reflected in the topics prioritized by the population, despite notable differences between Indonesia and the Philippines (**Table 1 + 2**).

The Southeast Asian nations' contemporary culture has started broadening their concerns to global challenges beyond their subsistence demands, such as increasing public support for human rights protection (White 2020: 32) and heightened criticisms of industries destructing the environment (Simpson 2018: 165). Societies like Malaysia, Singapore, and Thailand tackle these difficulties with a greater degree of individual autonomy compared to the rest of their Southeast Asian fellows, but in a pragmatic manner, and are not constrained by their social contexts. Other than the countries under scrutiny here, these three

Table 1: Priority ranking as perceived by Indonesians (WVS, wave 7, distributions in %)

No.*	Inquiries				
149	Most people consider both freedom and equality to be important, but if you had to choose between them, which one would you consider more important?	Freedom	Equality	Do not know	No answer
		34.3	64.9	0.5	0.3
150	Most people consider both freedom and security to be important, but if you had to choose between them, which one would you consider more important?	Freedom	Security	Do not know	No answer
		4.5	95.2	0.1	0.2
	People sometimes talk about what the aims of this country should be for the next ten years. On this card are listed some of the goals which different people would give top priority.	Growing economy	Strong defence	Getting things done	More beautiful cities/ countryside	Do not know / No answer
152	Would you please say which one of these you consider the most important?	45.8	9.3	29.9	14.7	0.3
153	Would you please say which one of these you consider the second most important?	25.4	22.6	26.3	25.2	0.6
		Maintaining national order	Having more says in government decisions	Fighting rising prices	Protecting freedom of speech	Do not know / No answer
154	If you had to choose, which one of the things on this card would you say is most important?	61	18.2	13.1	7.5	0.3
155	And which would be the next most important?	21.6	37.2	19.6	20.2	1.2
		stable economy	humane society	ideas count over money	Fighting against crime	No answer
156	Here is another list. In your opinion, which one of these is most important?	74.1	10.6	2.9	12	0.3
157	Here is another list. In your opinion, which one of these is most important? And what would be the next most important?	14.9	36.7	11.1	36.2	1.2

Source: Adapted from WVS (2020a: 40-42)

Note: * indicates the numbering of question items as appeared in the questionnaire book of WVS, wave 7

Table 2: Priority ranking as perceived by Filipinos (WVS, wave 7, distributions in %)

No.*	Inquiries					
149	Most people consider both freedom and equality to be important, but if you had to choose between them, which one would you consider more important?	Freedom	Equality	Do not know	No answer	
		48.2	51.8	0	0	
150	Most people consider both freedom and security to be important, but if you had to choose between them, which one would you consider more important?	Freedom	Security	Do not know	No answer	
		31.6	68.3	0	0	
	People sometimes talk about what the aims of this country should be for the next ten years. On this card are listed some of the goals which different people would give top priority.	Growing economy	Strong defence	Getting things done	More beautiful cities/ countryside	No answer
152	Would you please say which one of these you consider the most important?	43.6	22.6	24.8	8.8	0.1
153	Would you please say which one of these you consider the second most important?	19.8	24.5	33.8	21.9	0
		Maintaining national order	More says in government decisions	Fighting rising prices	Protecting freedom of speech	No answer
154	If you had to choose, which one of the things on this card would you say is most important?	52.7	20.8	17.6	9	0
155	And which would be the next most important?	19.9	25.2	31.5	23.3	0
		stable economy	humane society	ideas count over money	Fighting against crime	No answer
156	Here is another list. In your opinion, which one of these is most important?	44.9	24	12	19.1	0
157	Here is another list. In your opinion, which one of these is most important? And what would be the next most important?	20.7	23	24.9	31.5	0

Source: Adapted from WVS (2020b: 41-43).

Note: *indicates the numbering of question items as appeared in the questionnaire book of WVS, wave 7 nations were able to seek the fittest approach towards social and economic modernization from selected global models without being strangled by their traditional cultural roots. Pragmatism is the key to embrace cosmopolitan endeavours beyond national and geographical boundaries. This approach also entails prioritizing the role of individuals more than the community, corresponding their actions with recognized global best practices.

Right after separating from Malaysia, the Singapore government embarked on its economic modernization along with introducing bilingual education and has subsequently amplified its learning from the global development best practices (Savage 2015: 398-400). Despite their benign authoritarianism, Singaporean have maintained their leadership in governance and development by adopting their perceived finest policy lessons from a combination of former British colonial, American, and East Asian developmental models, and in turn, become a global model itself for an effective yet authoritarian modern regime (Thompson 2019: 40; compares to the whole argument by Springer 2009). Malaysia stepped into a lesser fortunate path by losing from mimicking Japan's developmentalism but has taken advantage of economic modernization spillover from its developments. Nevertheless, it keeps pursuing world-class education standards established in renowned democratic nations. This situation explains why it is easier for the people to restore democracy to the government in the wake of lengthy, protracted democratizations, despite concerns about future national growth (Ostwald & Oliver 2018). In contrast, a greater proportion of the younger population looks abroad for better social and economic prospects. In Thailand, the transition to democracy has not yet occurred. But the younger generation has shown resistance to the military administration since the aftermath of the 2014 coup demolished the democratically elected government even though the authoritarian regime employs both aggressive intimidation tactics and a hostile curriculum towards freedom of thought (Anamwathana & Thanapornsangsuth 2023: 152-153; Chambers 2015: 8). All three nations demonstrate enduring endeavours to promote democratization by mobilizing local aspirations and cosmopolitan orientation resources in alignment with global agendas, with the aim of countering authoritarian regimes.

The culturally Latin American Philippines and culturally African-Islamic Indonesia have preserved their religious and familial traditions. Religion and family-oriented values have been regarded for a long time as foundational to the spirit of national independence and national unity maintenance. Nonetheless, both failed to retain their government reform, in Indonesia since 2015 and in the Philippines since 2016, in the face of transition to democracy consolidation. Instead, both appear to be joining the rise of authoritarianism in the region (see for the Philippines: Juego 2017: 131; Teehanke & Calimbahin 2020: 71-72; and for Indonesia: Power 2018: 330; Wijayanto et al. 2021: 135-136). All conditions vary in these prominent Southeast Asian nations. Despite this, there is little indication that their established regional cooperation of the Association for South East Asian Nations (ASEAN) founded in 1967 plays any significant or at least intermediate roles in these social transformations and democratic processes.

Based on the above-mentioned sociocultural context specificities, we may evaluate the nations' commitment to democratizing their government systems by observing how they handle substantive and formal democratic transitions while abolishing the legacy of their previous authoritarian regimes. Undoubtedly, it is difficult for us to concentrate on the recurrent military junta regimes in Thailand and Singapore's benign autocracy. Malaysia's adamant efforts to obstruct democratization performance after a lengthy period of fluctuating democratization remains a persistent problematic situation. After the crucial regime shift from the Marcos period, the Philippines continues to struggle to reconstruct its democratic government (Hutchcroft & Rocamora 2003: 284; Quimpo 2009: 337). This regime shift also makes it the oldest democracy in Southeast Asia. Initial strategies include recalibrating check-and-balance mechanisms between state institutions and strengthening the authority and roles of the state auxiliary bodies. Governance actors currently handle drastic but still sluggish – steps toward full devolution, such as switching from unitary to federalism, easing restrictions on incoming foreign direct investment, and fostering a special autonomous Bangsamoro government in the South. Despite having completed considerable reforms at all levels of government following the fall of Suharto's authoritarian New Order regime, Indonesia stands in contrast to the Philippines. In the latter, the executive has predominantly coopted authority of some state auxiliary bodies under its feet, as it has also retracted power to local governments previously devolved in terms of regulation making, civil service appointments, and business permits. Indonesia was previously considered the most promising democracy in the region, prior to its current stagnation and decline (Mietzner 2015: 373).

5. Sociocultural implication on democracy transitions in Indonesia and the Philippines

Indonesia and the Philippines have exhibited democracy backsliding while their reform attempts of the government system have taken place. Moreover, Indonesian and Filipino sustainable societies are problematically viable. Political-economic growth and stability remain key survival ideals, in contrast to environmental conservation and humanism. The institutional modalities of the government system reform accomplished by their former administrations have remained, providing decent foundations for subsequent democratization attempts but not necessarily expedient to make sustainability a part of reform priority. The institutional modalities of the government system reform accomplished by their former administrations have remained, providing decent foundations for subsequent democratization attempts. Nevertheless, time-series data based on the Bertelsmann Transformation Index (BTI) 2010-2020 shows how the two countries have managed the transition.[10] Both countries have been under presidencies with once-promising reform advancement of the government system towards democracy consolidation, but later have proven otherwise.

Indonesia's Jokowi Administration takes a different approach from the Philippines, where authorities previously held by local governments in Indonesia have now been taken back by the central government. Benefitting solid support of almost all fractions in the legislative, the Indonesia's administration also modernizes state auxiliary bodies to capture them under the presidential authority domains. The government system reform progresses in the two countries facilitate drawbacks of democratization, with the Philippines performing the reform better than Indonesia.[11] The data of BTI indicates differences between two countries in terms of public participation in governance, consensus attainments, government capability, and public resource

---

10   It is parts of accumulated time series data within the BTI, which can be used with the interactive tool of the Atlas provided by Bertelsmann Stiftung through https://bti-project.org/de/atlas.

11   Although the governance index shown in the BTI across periods 2010-2020 depicts an inferior figure for the Philippines, its reform progresses better, upscaling from 4.07 (weak) to 4.89 (moderate), than the one for Indonesia which descaling from 5.87 (good) to 5.39 (moderate).

efficiency. Nevertheless, the two administrations still enjoy constant popular support from the majority of the people regardless of the democracy backslidings.

In the Philippines, Ferdinand "Bongbong" Marcos Jr. – the son of the late dictator President Ferdinand Marcos Sr. – took office after winning the national election in May 2022. The Duterte administration used its reform campaign to fulfil the unmet reform expectations of the former Aquino administration (Fernandez 2021: 3-5; Juego 2017: 133; see a close examination of the Aquino Administration in Holmes 2018: 33-35). The Duterte administration took a different trajectory from its predecessor, known as Dutertismo, which introduced policies of escalating peacebuilding attempts against the resurgence of radical communist entities and promoting extrajudicial killings of narcotics dealers while speeding up peacebuilding and development in the Mindanao region (Maboloc 2017: 4; Labastin 2018: 41-42). It has also undertaken measurable attempts for constitutional reform by devolving more authority to local governments, even by transitioning to federalism (Teng-Calleja et al. 2017: 64; Shair-Rosenfield, 2016: 160).

To address the ambivalent phenomena mentioned above, it is of utmost importance to look at how the societies regard their respective democratic transition trends based on their sociocultural underpinnings and their implications efforts on achieving sustainable societies. Furthermore, once the transition from the authoritarian system has come to be dismantled and embrace the Liberal Notions of Democracy (LNDs), it is necessary to assess the dynamics and long-term viability of the democratic transition and sustainability.

Figure 2 and **Figure 3** show the perception of procedural democratic practices held by Indonesians and Filipinos according to wave 7 of the WVS survey (2020a: 65-68; 2020b: 66-68). Both Indonesians and Filipinos believe elections are held reasonably abiding by the stipulated regulations and schedules. Election organizers, namely Komisi Pemilihan Umum (KPU, the General Election Commission) in Indonesia, and the Commission on Election (COMELEC) in the Philippines, are also considered relatively fair in carrying out their duties.

However, although the respondents' assessment is considerably close to the ideal principle of a democratic society, it is obstructed by perceptions of bad practices that deteriorate the quality of democracy with certain variations between Indonesia and the Philippines. **Figure 2** and **Figure 3** indicate that both countries are perceived to have many incidents that prevent candidates from the opposition from competing in elections. Such incidents are evident, especially in the election of members of the Senate (APHR 2021: 21). When comparing the result for Indonesia and the Philippines it becomes evident that Filipino voters more strongly feel to be offered genuine political choices for

In your view, how often do the following things occur in this country's elections? (Indonesia, WVS wave 7, distributions in %)

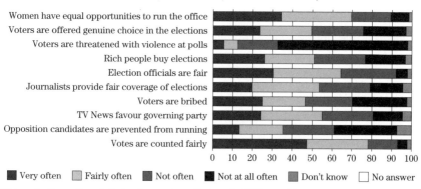

Figure 2: Perception of electoral procedures (Indonesia, WVS wave 7)
Source: WVS (2020a: 65-68)

In your view, how often do the following things occur in this country's elections? (The Philippines, WVS wave 7, distributions in %)

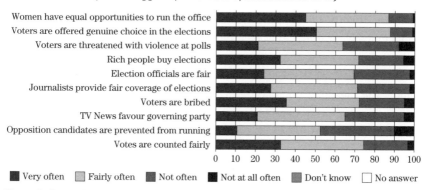

Figure 3: Perception of electoral processes (The Philippines, WVS wave 7)
Source: WVS (2020b: 66-68)

voting than Indonesian voters. At the same time, Filippino respondents feel more strongly than Indonesian respondents that journalists were able to report on the election freely[12] (BTI 2022: 10; Iannone 2022: 93). Genuine political choice offerings and journalists' freedom are considered insufficient enablers to make people in the Philippines articulate their aspirations better than those in Indonesia.

Nevertheless, as depicted in **Figure 3**, perceptions about constraints remain also in the Philippines, primarily with voter bribery seen as problematic. As acts of violence still occasionally occur in some areas in the Philippines outside of Luzon, voters also often feel threatened about using their voices. Compared to Indonesia, state-run television channels experience news bias favouring the ruling parties. However, overall, reporting is relatively balanced, due to non-governmental journalism, which is considered to report from a more objective stance. In Indonesia, on the other hand, the power circle controls even privately-owned media. While bribery, or the buying and selling of votes, often occurs in Indonesia, respondents perceive this vote-selling as less frequent than Filippino respondents.

6. Prevailing Authoritarian Notions of Democracy (AND) or Southeast Asian Democratic Notions of Authoritarianism (DNA) in the making?

The data of wave 7 of WVS indicate a strong AND (Authoritarian Notions of Democracy) tendency in Indonesia and the Philippines. The people of Indonesia and the Philippines support and consider their governments to be democratically governed. However, rather than an actual development towards AND, the resurgence of authoritarian features of recent government reform seem to indicate that the current administrations benefit from justifiable democratic means of democratic institutions. In this case, Southeast Asian nations develop from mere AND to Democratic Notions of Authoritarianism (DNA), and, therefore, away from the originally intended democratization. This

---

12 Despite civil society organizations in the two countries increasing critical journalism, a grand alliance of legislative and executive branch leaders controls the mainstream media in Indonesia. Meanwhile, ABS-CBN and Rappler news studios criticizing Duterte got their franchise extension permit disapproved by the administration in 2017. See Rappler (2021).

way, citizens perceive the government's authoritarian practices as democratic, like AND conceptualized by Welzel & Kirsch (ibid., p. 3) and advanced by Schmidt (2018: 10-12). But they also misunderstand authoritarianism, as the government actively creates manipulative narratives that use democratic means to achieve authoritarian goals. The controversial grand narrative *revolusi mental* (mental model revolution) campaigned by the President of Indonesia, Joko Widodo, and the *Dutertismo* pinpointed on the President of the Philippines, Rodrigo Duterte, exhibits exemplary DNA. It thus seems that most Indonesians and Filipinos perceive whatever the respective governments do as legitimate, including the governments' red-tagging of opposition and critics.

Both Indonesian and Philippine administrations manifesting DNA conforms with preferences of the general public. The WVS data seems to indicate that the citizens' satisfaction with the political system and their government is considerably high (2020a: 75-76; 2020b: 75-76, **Figure 4**). Other surveys conducted in Indonesia and the Philippines come to similar results. In Indonesia, the leading national mass media KOMPAS (2023) reports 79.2% respondents of a survey to be satisfied with law enforcement, security, and public affairs performed by the Joko Widodo Administration. Meanwhile, Social Weather Stations (SWS, 2022) – a social science research institute in the Philippines and survey partner of WVS for wave 7 survey – elucidates its survey result that approaching the end of the term of President Rodrigo R. Duterte, 88% of adult Filipinos expressed satisfaction with his performance.

Using the terminology of liberal democracy, the rights of citizens include human rights, such as the rights for protection and respect. Accordingly, electoral democracy in people's minds also refers to the freedom of the people to choose their leaders through a free, honest, and fair election. As shown in **Figure 5**, respondents from Indonesia and the Philippines considered civil rights protection from oppression by the state to be an essential characteristic of a democracy. Similarly, both Filippino and Indonesian respondents evaluate gender equality as an essential feature of democracy, including women's right to run for office.

In Indonesia and the Philippines, representative democracy in public accessibility is considered no less important hence they can participate in government administration. However, Indonesian and Filipino people consider the meaning of democracy differently from what is understood by Western

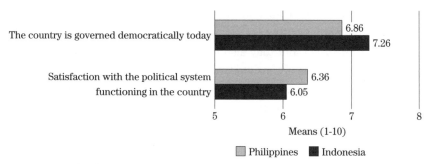

Figure 4: Perception of democratic processes and satisfaction with the political system (WVS, wave 7: Indonesia, the Philippines)
Source: WVS (2020a: 75-76; 2020b: 75-76)
Notes: Mean scores ranging from 1 = not satisfied at all/not democratic to 10 = satisfied/completely democratic.

society. This circumstance cannot be separated from the socio-cultural basis of the two societies with regards to democratic governments. We attest to what they really mean of democracy by examining their comprehension of essential characteristics of democracy and the rights of conduct, as depicted in **Figure 5**, **Figure 6**, and **Figure 7**.

As the value orientation between Indonesian and Filipino societies has been transitioning at differing paces (see **Figure 1**), so has the meaning of democracy according to their socio-cultural basis. In terms of democratic economic development, for Indonesia, civil rights protection is seen as more essentially democratic than taxing the rich and subsidizing the poor. While respondents in the Philippines showed higher support for unemployment insurance as an essential characteristic of democracy, Indonesian respondents might consider this type of social welfare as a burden on the public budget.

Both Filippino and Indonesian respondents simultaneously prioritize security above civil freedoms and equal distribution of economic growth. As shown in **Figures 5, 6** and **7**, a majority of Indonesians and Filipinos support public surveillance in public areas or monitoring of emails and other forms of online communication. Only when it comes to the unauthorized collection of personal information, support is somewhat weaker.

As depicted in **Figure 5**, Indonesians prefer people with military background to assume control of the country from an inept civilian administration. The safeguarding of citizens' civil rights is crucial in

Figure 5: Essential Characteristics of Democracy (WVS, wave 7: Indonesia, the Philippines)
Source: WVS (2020a: 70-74; 2020b: 70-74)
Note: mean scores (1 = not an essential characteristic of democracy, 10 = an essential characteristic of democracy)

democracies, even under military rules, which are still perceived as democratic, as expressed in **Figure 5**, with the logic of security delineated in **Figure 6** and **Figure 7**. Leaders with military origins have often been paired with civilian (non-military) leaders throughout Indonesia's political history, something we have not seen in the Philippines. Filipino support for the military taking over is just as high as for Indonesian respondents, in fact, people in the Philippines nearly always react to civilian incompetency by proposing more competent civilians or opting for a system that maintains civilian dominance over military power.[13] These tendencies are problematic for the Indonesian people, who still hold the military in high respect for maintaining order, discipline, and professionalism. These have long been seen as necessary for a healthy

---

13 Only retired Gen. Fidel Ramos, whose military background, became the president (1992-1986) since the government reform happened in 1986-1987 by the civilian populace, succeeding President Corazon Aquino (1986-1992). While carrying out his military service, President Ramos broke apart from former dictator President Marcos Sr., allowing civilian supporters of reform to rise and dismantle the authoritarian regime.

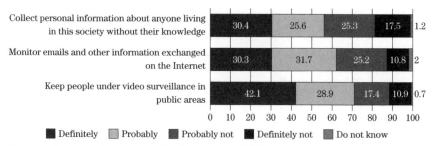

Figure 6: Support for the government's rights of conduct (WVS, wave 7: Indonesia, distributions in %)
Source: WVS (2020a: 58-59)

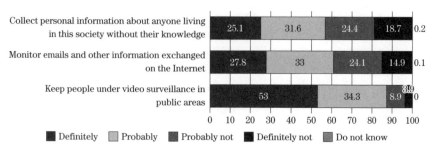

Figure 7: Support for the government's rights of conduct (WVS, wave 7: the Philippines, distributions in %)
Source: WVS (2020b: 59-60)

democracy.

Technocrats are the best option for political leadership that is supposed to be not typically military for most Indonesians and Filipinos. The preferred technocracy marks a feature of modernity that reaffirms that it is also prone to authoritarian regimes. Positive evaluation of the statement "Having experts, not government, make decisions according to what they think is best for the country" in the WVS, affirms this tendency. Of Indonesian respondents, 19.5% thought this was a very good and 48.6% a fairly good way of governing a country. Respondents from the Philippines agreed to a similar extent that this was a very good (15.5%) or fairly good (50.2%) way to govern a country. Indonesia experienced the rise of professional technocrats as a foundation for an authoritarian regime (Prasojo & Holidin 2018: 56). For more than three decades, President Suharto's authoritarian New Order regime included a willingness to send citizens to study abroad in order to benefit from their expertise. Civil service was also considered part of Suharto's political vehicle under the umbrella of the *Golongan Karya* (GOLKAR), which was not a political party. It was the only professional organization – including civil servants – that is legally legitimate to contest in elections until the end of his term of office. Entering the reform period in 1998, Indonesia managed to emerge from the 1997 financial crisis under the one-year leadership of President Habibie, a reliable technocrat nurtured under the Suharto administration, who was a member of GOLKAR, and a favoured subject of President Suharto but at the same time a reformist figure.

The desire of the Indonesians and Filipinos for a strong leader, which is anchored in the traditional values of familism and collectivism, together with hierarchical social culture, affirms their definite preference for leadership competency. Results from the WVS (2020a: 68; 2020b: 69) show that there is widespread support of "Having a strong leader who does not have to bother with parliament and elections" among Indonesian (24.4% and 34.6% evaluate this as very good and fairly good respectively) and Filipino (22.7% and 52.4% evaluate this as very good and fairly good respectively) populaces for a strong leadership unaffected by parliament/legislature and elections. While patronage politics in Indonesia is not solidified based on family networks, it is contrary to that of the Philippines (Porio 2017: 33). Patronage politics develops under the primordial sturdiness of political dynasties. Although the Duterte administration has outlawed dynastic politics in government,[14] the fundamental political infrastructure still permits it and cannot escape from legislations enacted under the Marcos Sr. dictatorship.[15] Within the party system, individuals can switch parties (Aceron 2009: 9; Montinola, 1999: 742). This method retains the option to prioritize a party-list candidate for a seat in the legislature. Without a strong

---

14 It is, however, interesting to note that in the May 2022 national elections, Duterte and Marcos families joined forces in campaigning for the winning candidates of Ferdinand "Bongbong" Marcos Jr. and Sara Duterte, daughter of former President Duterte and former mayor of Davao City, consolidating their electoral support from primordial bases in the southern and northern parts of the Philippines respectively, significantly defeating alliances made by reformist *cum* opposition led by the Liberal Party and Aquino Family's supporters that campaigned for former Vice President Maria Leonor "Leni" Gerona Robredo and former Senator Francis Nepomuceno „Kiko" Pangilinan.

15 Article II Section 26 of the reformist 1987 Constitution abolishing the Marcos regime even use softer phrases that state "The State shall guarantee equal access to opportunities for public service; and prohibit political dynasties as may be defined by law".

ideological basis of political platforms and alignment between political parties and voters' aspirations, those party-switching and the presence of party-list in the Philippine representative systems favour personalist politics and political patronage under certain ruling dynasties. All of these problems are even tougher to eliminate at the local level. Local government selections continue to be dominated by family networks, hence institutionalizing political dynasties.

The preferred values of familism and strong leadership mentioned above offer a solid basis for a strong authoritarian inclination and are justified by the citizens themselves as if they were indicative of a functioning democratic governance structure. The value trend entails the concept of the unitary state for both Indonesia and the Philippines, as well as the selection of a presidential system therein. Since the increase in electoral and parliamentary thresholds, the current Jokowi Administration in Indonesia has secured concentrated power under its feet, undermining the legislative oversight, and obstructing the check-and-balance mechanism. Sociocultural upbringings of this situation matter. Aspinall et al. (2018) and Pepinsky (2019: 58-59) agree that voters' dealignment from competing political parties, both point to the rise of identity politics and the popularity of reforms with a nationalist orientation. In contrast, Warburton (2019) argues that religious dogma and party divide have intertwined themselves with pragmatic procedures, posing an escalated threat to Indonesian democracy.

The Philippines' basis is distinct. Despite the reported value preferences, the structure of a unitary state inextricably links to the regional stability policies pursued by the United States, which colonized the Philippines in the aftermath of the Spanish era. While Filipinos inherit liberal values from the US colonial master, ethic-cultural norms they have embraced from the Spaniards prevail. In the current modern Philippines, amidst heightened debates over constitutional reform proposals for turning the state into a federal-parliamentary government system, democratic features of good and responsive government are upheld as a mainstreaming bent. For this sake, even the authoritarian leadership style of local or national leaders still becomes the preference of Filipinos (Brillantes & Perante-Calina 2018: 161).

The presented WVS data also reflects prioritizing the value of economic stability over a humanist society and the value of sustaining national order over participation in government. These two patterns of value inclinations mutually validate one another and explain the continuance of the authoritarian type of institutional control that uses democratic principles as justification. The patterns, however, are typical Southeast Asian polities whose state-society relations are built on a strong hierarchy culture standing upon stability and control (see also the multiple comparisons across the nations explained by Berenschot et al. 2017).

7. Conclusion

Efforts to realize sustainable societies in terms of peace, justice, and strong institutions need an augmented, closer scrutiny beyond the formal institutional setting of the system and organization of the societies. They also need to be grounded in shared values of the citizens. Based on WVS data, we investigated the influence and strength of the cultural-religious background on preferences for types of governance and leadership. The starting point of this chapter was Western research on value change, developed especially by Inglehart and others. Next, we discussed a possible connection between the trajectory of value change and ethic-religious background on attitudes towards democracy.

According to the Western discourse on value change, a value change from traditional-religious to secular-rational values took place in the "first" modern age, which, however, did not necessarily lead to democracy. For the "second" modern age, a shift from materialistic to post-materialistic values and an intensification of the demand for self-expression values were predicted. Triggered by rising levels of education, this was expected to also lead to increasing support for democracy.

While Confucian countries show high support for secular-rational values, citizens of these countries show only low support of post-materialistic and self-expression values. As a result, democracy finds relatively little support in these countries. Especially in Japan, where the level of education is as high as in Germany, our previous research has shown that support for liberal ideas of democracy was comparatively low, which can be described as a "second paradox".

Extending the existing literature, we then discussed Southeast Asian societies, specifically Indonesia and the Philippines. Representing different cultural backgrounds and with lower educational levels than their East Asian counterparts, we found a similar tendency of valuing economic stability over a humanist society and sustaining national order over participation in government. Regardless of the cultural differences between Indonesia and the Philippines, both societies have pragmatically moved closer to democratic values, but authoritative tendencies remain. These Authoritarian Notions of Democracy (AND) which we find in Southeast Asian countries are similar to East Asian Countries. Moreover, because they have only inherited the institutional and socio-cultural imprints of their colonial masters and have never developed an idea of what true democracy in today's Western sense is, the tendency towards ANDs may be an inevitable consequence.

Therefore, we refute the Western value change discourse that expects a universal value change towards sustainable democracy in the second modernity. We point to the importance of the cultural-religious background driving value change in different ways during democratization in East and Southeast Asian societies. Moreover, in all these Asian countries, the concept of democracy in the Western sense is not indigenous. It should be emphasized that this leads to a diverging understanding of democracy in Asia and Europe. In Asia, we may even speak of democratic notions of authoritarianism (DNA), which leads to authoritarian government practices. Therefore, we do not expect to see the development of sustainable democracies, as defined above, in Southeast Asia in the near future.

References

Aceron, Joy. (2009): It's the (non-) system, stupid!: Explaining 'mal-development' of parties in the Philippines. In: Friedrich Ebert Stiftung, *Reforming the Philippine Political Party System ideas and initiatives, debates and dynamics*, Metro Manila, 5-22, library.fes.de/pdf-files/bueros/philippinen/07131.pdf, [Accessed 10 October 2023].

Anamwathana, Panarat/Thanapornsangsuth, Sawaros (2023): Youth political participation in Thailand: A social and historical overview. In: *International Journal of Sociology* 53 (2): 146-157. DOI: 10.1080/00207659.2023.2167381.

APHR (ASEAN Parliamentarians for Human Rights) (2021): Parliamentarians at risk: Reprisals against opposition MPs in Southeast Asia in 2021. ASEAN Parliamentarians for Human Rights and the Hanns Seidel Foundation, aseanmp.org/2021/12/02/parliamentarians-at-risk-reprisals-against-opposition-mps-in-southeast-asia-in-2021/, [Accessed 10 October 2023].

Aspinall, Edward/Fossati, Diego/Muhtadi, Burhanuddin/Warburton, Eve (2018): *Elites, Masses,*

And Democratic Decline in Indonesia, NewYork: Routledge.

Beck, Ulrich/Bonß Wolfgang/Lau, Christoph (2001): Theorie reflexiver Modernisierung – Fragestellungen, Hypothesen, Forschungsprogrammen. In: *In Die Modernisierung der Moderne*, ed. Ulrich Beck and Wolfgang Bonß, ed., Frankfurt Main: Suhrkamp, 11–59.

Berenschot, Ward/Nordholt, H.G.C. Schulte/Bekker, Laurens (2017): *Citizenship and democratization in Southeast Asia*, Leiden: Brill.

Brillantes, Alex B./Perante-Calina, Lizan E. (2018): Leadership and public sector reform in the Philippines. In: Evan Berman & Eko Prasojo, eds., *Leadership and public sector rform in Asia (Public Policy and Governance* 30), Bingley: Emerald Publishing Limited, Bingley, 151-178. DOI: 10.1108/S2053-769720180000030007.

BTI (Bertelsmann Transformation Index) (2020): *Country Report 2020: Indonesia*, Gütersloh: Bertelsmann Stiftung.

BTI (Bertelsmann Transformation Index) (2022): *Country Report 2022: the Philippines*, Gütersloh: Bertelsmann Stiftung.

Chamber, Paul (2015): Civil-military relations in Thailand since the 2014 Coup: The tragedy of security sector 'deform'. In: *PRIF Report* 138, Frankfurt am Main: Peace Research Institute Frankfurt, www.hsfk.de/fileadmin/HSFK/hsfk_publikationen/prif138.pdf, [Accessed 10 October 2023].

Cheung, Anthony B.L. (2013): Can There be an Asian Model of Public Administration? In: *Journal of Public Administration and Development* 33 (4): 249-261. DOI: 10.1002/pad.1660.

Eisenstadt, Shmuel Noah (2000): Multiple Modernities. In: *Daedalus* 129: 1–29.

Fernandez, Artchil B. (2021): Disrupting Liberal Democracy: The Phenomenal Rise of Duterte. In: *Mabini Review* 10: 1-19.

Haerpfer, C./Inglehart, R./Moreno, R. A./ Welzel, C./Kizilova, K./Diez-Medrano, J./Lagos, M./ Norris, P./Ponarin, E./Puranen, B. (eds.) (2022): *World Values Survey: Round Seven - Country-Pooled Datafile Version 4.0*, Madrid, Spain & Vienna, Austria: JD Systems Institute & WVSA Secretariat. DOI: 10.14281/18241.18.

Hill, Hal. (2014): Is There a Southeast Asian Development Model? In: Schulze, Günther G., ed., *Discussion Series Paper*, Dept. International Economic Policy – University of Freiburg, Freiburg.

Holidin, Defny (2022): Persistent Developmental Limits to Devising Policy Innovation for Innovation Policies in Emerging Economies. In: *Policy & Governance Review* 6 (1): 1-16. DOI: 10.30589/pgr.v6i1.386.

Holmes, Ronald D. (2018): Can the Gains be Sustained? Assessing the First Five Years of the Aquino Administration. In: P. D. Hutchcroft. *Mindanao: The Long Journey to Peace and Prosperity*, Singapore: World Scientific Publishing, 3-35.

Hutchcroft, Paul/Rocamora, Joel (2003): Strong Demands and Weak Institutions: The Origins and Evolution of the Democratic Deficit in the Philippines. In: *Journal of East Asian Studies* 3: 259-292. DOI: 10.1017/S1598240800001363.

Iannone, Aniello (2022): Democracy Crisis in South-East Asia: Media, Control, Censorship, and Disinformation during the 2019 Presidential and General Elections in Indonesia, Thailand and 2019 Local Elections in the Philippines. In: *Jurnal Ilmu Sosial dan Ilmu Politik* 26 (1): 81-97. DOI: 10.22146/jsp.71417.

Inglehart, Ronald/Welzel, Christian (2010): Changing mass priorities: The link between modernization and democracy. In: *Perspectives on Politics* 8 (2): 551–567.

Inglehart, Ronald (1971): The silent revolution in Europe: Intergenerational change in post-industrial societies. In: *American Political Science Review* 65: 991–1017.

Inglehart, Ronald (1990): *Cultural shift in advanced industrial society*. Princeton: Princeton University Press.

Inglehart, Ronald/Welzel, Christian (2010): Changing mass priorities: The link between modernization and democracy. In: *Perspectives on Politics* 8 (2): 551–567.

Juego, B. (2017): Duterte-led authoritarian populism and its liberal-democratic roots. *Asia Maior* 28: 129-164.

Kim, Pan Suk (ed.) (2010): *Public Sector Reform in ASEAN Member Countries and Korea*, Seoul: Daeyoung Moonhwasa Publishing Company.

KOMPAS (2023) Survei Terbaru Litbang 'Kompas': Kepuasan Publik atas Kinerja Jokowi Meningkat, Citra TNI Dinilai Paling Baik, 22 February, nasional.kompas.com/read/2023/02/22/06125961/survei-terbaru-litbang-kompas-kepuasan-publik-atas-kinerja-jokowi-meningkat, [Accessed 22 February 2023].

Labastin, Benjiemen A. (2018): Two Faces of *Dutertismo*: Two Visions of Democracy in the Philippines. *Social Ethics Society Journal of Applied Philosophy*, special issue (December), 31-54.

Maboloc, Christopher Ryan (2017): Situating the Mindanao Agenda in the Radical Politics of President Duterte. In: *Iqra: Journal of AlQalam* 6: 3-24.

Marilang, Muammar Bakry/Arbani, Tri S./Syatar, Abdul/Amiruddin, Muhammad M./Ishak, Nurfaika (2021): Establishing omnibus law in Indonesia: Strict liability in environmental law. In: *Journal of Legal, Ethical, and Regulatory Issues* 24 (1): 1-9, www.abacademies.org/articles/establishing-omnibus-law-in-indonesia-strict-liability-in-environmental-law.pdf, [Accessed 10 October 2023].

Mendoza, Ronald U./Yap, Jurel K./Mendoza, Gabriella A.S./Jaminola III, Leonardo/Yu, Erica C. (2022): Political dynasties, business, and poverty in the Philippines. In: *Journal of Government and Economics* 7 (100051): 1-10. DOI: 10.1016/j.jge.2022.100051.

Mietzner, Marcus (2015): Indonesia: Democratic Consolidation and Stagnation under Yudhoyono, 2004-2014. In: W. Case (Ed.). *Routledge Handbook of Southeast Asian Democratization*, New York, NY: Routledge, 370-383.

Montinola, Gabrielle R. (1999): Politicians, Parties, and the Persistence of Weak States: Lessons from the Philippines. In: *Development and Change* 30: 739-774.

Ngarayana, I Wayan/Sutanto, Jepri/Murakami, Kenta (2021): Predicting the future of Indonesia: energy, economic and sustainable environment development. In: *IOP Conference Series: Earth and Environmental Science* 753 (012038): 1-7. DOI: 10.1088/1755-1315/753/1/012038.

Ostwald, Kai/Oliver, Steven (2019): Four Arenas: Malaysia's 2018 Election, Reform, and Democratization. In: *Democratization* 27 (4): 662-680. DOI: 10.1080/13510347.2020.1713757.

Pepinsky, Tom (2019): Islam and Indonesia's 2019 Presidential Election. In: *Asia Policy* 46 (4): 54-62, www.jstor.org/stable/26867614, [Accessed 10 October 2023].

Porio, Emma (2017): Citizen Participation and Decentralization in the Philippines. In:

Berenschot, Ward/Nordholt, H.G.C. Schulte/Bekker, Laurens Citizenship and Democratization in Southeast Asia, Leiden: Brill, 29-50, www.jstor.org/stable/10.1163/j.ctt1w76ws5.6, [Accessed 10 October 2023].

Power, Tom P. (2018): Jokowi's Authoritarian Turn and Indonesia's Democratic Decline. In: *Bulletin of Indonesian Economic Studies*, 54 (3): 307-338. DOI: 10.1080/00074918.2018.1549918.

Prasojo, Eko/Holidin, Defny (2018): Leadership and public sector reform in Indonesia. In: Evan Berman & Eko Prasojo, eds., *Leadership and public sector reform in Asia (Public Policy and Governance* 30), Bingley: Emerald Publishing Limited, 53-83. DOI: 10.1108/S2053-769720180000030003.

Quimpo, Nathan G. (2009): The Philippines: Predatory regime, growing authoritarian features. In: *The Pacific Review* 22 (3): 335-353. DOI: 10.1080/09512740903068388.

Rappler (2021): Revive ABS-CBN franchise? Wait until after Duterte term, February 11, www.rappler.com/nation/speaker-velasco-says-calls-revive-abs-cbn-franchise-have-to-wait-after-duterte-term/, [Accessed 10 October 2023].

Savage, Victor R. (2015): Singapore's global city challenges: National identity, cosmopolitan aspirations, migrant requirements. In: Singh, R. (ed.): *Urban development challenges, risks and resilience in Asian mega cities (Advances in Geographical and Environmental Sciences)*, Tokyo: Springer, 395-408. DOI: 1007/978-4-431-55043-3_20.

Schmidt, Carmen E. (2018): Values and democracy in East Asia and Europe: A comparison. In: *Asian Journal of German and European Studies* 3 (10): 1–16. DOI: 10.1186/s40856-018-0034-9.

Sembiring, Raynaldo/Fatimah, Isna/Widyaningsih, Grita A. (2020): Indonesia's omnibus bill on job creation: A setback for environmental law? (Note on recent developments). In: *Chinese Journal of Environmental Law* 4: 97-109. DOI: 10.1163/24686042-12340051.

Setyaningrum, R/Wijaya, Andi R./Subagyo (2018): The comparison of cultural dimension between Sulawesi, Indonesia and Philippines: a measurement of five Indonesian islands. In: *IPTEK Journal of Proceedings Series* 3: 107-115. DOI:10.12962/j23546026.y2018i3.3715.

Shair-Rosenfield, Sarah (2016): The causes and effects of the local government code in the Philippines: Locked in a status quo of weakly decentralized authority? In: *Journal of Southeast Asian Economies* 33 (2): 157-171.

Simpson, Adam (2018): The environment in Southeast Asia: Injustice, conflict and activism. In: Alice D. & Beeson, Mark (eds.): *Contemporary Southeast Asia: The politics of change, contestation, and adaptation.* 3rd Edition, London: Palgrave Macmillan, pp. 164-180.

Springer, Simon (2009): Renewed authoritarianism in Southeast Asia: Undermining Democracy through Neoliberal Reform. In: *Asia Pacific Viewpoint* 50 (3): 271–276.

SWS (Social Weather Stations) (2022) Second Quarter 2022 Social Weather Survey: Pres. Rodrigo Duterte's final net satisfaction rating at +81, 23 September, www.sws.org.ph/swsmain/artcldisppage/?artcsyscode=ART-20220923101814, [Accessed 10 October 2023].

Teehanke, Julio C/Calimbahin, Cleo Anne A. (2020): Mapping the Philippines' defective democracy. In: *Asian Affairs: An American Review* 47 (2):97-125. DOI: 10.1080/00927678.2019.1702801.

Teng-Calleja, Mendiola/Hechanova, Ma Regina M./Alampay, R.B.A./Canoy, N.A./Franco, Edna

P./Alampay, E.A. (2017): Transformation in Philippine local government. In: *Local Government Studies* 43 (1): 64-88. DOI: 10.1080/03003930.2016.1235561.

Thompson, Mark R. (2019). Singapore and the lineages of authoritarian modernity in East Asia. In: L. Rahim, M. Barr, (eds.) *The Limits of Authoritarian Governance in Singapore's Developmental State*, Singapore: Palgrave Macmillan, 29-48. DOI: 10.1007/978-981-13-1556-5_2.

Warburton, Eve (2019): Polarization in Indonesia: What if perception is reality? *New Mandala*, www.newmandala.org/how-polarised-is-indonesia, April 16, [Accessed 10 October 2023].

Welzel, Christian/Kirsch, Helen (2017): Democracy misunderstood: Authoritarian notions of democracy around the globe. In: *World Values Research (WVR)* 9 (1): 1–29.

White, Michael J.V. (2020): National human rights institutions: From idea to implementation. In: Gomez, James, & Ramcharan, Robin, (eds.): National human rights institutions in Southeast Asia: Selected case studies, Singapore: Palgrave Macmillan, 21-36.

Wijayanto/Budiarti, Aisah Putri/Wiratraman, Herlambang P. (2021): *Demokrasi tanpa Demos: Refleksi 100Ilmuwan Sosial Politik tentang Kemunduran Demokrasi di Indonesia*, Jakarta: LP3ES.

WVS (World Values Survey) (2020a): World Values Survey Wave 7 (2017-2020): Indonesia. Study # WVS-2017 v2.0. In: Haerpfer, C./Inglehart, R./Moreno, R. A./Welzel, C./Kizilova, K./Diez-Medrano, J./Lagos, M./Norris, P./Ponarin, E./Puranen, B. (eds.): *World Values Survey: Round Seven - Country-Pooled Datafile*. Madrid, Spain & Vienna, Austria: JD Systems Institute & WVSA Secretariat, www.worldvaluessurvey.org/WVSDocumentationWV7.jsp, [Accessed 10 October 2023]. DOI: 10.14281/18241.13.

WVS (World Values Survey) (2020b): World Values Survey Wave 7 (2017-2020): Philippines. Study # WVS-2017 v2.0. In: Haerpfer, C./Inglehart, R./Moreno, R. A./Welzel, C./Kizilova, K./Diez-Medrano, J./Lagos, M./Norris, P./Ponarin, E./Puranen, B. (eds.): *World Values Survey: Round Seven - Country-Pooled Datafile*. Madrid, Spain & Vienna, Austria: JD Systems Institute & WVSA Secretariat, www.worldvaluessurvey.org/WVSDocumentationWV7.jsp, [Accessed 10 October 2023]. DOI: 10.14281/18241.13.

WVS (World Values Survey) (2023): The Inglehart-Welzel World Cultural Map: World Values Survey wave 7 (2017-2022), www.worldvaluessurvey.org/WVSContents.jsp?CMSID=Findings, [Accessed 10 October 2023].

Epilogue

Sustainable Societies: Moving Forward With No Time to Waste

Masato Kimura
Carola Hommerich

We are no longer left with a long reprieve before the challenge of creating a sustainable world for all needs to be completed. In 2015, the UN Sustainable Development Summit adopted the 2030 Agenda for achieving the concrete 169 targets embodying the 17 goals, which include poverty and hunger eradication, quality education, gender equality and climate change action. The year of 2023 marked halfway to the deadline. While early efforts showed positive trends, the past three years made clear that much of this progress was fragile and too slow.

In July 2023, the UN published a special report stating that at the current pace achieving the 2030 Agenda is unlikely (UN 2023). According to the report, of the 140 targets for which trend data is available, only 15% are on track to be met; 48% are off track, and 37% have stagnated or gone into reverse since 2015 (ibid.: 11). The Sustainable Development Goals are in peril. As we have entered a new age of polycrisis, the SDGs are 'disappearing in the rear-view mirror, as is the hope and rights of current and future generations' (ibid.: 4).

In 2022, about 735 million people, equivalent to 9.2 % of the world population, were still facing chronic hunger (ibid.: 14), with the impact of the COVID-19 pandemic and Russia's invasion of Ukraine reversing some of the progress that had been made. If the current trend continues, 575 million people – an estimate of 7% of the world population – will still be living in extreme poverty in 2030 (ibid.:12).

Global environmental change is also critical. In response to the hottest summer ever recorded in 2023, UN Secretary-General Antonio Guterres announced at his press conference in New York, 27 July 2023, that 'the era of global warming has ended. The era of global boiling has arrived'. The World Meteorological Organization similarly warned in its State of the Global Climate 2022 report that this was not a single heat wave, but a longer trend, with the years 2015 to 2022 having been 'the eight warmest in the 173-year instrumental record' (WMO 2023: 4). The Paris Agreement, adopted by 196 Parties at the UN Climate Change Conference (COP21) in 2015, set the goal to limit the global temperature increase to 1.5 degrees Celsius above pre-industrial levels. To achieve this, by 2030, global greenhouse gas emissions must be cut by 45% compared to 2010 levels. Instead, global greenhouse gas emissions increased to a record high in 2022 (UNEP 2023: 4).

All of this indicates that we have a stony path ahead of us. The current evaluations are likely to render us pessimistic and disillusioned, but we cannot give up. Only a fast and ambitious change of course can enable us to achieve a future that is peaceful, inclusive and sustainable. Developed countries, in particular, have a significant role to play in this.

In this volume, we have presented research on a limited number of topics and cases concerning SDGs from the developed countries of Germany and Japan. The different chapters all present original research, utilizing different methodologies, ranging from theoretical and empirical analyses of case studies to community-based initiatives and comparative statistical data analysis.

Three key areas were covered. A first topical focus circled environmental sustainability, discussing policy attempts by local authorities for waste sorting and reduction, school education on climate change, as well as changes in environmental attitudes and behaviour.

A second focal point highlighted sustainability approaches in regional and urban planning, presenting recommendations for the creation of resilient and sustainable communities, and discussing the rationale of the smart city concept based on comparative research from Japan and Germany.

Lastly, the topic of social inclusion was examined by looking into hardships experienced by the urban poor in Japan during the COVID-19 pandemic, who were not sufficiently supported by social policy measures; as well as by an international comparison of the current situation and factors behind cyberbullying; and with an analysis of democratic and authoritarian values in East and Southeast Asia, the balance of which can play a big role in realizing a society where no one is left behind.

There are, of course, many more issues subsumed under the SDGs, including gender, peace and justice, energy and water supply, land issues, etc., which were not covered here. What is more, Germany and Japan are societies with declining and ageing populations, which means that domestic demographic structures as well as questions of financial sustainability must also be further considered. These topics remain the subject of further research. In any case, we hope that the analyses of the concrete local initiatives and the empirical data presented in this volume can contribute to documenting our journey towards a sustainable future. While the path is stony, we must move forward with no time to waste.

References

UN (United Nations) (2023): *The Sustainable Development Goals Report: Special edition*, UN.

UNEP (United Nations Environment Programme) (2023): *Emissions Gap Report 2023: Broken Record – Temperatures hit new highs, yet world fails to cut emissions (again)*, Nairobi: UN. DOI: 10.59117/20.500.11822/43922.

WMO (World Meteorological Organization) (2023): *State of the Global Climate 2022*, Geneva: WMO.

Sustainable Societies in a Fragile World :
Perspectives from Germany and Japan

2024年3月28日　第1版第1刷発行

編　者：Carola Hommerich
　　　　Masato Kimura

発行者：アガスティン　サリ

発　行：Sophia University Press
　　　　上　智　大　学　出　版
　　　　〒102-8554　東京都千代田区紀尾井町7-1
　　　　URL：https://www.sophia.ac.jp/

制作・発売　株式会社 ぎょうせい
〒136-8575　東京都江東区新木場1-18-11
URL：https://gyosei.jp
フリーコール：0120-953-431
〈検印省略〉

印刷・製本　ぎょうせいデジタル㈱
ISBN978-4-324-11375-2
(5300340-00-000)
〔略号：（上智）Sustainable Societies〕

Sophia University Press

　上智大学は、その基本理念の一つとして、
「本学は、その特色を活かして、キリスト教とその文化を
研究する機会を提供する。これと同時に、思想の多様性を
認め、各種の思想の学問的研究を奨励する」と謳っている。

　大学は、この学問的成果を学術書として発表する「独自
の場」を保有することが望まれる。どのような学問的成果
を世に発信しうるかは、その大学の学問的水準・評価と深
く関わりを持つ。

　上智大学は、（1）高度な水準にある学術書、（2）キリス
ト教ヒューマニズムに関連する優れた作品、（3）啓蒙的問
題提起の書、（4）学問研究への導入となる特色ある教科書
等、個人の研究のみならず、共同の研究成果を刊行するこ
とによって、文化の創造に寄与し、大学の発展とその歴史
に貢献する。